My Mother Ruth

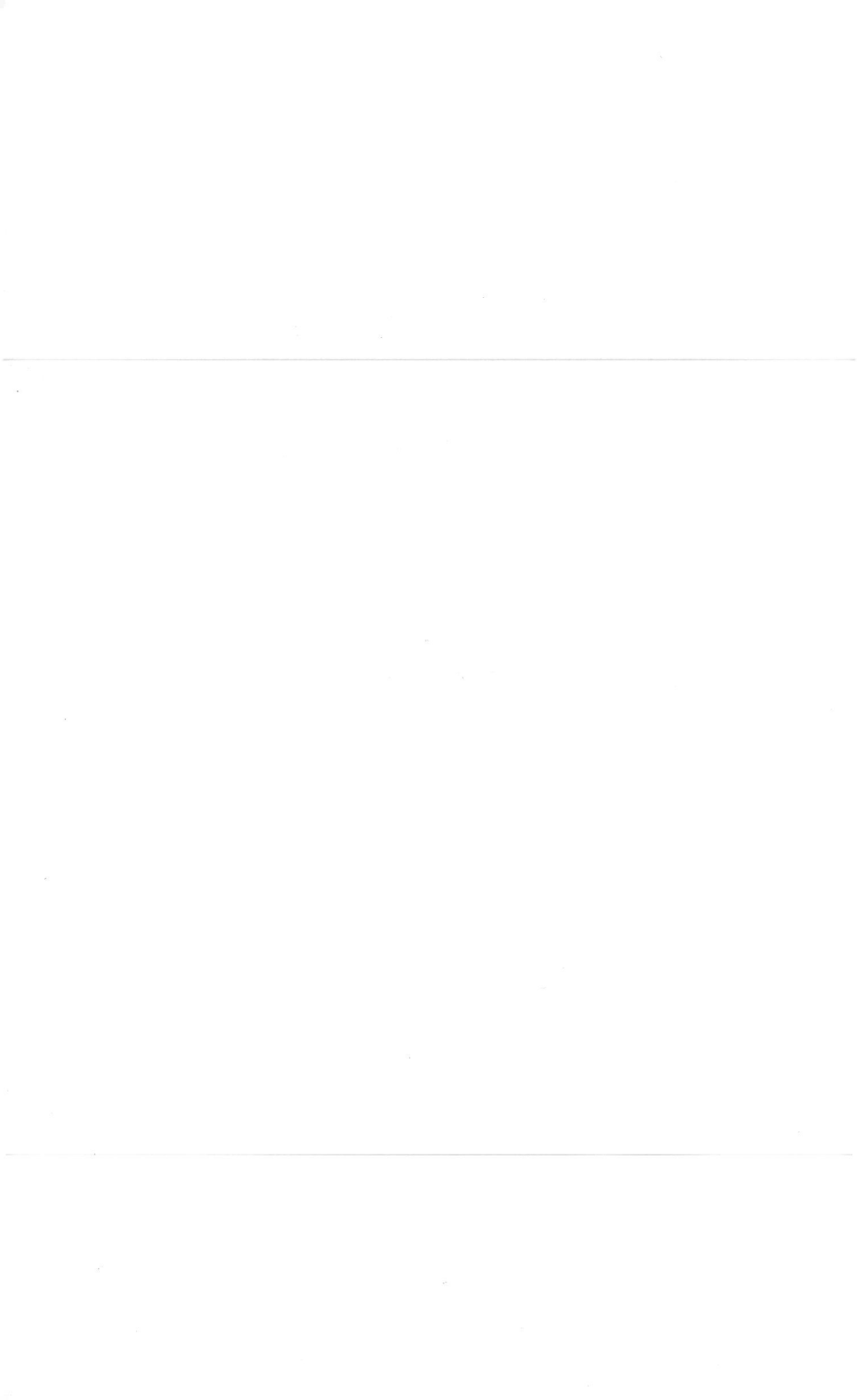

My Mother Ruth

HILLARY JOHNSON

ART BY RUTH JONES

ST. MARTIN'S GRIFFIN ❧ NEW YORK

For Susan Waterman

Book design by Gretchen Achilles

www.stmartins.com

Library of Congress Cataloging-in-Publication Data

Johnson, Hillary.
    My mother Ruth / text by Hillary Johnson; art by Ruth Jones.
        p. cm.
    ISBN 0-312-19930-9 (hc)
    ISBN 0-312-26763-0 (pbk)
    1. Jones, Ruth. 2. Mothers—United States—Biography. 3. Mothers and
daughters—United States—Case studies. I. Jones, Ruth. II. Title.
HQ759.J63 1999
306.874'3—dc21   99-19236
                                                              CIP

First published under the title My Mother Dying

FIRST ST. MARTIN'S GRIFFIN EDITION: OCTOBER 2000

10 9 8 7 6 5 4 3 2 1

ACKNOWLEDGMENTS

I am beholden to my mother's friends, relatives, and teachers for their assistance and encouragement. I thank especially Fran and Robert Schmidt, Shirley and Ken Olson, Anne DeCoster, and Jennifer Bong, who lent pieces of my mother's art for reproduction in this book.

Kitty Ross posed tough questions in a gentle manner, and offered important counsel, early in the writing.

I am deeply grateful to my literary agent and friend, Michael V. Carlisle, who listens carefully, who sees people with unusual clarity, and who urged me to write this book. I am equally grateful to my talented and tireless editor, Michael Denneny at St. Martin's. I doubt I could have written this story, this way, for anyone else. Thank you, Michael D.

What follows is a personal, subjective account. I have given some of the people who figure in this story pseudonyms in order to protect their privacy, although the headmaster of the Northfield School for Girls is not one of them.

Prologue

Ruth, late 1950s

A woman, barely twenty-two, is lying in a room in a small brick maternity hospital in Minneapolis. She has given birth to her second child. When she was pregnant, she satisfied her cigarette habit by rolling her own; she used her enormous belly as a kind of shelf on which to manufacture these nicotine bombs, and now she has pneumonia. She has waited so terribly long for this baby. Her first child, who is three, was an anxious, unhappy infant who cried and could not be consoled; his babyhood left her feeling helpless. She is unable to focus on these thoughts for very long. With the new child, this fat, nearly bald baby with hazel eyes, life will be different. She knows this with a certainty as profoundly held as some people's belief in God. She has always wanted a girl.

There is a problem, however. The nurses won't let her hold the infant. "Please—bring me my baby!" the young woman pleads. The nurses are stoic; they have their orders. When the pneumonia passes, they assure her, they will bring her the baby. On the second day, the young woman tries to dupe the staff; she is perfectly well now, she notifies them. She smiles her most confident, reassuring smile. Do the nurses waver—even a little? Perhaps they hear the new mother coughing when they stand outside the room. They continue to withhold the baby.

On the fourth day, the twenty-two-year-old is frantic, but she has a plan. She dresses. She walks to the nursery and finds her baby; she lifts the infant and presses it to her chest. She takes shallow breaths to keep the air from catching in her lungs, but her heart is pounding and it is very difficult. She walks with her newborn directly to the lobby and calls her husband. She demands that he come for her and their child immediately. She furnishes no details. When a passing nurse questions her, she smiles again, a false smile.

She comments that all is well and—isn't it wonderful?—she and her baby are being released. After that, the young mother decides to wait outside the hospital doors.

She envelops the baby in her coat. When she fastens the buttons, she discovers that the baby stays nicely tucked against her upper body. With one hand, she protects the top of its head from the chill of the last days of October. With the other, she reaches into her pocket for a cigarette. It is October 25, 1950.

Three decades later, when she is fifty-two, she finds herself telling her daughter the whole story. Unmarried, childless, her thirty-year-old girl child is watching her disapprovingly. Certain canned phrases are running through the daughter's head: secondhand smoke; rolling your own; walking pneumonia. "I *needed* you," the mother says. The words come out in a whisper, as if she's suddenly afraid. The comment merely serves to annoy the daughter further: Wasn't it the other way around? the daughter is thinking. Struck by her daughter's brooding face, the mother brings her tale to a sudden close.

This same woman is sixty-four, both her children have grown to middle age, and she has recently lost her moorings. She is receiving regular doses of morphine through a thin plastic tube that enters her body through an opening below her left clavicle. Liquid nutrition is being pumped directly into her stomach in an around-the-clock succession of droplets the size of tears. A malignant tumor has nearly occluded her throat and a metal tube has been inserted directly into her trachea to allow her to breathe; an oxygen mask covers the opening in her neck. Lately, she has forgotten the events—the intolerable pain, the parade of incompetent or indifferent doctors, the "nursey ladies," the hospitals, the surgeries, the drugs, and her final, non-negotiable decisions—that delivered her into this nadir of existence.

She is merely acutely aware that she is in a hospital bed. Perplexingly, the stainless-steel structure is in her own bedroom, in plain view of the carved mahogany antique upon which she and her second husband have slept throughout the twenty-five years of their married life, and frequently before their married life. There is also a woman moving around her, sponging her, toweling her dry, jabbing thermometers in her mouth or under her arm with compulsive frequency, attending hourly to some bloody sore at her throat, sitting by her side reading magazines and newspapers late into the night, refusing her permission to leave her own house, refusing her permission even to rise from the bed. This woman must be a nurse, the sixty-four-year-old muses, one of those nurses who, like the new breed of nuns, wears no uniform. In fact, this nurse, who dons jeans and men's work shirts every day, wears no makeup, and barely combs her hair, is clearly quite disturbed. Occasionally she leaves the room; when she returns, one would almost think she has been crying. Whatever she is, the older woman's dubious expression readily communicates, she's not much of a professional.

One morning, the sixty-four-year old is suddenly sharply cognizant of the fact that she has lost her speaking voice. Eyes wide with fear and puzzlement, she demands by means of eloquent facial expression, What on earth is going *down* here? When the nurse looks at her but fails to reply, the woman writes in ballpoint pen on the yellow legal pad in her hands, "I feel like I have a bad, bad illness." She gives the legal pad to the nurse, awaiting explication. Yes, the nurse nods in acknowledgement, but fails to elaborate. The nurse returns the notepad. Then, a few moments later, as if the older woman has finally come to understand the problem, the crux upon which this entire nightmare rests, she writes in frantic, enormous letters that nearly careen off the page: "Bring me my baby."

The nurse, strangely troubled, unkempt, responds tentatively: "I am your baby." The sixty-four-year-old is dumbstruck, then angry. What new outrageous sham is this? Her eyes look away, their gaze fixing on the sliding glass doors leading to an aged cedar deck outside, slick with rain. If only she had the strength to raise herself from this preposterous bed.

She begins writing anew. "Please! Bring me my baby now." She underlines the word *now*, then taps her pen on the word and stares sharply at the nurse. "Mom," the nurse says again, "I am your baby girl. I grew up."

The sixty-four-year-old stares incredulously at this dissembling paraprofessional in her bedroom—a nurse who doesn't even own a uniform, for Christ's sake—then looks away. Long, silent moments pass; chipmunks scurry across the deck and dive into the woodpile. The sixty-four-year-old, who once attended their activity with near catlike, if affectionate, fascination, is unseeing. An hour passes. There has been no writing, no physical movement, but the woman is awake. She looks at her phony nurse again. Now, the older woman wears a false smile—charming, loaded with wattage, in fact—but utterly false. She blinks girlishly a few times as if to establish her innocence. When the obstinate girl just stands there, failing yet again to produce the infant, the older woman withdraws into some private place, her helpless rage filling the room. "Are you sleeping with my husband?" she demands to know.

"Bring me my boots and my fur coat," the woman writes as evening falls. "Put them on my bed. I'm going away tonight." The daughter complies and the patient is appeased. The sheepskin-lined, suede-soled boots, meant to be worn in fresh snow, coupled with the heavy coat, sit in a mound like religious totems at the end of the bed throughout the night. Whenever the older woman wakes, she seems consoled by the sight of them.

By morning, her handwriting has deteriorated badly. "Baby. Pleeeese," she writes. In fact, for the next several days, she writes little that is legible. She draws curlicues and straight lines and scribbles layered-over scribbles until the page is nearly blackened, and even a series of sudden sharp angles as if her hand was simply registering her brain waves. She works hard. At times, her effort borders on the frantic. She has much to say and appears to understand she has increasingly little time in which to say it. Just one word, sometimes encompassing the entire page with its four letters, continues to be legible: *baby*.

It is mid-August 1993.

Early one morning two weeks later, the sixty-four-year-old stops breathing. Her pulse races for a few seconds, then it stops as well. The daughter is unable to relinquish her nursing duties with a suddenness akin to her mother's dying. She keeps her mother warm by tucking a blanket close to her sides, and sits just inches from her mother's body until evening, when her brother arrives. He has come from Los Angeles. By then, their mother's face has relaxed into peaceful repose. During the day, the woman's expression seemed to have changed every time her daughter looked. Sometimes there was even a hint of a smile. In fact, sitting in her mother's bedroom, which for the first time in six months was absent the steady hiss of the oxygen pump, the daughter had been taunted by faint echoes of her mother's breathing. The sounds came to her like whispered phrases too low to be deciphered. As if in a dream state, the daughter listened intently throughout the day, struggling to hear whatever final words her mother might be seeking to impart.

The woman's son takes his sister's hand and his stepfather's hand in each of his, and they stand at the bedside, their arms creating a circle above the body of the woman. The son says a prayer, one he invents as he goes along. "Death is our common enemy," is one of the remorselessly true things he says. He expresses his hope that his mother will be revived in the paradise to come.

Soon after, two mortuary attendants arrive and begin to lift the woman into a black plastic bag with a wide steel zipper down its center. As the zipper nears her mother's face, the daughter begs them to stop. Enfolding his sister in his arm, the son gives the strangers permission to continue, but the daughter is knock-kneed and incredulous as she watches her mother's face disappear behind the steel and plastic.

The strangers carry the shrouded woman down the stairs toward the front door. She was a tall person, and there are three turns in the stairway. The husband, exhibiting the lost, awkward stance of a blind man, hovers at the top of the landing watching the intricate procedure. The strangers halt their efforts for a moment, awaiting direction, their faces a study in blankness. The son offers them encouragement, and afterward thanks them with such formality it sounds as if someone other than he is speaking.

The strangers drive away in a white Cadillac hearse with enormous chrome-edged fins and white velvet curtains. Alone suddenly on the sidewalk, the daughter senses the presence of her mother's neighbors at their windows along the dark street. She cannot turn her head to meet their eyes, to acknowledge that "Yes, as you can see, Ruth has died." The moment is too private, too horrible. And she is embarrassed. She has stood by, helpless, as her mother was carried away forever in this appalling contraption.

There is no funeral or burial, just a new, terrible silence. After two days, a mortuary attendant presents the daughter and son with a brass box. Its shape resembles a large hardcover book, but it has the heft of a brick. In fact, it quickly rips through the small white shopping bag in which it is proffered. The son returns to Los Angeles. The daughter tucks the box away amid the pencils, paper clips, manuscripts, and reference books of her office armoire.

The discussion between herself and her mother about who would be allowed to keep the ashes, and in what container, and where, had gone on for hours one day months before. "My dear, I'm yours, literally, from now on. Just don't make a shrine," her mother had said finally. Now the daughter is surprisingly unmoved by the heavy brass box. She simply cannot find it in her heart to believe that her mother's ashes are inside. It's the journalist in her, she knows: She once met a lawyer who successfully prosecuted a California funeral home for just such an offense. But the person who was her mother—even her ashes—could not possibly have been compressed into the box now sitting atop the laser printer paper.

Part One

My mother lived in a house by Cedar Lake, a deep, well-fed body of water in Minneapolis, for the last twenty-six years of her life. As a child, I swung from a heavy rope looped around a tree branch and allowed myself to fall into this cold black lake filled with snapping turtles and evil-looking fish I knew to be as large as myself. As an adolescent, I tanned myself on its public beaches in a bikini with pink polka dots, my skin slathered with cocoa butter, my hair drenched with lemon juice. From my place inside a wobbly canoe on this lake, I hit a handsome boy named Jimmy full on the head with the broad side of my wooden paddle as he reached up from the dark water below me and tried to flip my narrow boat. The sound of his skull colliding with the paddle reverberated across the lake, causing a momentary hush, as if I had stopped time. For a middle-class American girl born at the precise middle of the century, growing up in an era when women still wore white gloves and hats on formal outings, I believe I was both witness to and committed more violence than might be usual.

My mother's name was Ruth. For me, the sound of the word will forever conjure not the rustic, biblical associations, but the singular emotional jolt that is felt upon entering an unusually elegant, stylish room. "Is your mother English?" a friend once inquired when I was a child. My friend had been a passenger on a city bus when my mother stepped aboard and asked the driver the fare. Ruth had a curious ethereal aspect, a manner of elocution, as well as a seemingly heightened sense of her own physical presence, that caught the eye and the ear, especially in Minneapolis, in the 1950s.

She herself wore neither white gloves nor hats; too conventional, too Republican, I imagine. At home, her manner of dress would have been classified as Bohemian in those years. Her wardrobe consisted of jeans and sweatshirts, or perhaps one of my father's sheer cotton shirts, its tails manipulated into a square knot at her navel. She never wore a bra, which embarrassed me when I noticed men staring. She often embarrassed me. Our groceries rung up, we would stand in the Red Owl checkout line, she in Capri pants and a halter top, me in a sundress and bare feet, my head tipped against her body. With what was, in my opinion, undue drama, she would draw her pen and checkbook from her hip pocket and, like a merciless schoolmarm, demand to know, "Hillary, how many humps in Johnson?" When, as usual, I began stammering in shame—after all, everyone else's mother knew how to write their last name—Ruth shrugged her shoulders in defeat for the benefit of the checkout girl, as if to say, "I was hoping for some help. You'll just have to accept the signature as it is." It was Ruth's way of letting the Red Owl staff know on a regular basis that she had married the wrong person.

Dressed up, Ruth was sleek and impressive in silk suits of a spare design, a strand of fat pearls circling her neck, her baby-fine hair inevitably cropped as short as a man's. Sometimes she wore a black sheath, cut high at the neck but leaving her shoulder blades exposed. She had achieved her height of five feet eight inches by the time she was twelve, a trauma that haunted her for most of her life. It's fair to say, in fact, that my mother considered being tall in the same league as affliction with a club foot. During my childhood, she rarely weighed more than a hundred and ten pounds. I believe she tried to diminish what she considered to be her extravagant height by minimizing her body mass, or else she simply lacked an appetite. She was quick to admit that her legs were the only aspect of herself about which she was vain. It was simply that she had the greatest legs in the Western world, she would add in a tone suggesting that honesty was the best policy on this particular matter. Surely, the magnificence of her legs was a fact too important to go unremarked upon out of deference to silly parlor manners. After her legs, straightforwardness was among Ruth's most striking attributes.

My mother dwelt in her house by Cedar Lake without me. When I was nineteen, she moved there with her second husband. My childhood playground was now my mother's idyllic retreat, the place where she would mend the self that had been bruised in a harsh, chilly first marriage, the place where she would become, in the formal, or literal, sense of the word, an artist. Ruth couldn't have known then that such things were about to happen, of course, but she was optimistic and had at least one arching plan. She immediately began supervising the gutting of the house, a project concluded only when the structure was reduced to a shell through which plaster dust traveled unimpeded by walls or ceilings. Then she invited all her friends over to celebrate the place—not for what it was at that moment, but for what it would become under her stewardship. People stood about uneasily, drinking champagne and sampling Melba rounds topped with sour cream and caviar, hoping their next step wouldn't send them crashing through the floor.

In the years that followed my mother's new marriage and her move to Cedar Lake, I was solidly launched on my own life, the highs and lows of which I would impart to Ruth via telephone lines from Berkeley, Washington, D.C., New York, Rome, Jamaica, Los Angeles, wherever I might be, day after day, year after year. I negotiated the steep face of that terrain for twenty years until one summer evening in 1989 when my mother called me and, without meaning to, closed the gap.

❖ ❖ ❖

My mother began collecting art when I was still quite young. When she was in her late twenties, she became friends with a local artist named Carol Pinsky. At a show held by the artist, Ruth gravitated to a painting of a woman in a lipstick-red dress with a low neckline and bouffant sleeves. The subject's skin was painted an exotic pale green. Medusa-like, her hair filled the background; she wore an expression of unflagging self-assurance. "What will you take?" Ruth asked the artist. "What are you offering?" the artist responded. "I'll give you twenty-five dollars a month." "For how long?" the artist asked. "Until I've paid you what it's worth," Ruth said. My mother sent checks on a monthly basis for nearly two years, then stopped. Pinsky called her: Where was the check? "I've paid in full," Ruth responded. "Okay," the artist said.

Ruth met a roguish painter named Tom Sewell, who had a gallery in downtown Minneapolis before he moved to Venice, California, in the mid-Sixties. From him she bought, in another installment deal, a five-foot-by-five-foot canvas of an elaborately decorated hot-air balloon floating slightly off center in a pink sky. Sewell had pasted a rotogravure image of a bosomy Victorian woman into each of the three gondola windows. High in the troposphere, these Victorians seemed to be dreaming of forbidden pleasures.

Ruth's transition from art consumer to artist was gradual—so gradual I barely noticed, even though, as she grew increasingly accomplished, my inability to recognize the transformation could be compared to that particular form of blindness in which peripheral vision remains intact but the sufferer cannot see that which is directly in front of her. It was only after Ruth died that I began piecing it all together—my blindness, her artistry, our failure to connect on this signal matter.

With a fixedness of mind that astonishes me now, I had thought I knew everything that could be known about my mother. Instead, after her death, I was compelled to learn about someone I barely knew, an artist who also happened to be my mother. I was forced to conduct "research" on that portion of Ruth's life I had missed, exactly like an inexperienced reporter who, at the moment she sits down to write, makes the dismaying discovery that merely interviewing the subject hadn't been sufficient. She had thought her reporting technique to be impeccable. Now she discovers the "holes," the great, gaping spaces in the story she was poised to tell—those opaque, unexplored regions of her subject's life that harbor clues and symbols of larger importance even than the linear "facts" so well and dutifully recorded.

❖   ❖   ❖

When I was a little girl living in Minneapolis in what was, by outward appearances, a perfect nuclear family of four, one of my mother's favorite ways to begin a sentence was with the words "When I am rich and beautiful and live in New York . . ." When these events came to pass, she implied, our lives would be better. She never really expected such things to happen; the line was a demonstration of comical grandiosity. Nevertheless, solvency, living in a city of sophisticates instead of a town where the word *toast* was pronounced with two syllables, were among the most treasured of her fantasies. Her beauty was a given.

By some miracle, twenty years later, her daughter—the me that was some kind of Ruth-Hillary hybrid, my mother's surrogate in the professional world, if you will—was living in New York and oftentimes well-heeled. Although one of my editors once affectionately observed that I looked like a cross between Jean Arthur and the young Clare Boothe Luce, I was hardly one of those raving New York beauties as my mother might have been. I was a smartly attired female with pleasing, symmetrical features, no more, no less. My childhood in Minneapolis was not forgotten, but I could draw no solid connection between it and the life I was leading then. Ruth was the only constant: My knowledge of her, my sense of her, was like a light breeze forever blowing in my direction.

In the summer of 1989, when she was sixty, and some seventeen years after my move to New York, Ruth called me one day and reported uncharacteristically that she had felt strangely ill for some time, that she found herself increasingly disenchanted with her husband of twenty-one years. He had become simply a "great toad" in her beautiful house who did nothing but sleep, eat, and watch television. She was loyal enough to note, however, that when she confronted him with her grim appraisal, her husband—unfazed—had responded, "I was a prince until you kissed me." She told me she felt like spending the night in the Lakeland Motel—a real place but one that for practical purposes existed more in the minds of my mother and stepfather; it was where one or the other threatened to go on the rare occasions when they were mad at each other.

Maybe it was the hint that she might leave her husband, if only temporarily; maybe I was at last on my way to becoming a human being. I spontaneously invited her to come and stay with me for a while. "I will give you a party and introduce you to all my friends," I heard myself saying. "We will spend our afternoons at the Met, and we will spend our mornings at the Whitney. I will buy you a hundred-dollar haircut from my guy on East Fifty-seventh Street. We'll have blinis at the Russian Tea Room and tea at the Stanhope. Will you come?" I knew she was startled—after all my years away, this was her first invitation to visit me—and more than intrigued. "Thank you, darling. Let me think about it a day," she said. By that she meant, I believe, "*You* think about it."

Ruth called me the following day. I could barely hear her. The street outside, Madison Avenue, had collapsed into itself, forming a crater that looked, from my vantage six stories up, like a great toothless grin. Con Edison had been jackhammering around the clock for days. The week before, Ruth had air-expressed me a pair of bright orange ear muffs designed for people who stand on airport tarmacs and direct jet traffic. I carried the phone as far away from the windows as I could—eighteen feet—and leaned into my tiny kitchen. Ruth's voice was measured and sad, as if she was about to say something that would hurt my feelings—and it had always caused her great pain to have to hurt me. She would not be coming, she said. She had just received a diagnosis of esophageal cancer. The outline of this tumor had been overlooked by radiologists for quite some time, possibly two or three years. She allowed as how she was dying and could not be saved. She and her husband planned to spend the evening holding hands and crying, she told me. Did I have a friend—anyone—I could stay with that night? she asked. Trying desperately to help me find a way to avoid suffocating in my own stunned despair and terror, she employed a voice she had used when I was very young, the baby-soft voice with the New Orleans lilt, the voice of her own mother: "Darlin', I don't believe a girl should be alone when she realizes she's about to lose her mamma."

I felt sick. I was thirty-eight. I had nothing but a dented file cabinet full of magazine clips, a few snapshots of men who had never loved me scattered about the one-bedroom apartment where I had lived entirely alone for twelve years, and now Ruth was dying. A radio station played big-band songs from the 1940s all night; I listened to them as if for the first time and imagined my mother, a beautiful teenager, dancing the lindy, her face a blaze of pleasure. By dawn, I was dizzy and disoriented. I had been crying for hours. It seemed as if my bed, indeed, the world's surface, was slowly sinking, inch by uneven inch, into a stratum of lava. Perhaps we will all be dead soon, I thought with something approaching hope.

I went back then, to Minnie-No-Place.

❖ ❖ ❖

I have been in Minneapolis just three days. I am at the beginning of what will be a stay of seven years, though Ruth will be gone in exactly four. We are in a patient room in Abbott Hospital. An impassive woman in white is forcing the contents of a syringe one and one-half inches in diameter into an ambivalent vein inside Ruth's elbow. Two years earlier, Ruth had undergone surgery for a small white tumor in her mouth and another in a lymph node situated next to her jugular vein. The surgery was considered high risk. The night before that operation, which was scheduled for 7 A.M., my mother called the surgeon at home and let him know he was allowed just one glass of wine with his dinner.

The recent discovery of a large tumor in her esophagus inspired a profound therapeutic nihilism in Ruth's doctors. It was a deadly, inoperable cancer. Since her terrifying call to me, however, a new doctor has emerged to say something can be done. He has proposed courses of radiation and chemotherapy.

Ruth wanted to celebrate my arrival with a picnic on the park-like grounds of the city's racetrack. At their first meeting the day before, however, the new doctor told Ruth she needed to be hospitalized for chemotherapy immediately. Ruth protested: She had planned a picnic! She asked the doctor if she could postpone the treatment for a day. She desperately wanted a reprieve, a sunny day at the races where she could pretend for a few hours that everything was as it should be: I was home, she was not dying. She outlined the party she had planned for her daughter, just returned from New York after a long absence. Her eyes were boring into the doctor over her half-moon reading glasses; her long legs were crossed comfortably, like a man's; her feet were shod in khaki tennis shoes without socks. Outside, in the chrome-and-glass waiting room, taut-skinned cancer sufferers sat silent and alone as if in a chapel. In this little room, flanked by her husband and daughter, Ruth was talking about fried chicken and chocolate cake, as if these happy phrases could ward off certain dire realities.

The doctor looked in my direction, annoyed. He was a famous practitioner, a white-haired patrician man, expensively attired. Listening to my mother, one would think that his plan to prolong her life was a serious inconvenience. His response to her was unequivocal and devoid of sentimentality. "No."

The chemical is the most astonishing color: an iridescent cobalt blue, like a liquid form of the glass. Together, my mother and I have been studying this bolus of poison befitting a horse in frightened silence. I am trying to think of something to say, something to distract us from the fact that she is just then being treated for a disease that will likely end up killing her. Ruth turns her gaze toward me, away from the battleground at her elbow. We remain locked in focus on each other's face, nearly speechless with emotion.

My heart is pounding wildly. Ruth appears to me like a felled tree, like something awesome that has been wickedly brought low. I am, in that instant, cognizant of the fact that I will not be leaving. For what seems like the first time in my life, there is nothing to decide.

❖ ❖ ❖

Ruth is lying on her back on the bottom of the ocean, the only life in a vast expanse of black. A machine hovers directly above her like a battleship preparing to drop anchor. A dull mechanical purr fills the cavernous space, but in her head, the books of the Old Testament are racing along, coming out in a frantic whisper too low to be heard: "Genesis, Exodus, Leviticus, Numbers, Deuteronomy, Joshua, Judges, Ruth, Samuel, Kings, Chronicles, Ezra, Nehemiah, Esther, Job"—all the way to Malachi, at which point she starts over. She had demonstrated a superior facility for memorization in her one-room Lutheran grade school in Englewood, Colorado. At last, she has discovered a use for this formerly useless information.

Two pieces of surgical tape applied in a St. Andrew's cross mark the place, approximately three inches below the base of her throat, where the radiation is to be directed. A technician watching her from outside a window in the wall focuses the beam at the center of the X and presses a red button. The machine makes a funny humming noise for a few seconds, then stops. Ruth has been zapped; she won't need to be zapped again for a few days.

She is an outpatient now. She left the hospital after three days, less than forty-five minutes after a nurse mentioned she could continue to receive her chemotherapy at home if she kept a small computerized pump full of the liquid cobalt near her. She was dizzy and weak, but she stood in a wobbly fashion and began to dress the minute she heard. She was upset. Why hadn't anyone told her until now? She could sling the pump over her shoulder like a small handbag, or attach it with Velcro to a belt at her waist; the line would run directly into a vein.

When a nurse arrived at her house a few days later bearing the little pump and the chilled cassettes of poison, Ruth was polite but distant. She was dressed up, attired in a long white denim skirt, neatly belted, and a white turtleneck; she wore mascara and lipstick. She arrayed herself in a languorous pose on the black lacquered daybed she had recently slip-covered in mattress ticking. There were cut flowers—lilacs, daisies, peonies, lilies—in vases all over the room. She focused her attention on her daughter, asking her questions, drawing her out, pretending the nurse wasn't there. It was a facility she had.

The nurse left with hurt feelings. She took pride in her work and she wasn't used to cancer patients exhibiting the cavalier lack of interest this one had just demonstrated, or of being made to feel invisible.

Without really thinking about it, Ruth nearly slammed the door on her when she left, resuming her conversation with her daughter as if an anonymous UPS man had just departed the premises. Ruth regarded the nurse as one of *them*—a tormentor; she had not been welcome at this party.

❖   ❖   ❖

While she was still hospitalized, I spent an afternoon in my mother's art studio, a cheerful whitewashed room in the basement she shared with the laundry machines. I had been home less than a week. Her printmaking press sat silent and imposing at one end of the room. Ruth used it to make art, of course, but I associated it with something else: an artifact one might find in an old-time newspaper office. Absurdly, I imagined a few hundred copies of a small-town paper, rich with ingenuously composed local news and gossip, being generated from its gray steel frame each day. One wall of the studio was lined with shelves, their surfaces packed with squat tins of powdered paint and handsomely shaped jars of ink. I also saw palette knives seasoned with patinas of rich colors; my mother's fingerprints were embossed on the wooden handles in interesting hues. Paintbrushes of every size and in every condition, brand new and worn to nubs, stood upright in jars like bouquets of dried flowers. In the center of the space, free-standing shelving units topped with Plexiglas surfaces stood like small monuments.

With a presumptuousness that sickens me now, I thought I might tidy up the place while she was gone. I thought that might please her.

I swept and washed the floor; I straightened stacks of heavy white lithography paper in the shelving units; using a razor, I scraped all the dried paint off the Plexiglas. I actually tossed some random-seeming scraps of paper away. I desperately want to believe there was nothing on those scraps—that they were blank—but I cannot recall precisely, and I find that the harder I struggle to remember, the more confused and uncertain I become.

The job took an entire afternoon, much longer than I had expected. Every time I turned around, it seemed, I came upon something fascinating that stopped me in my tracks. I distinctly recall several large, fully executed and strikingly beautiful pieces of art, richly painted with strong lines and colors. I remember feeling impressed by the artist's powerful graphic sense. Those paintings held me temporarily spellbound. I sighted, as well, a number of ink sketches enhanced by watercolors. I examined them closely, finding them highly unusual and imaginative.

I was frankly puzzled. I wondered who among Ruth's artist friends had created these stirring pieces, and why Ruth hadn't framed them or displayed them in some manner; why she had simply left them, unappreciated, in this disorganized fashion in her studio. I made a mental note to ask Ruth whose work she was storing down there, and why, but the immediacy of her deadly medical problems quickly overtook me, and I forgot.

❖ ❖ ❖

My mother's search for formal training in art began with drawing classes offered here and there in Minneapolis and St. Paul. In the summer of 1974, when she was forty-five, she took a basic painting class at Macalaster College. She learned how to stretch canvases over frames and studied techniques for applying pigment to canvas. She painted abstracts and still lifes and drew sketches of nudes. "Mostly, she did lots of funny little people," recalled a woman Ruth befriended in the class. "That was her territory. She also had very witty titles for her pieces." The instructor, artist Jerry Rudquist, remembered Ruth's appearance in his classroom that summer vividly. He recalled feeling that Ruth exhibited a certain polite tolerance for the basics he sought to impart to all beginning artists— "the methodical stuff"—but he also sensed that "she clearly had a fund of ideas that she wanted to do. She was impatient to get on with it. . . . She had a great sense of wit," he continued, somewhat ruefully, "and I'm not sure I allowed that. . . . I didn't bring that up—that one could take on subjects as a source of wit."

When the class ended, Ruth had a party at her house for the students and her teacher, a pattern she would repeat again and again as she took more courses and met more artists. Her parties, at bottom, were an expression of her exuberance, her optimism; little in life gave her more pleasure.

The following summer, when she was forty-six, Ruth sent me a letter. She announced she had enrolled in a drawing class offered at a local public school. "Now that I know *what* I want to draw, it couldn't be all bad to find out *how* to draw it, right?" she posited. She expressed her view that art could be "accessible" without being "banal or trite." Unlike her painting professor of the year before, she wrote, whose work was "complex and very serious and, if one is to believe the titles, exposes the human condition, explores its complexities, and offeres solutions—all in mysterious allegory," she wished only to amuse.

My mother's art was indeed amusing, but, as I was to learn, first impressions were often deceiving. Immediately after her death, I found seven of her etched copper and zinc plates in her garage, stacked haphazardly against a wall behind some old boards. They were covered with dust. The design on one of these plates appeared to depict a busy menagerie, most likely rats or mice. A few years later, I was afforded the opportunity to witness a wholly unexpected image emerge when a master printmaker from Pratt cleaned the plate and made a print for me. Initially, we did indeed see a curious conclave of rats and mice. But as we continued to study the work, we realized it was Holocaust imagery—large, evil white rats—Nazi rats—herding a stream of innocent, multitextured mice along their way toward an ominous end: rail cars to Austria or Poland—or big rat ovens where innocent mice were broiled on spits. The work was executed years before the emergence of *Maus*, the dark rendition of the Nazi Holocaust in a cartoon serial populated by rodents.

Since then, I have often wondered when studying certain pieces among my mother's art whether she intuited the precise nature of her own death and expressed it through her imagery, even though nearly all of her art was created some years before her cancer diagnosis. Perhaps not surprisingly, as I have studied this print, it has been transformed in my mind into an entirely different kind of metaphor, arising from the years I spent with my mother clumsily attempting to help her through what became a nightmare maze of cancer medicine. The print no longer strikes me as a Holocaust image. Instead, the rats are doctors, the mice are cancer patients.

These trusting, unknowing little creatures are being herded along their way toward multitudinous horrors from which they are unlikely to emerge.

Cancer was certainly on Ruth's mind. An ink-and-watercolor drawing my mother executed in 1979, almost a decade before the first instance of her cancer appeared, portrayed a serenely self-satisfied woman who perhaps fancies herself an aristocrat, what with her long, elegant nose and her proud posture. She is seated on a park bench, snoozing. All is well, her expression seems to imply. On closer examination, however, one notices that a strap of the woman's dress has fallen, leaving a naked breast exposed to the world. My mother called this piece *Cat Scan*.

Cat Scan

My abandonment of New York in favor of Minneapolis, the very place I had once assured her I would never live again, frightened Ruth initially. The act was so stunningly noncareerist of me; so apparently selfless. I knew she was worried I might come to resent her if the move destroyed my painstakingly crafted New York life, if somehow, by moving away, I might never find the resources, the stamina, to get back, and I would hold it against her, long past her death.

As the months wore on, however, New York, once my Emerald City, began to symbolize loneliness, the clenched-jaw anxiety of needing to outperform whoever was quietly climbing up your back in the workplace, men who wanted sex but not love, parties where everyone was looking over everyone else's shoulders, legions of otherwise healthy young women whose only prayer of long-term sanity was an infinitely refillable Valium prescription. I pondered, too, my own complicity in what increasingly seemed, at bottom, an unhappy life, one ruled by misguided, myopic notions about what mattered. I continued to read *The New York Times* out of habit, but for the first time in memory I didn't particularly care whether or not I ever worked for that publication. The sight of a new byline on the front page used to give me the willies; someone, obviously not me, was making it! Now the appearance of a new byline just made me sad for the poor ambition-riddled sot. The contempt I had held for Minneapolis from a young age was melting away, too; begrudging admiration took its place. So this was how the rest of America lived, I marveled: in houses shaded by trees; inhaling air that didn't sting the nostrils; insensible to daily bulletins about the vicissitudes of Ivana and Donald Trump.

I rented a small apartment downtown, but my radically revised definition of success in life was owning my own house, one with a yard for planting tomatoes in the summer. I thought a yellow bedroom would be nice. I dreamt of a cozy room I could call my office, the kind of room Virginia Woolf insisted a woman such as myself required. Mine would be wallpapered in red *toile de jouy*. I wanted to learn from my mother how to make an eight-layer burnt sugar cake from scratch.

As my newly discovered antipathy for New York unfurled itself, Ruth relaxed. I was in Minneapolis because I *wanted* to be there. Eventually we fell into the habit of looking at open houses on Sunday afternoons. It was all fantasy, of course, though we never saw it that way. The main body of the fantasy, left unarticulated since we were in full agreement on the matter, was that I would live in a house in the same city she lived in and that she would not die. We would start over and do everything properly this time. When we at last found the right house, we were flung into reality like some large vehicle catapulted over a guardrail and dropped in a canyon: I hadn't a penny with which to buy a house, she hadn't a penny to give me, and in spite of diversionary tactics like house hunting, her cancer wasn't going away.

❖ ❖ ❖

Death is our common enemy.

In the profound silence of her absence, my mother's art keeps up a conversation with me. The images offer condolence, they embolden me, they quiz me, just as my mother once did. "Here, my darling girl," a piece of her art might suggest to me, "look at this funny cat. See how very droll it is. This cat has known sadness, that is true. But look again. The cat is very clever. It is undefeated. It harbors a great secret. What is that secret?"

My mother drew animals, sometimes inventing her own peculiar primordial species, and she drew women, or, as she would have

preferred, "ladies." In all her creatures, there are certain commonalities to be found in their expressive eyes. Only rarely are they unabashedly happy. Occasionally they are self-deluded. More often than not, they are wistful, but they harbor a certain powerful knowledge that allows them to continue, in spite of the hardships they have endured. They have faced conflicts bravely, made choices, and soldiered on. It was a quality for which Ruth had deep respect. Occasionally, my mother refused to draw faces at all, letting the relationships among her subjects, communicated by the way they postured themselves, tell their stories—tell how they had avoided being crushed by life.

I have no doubt that my mother began her own life with an uncommon sense of joy, even glee, her only birthright. A photograph of her at five reveals her to be an impish, towheaded youngster in a jumper, a white blouse, and leather tie shoes, standing on a dusty plain in Colorado during the Great Depression. Her cotton leggings have fallen below one knee and are beginning to slide down the other. She stands unself-consciously, her hands comfortably at her sides. Already, her limbs have a languid elegance to them. She is peaceful, exhibiting neither defiance nor embarrassment. She looks at the world with eyes that seem actually to twinkle. Her mouth is shaped in a sly, knowing grin, as if she carries a delightful secret, one she may or may not choose to reveal.

"I wish I knew now what I knew then," Ruth would say, studying the photo carefully, when she came upon it a half-century later.

❖ ❖ ❖

During those years that I spent with her, years during which she presumably was looking down death's jaws, Ruth was not an angry, resentful, or even depressed person. She was, instead, someone with an uncommon capacity for delight, someone who chose to see mostly beauty and who spent the lion's share of energy remaining to her creating it.

Perhaps when the person we love the most, who loves us the most, is facing certain death, there is little about them that doesn't glow with an almost magical grace we have somehow failed to see before. Nonetheless, I believe the woman I encountered in Minneapolis in the summer of my thirty-eighth year was someone quite different from the woman I had known only as my mother. She was gayer. She would lean against a doorway in her house and smile at me and her husband with the grin she wore in the photograph when she was five, just watching us, and we would watch her with equal parts fascination and admiration. Her high spirits were like those of an untroubled child. I am not talking about naïveté, but rather openness and undiluted good cheer. She seemed more powerful as well. After the early, difficult years of courtship, she had achieved mastery in her marriage. She had emerged the strong one, the one in constant motion, the one who defined how life would be lived in her household from day to day.

I felt myself in a perpetual conundrum: Was this Ruth as she always had been, someone I simply hadn't seen clearly when I was a child? Or was this the original Ruth, the mirthful, buoyant being, restored? It was a doleful riddle I never solved to my satisfaction, though if I had to guess, I would vote for the latter. My brother, Ethan, felt it, too, at the end. "Her remarriage ended the family I had been raised in," he wrote in a brief eulogy after her death, adding, "and from then on we were individuals with a common history and a shared personality. The person that so many people know today as Ruth Jones was the reformation of my mother according to her aspirations, a re-creating of herself according to her artistic sensibilities." Either way, it was obvious to me that by living in New York I had missed a crucial portion of my mother's life, a brilliant life in which I had always been welcome to share.

❖ ❖ ❖

Cancer offers time, its only kindness. With any luck, the patient decides how that time is to be used. Those who love that person must find their way in the expanse of time as well. The difficulty is that neither party knows precisely when the time will end, and if one is confused or frightened, one begins grieving too soon. When I returned to Minneapolis at thirty-eight to be with my terminally ill mother, I found it impossible to accept the terrible outcome that was so clearly beyond my control. I felt like I was sitting on my hands in a burning house. I don't believe I ever really stopped trying to somehow slow the process down or change the outcome. I can see now that my efforts often interfered with Ruth's choices and may have compromised the peaceful, clear headed way she was trying to die.

In the beginning, armed with no special wisdom or insight, certainly without pamphlets or platitudes from the "death and dying" industry, I simply went to my mother's house every day and spent time with her. I brought her chocolate-covered cherries, magazines about fabrics and furniture and decorating, fat hardcover books, flowers, wool throws. To my stepfather's dismay, I persuaded her to buy a dog. She wanted a standard poodle because she had heard they were the smartest breed. She claimed she wanted a dog that was so smart it could drive her places, as well as compose letters to the editor, saving her the trouble. She added she would like a Volkswagen convertible—white, if you please. She began talking about a lot of things she would have liked, things I had no idea she might have wanted. The notion of Ruth, who hadn't driven in twenty years and hated to leave her house, independently tooling around town in a little convertible was a wonderful, incredible image. It was heartbreaking, too. I wanted her to have another chance at life, a life during which she could take up driving again, accompanied in the passenger's seat by her smart poodle, its ears flung back, eyes forward, long nose pointing the way. I wanted her to have years and years of time during which she could continue her fascinating process of *becoming*.

Ruth ended up with a Yorkshire terrier puppy, the first dog we saw. She named him Rodger. It was my duty to walk the dog each day, out to the docks and along the edges of the lake, where every tree and rock seemed to have a place in my history. We were both heartened by the earnestness of this tiny creature as he sallied into the natural world, each day more eagerly. A life was just beginning. I had never presented Ruth with a grandchild, but we raised the hilarious little puppy together and treasured him as we might have treasured a human infant. "We *share* him," Ruth would say to anyone who was confused about the dog's ownership. Rodger learned enough parlor tricks to please Ruth. "Go hump your teddy," she would whisper to Rodger when the guests at her dinner parties had eaten and were now arrayed in her living room with their brandies, awaiting the next development. The little dog would go off in search of his stuffed companion, later prancing into the center of the room with his teddy in his mouth, where, with an encouraging word from

Ruth, he would begin frantically humping the toy. When the dog finished, he lay on his back, panting, the picture of Yorkie ecstasy. "Somebody give that dog a cigarette," Ruth would say.

It was early spring by then. Ruth had survived the fall and winter; the tumor was reduced in size. We cheered the news, but didn't speak of it further. It was a temporary fix; the five-year survival rate for esophageal cancer was eight percent. We talked freely about everything but the fact of her dying. She chose to avoid the subject and I took my cue from her. At night I returned to my apartment downtown and cried in solitude. Ruth was dying! The thought filled my brain up, pushing everything else out of the way. A friend coun-

seled me long distance: Ruth is alive *today*, she will be alive *tomorrow*. Celebrate! I recognized the prudence of that counsel. I found it difficult, nevertheless, to sublimate for very long the looming catastrophe of Ruth's death. The fact that I was unable to lay my most profound terror at her feet as I had done with lesser terrors all my life, giving her the opportunity to wave her magic wand over it, was the most difficult exercise in self-composure, perhaps the hardest thing I have ever had to do. The uneasy dreams I experienced for so long after Ruth died were never about her final illness and death, they were about the lengthy period during which I lived with the certain knowledge that she was going to die.

Ruth decided how she would use her time. What she chose to do first, even before her courses of radiation had officially ended, was commission an architect to design an addition to her house, one that would include a very grand bedroom and a glass elevator to ferry people between the ground-floor entrance and second level. She soon fired the architect and took over the project, working out the configuration of the rooms herself. She spent the first several months after my return supervising building contractors and their crews, watching as massive slices of earth were excavated from her yard, and volunteering me to chauffeur her on ambitious drives through thriving Minneapolis suburbs I hadn't even known existed in search of carpets and textiles. One day we went to look at sofas. A saleslady in one store assured Ruth that the sofa she had admired was guaranteed for life. Ruth looked at me to be sure she had my attention, and then she brightly inquired of the saleslady: "Whose life? Yours or mine?"

When an awkward patch of old wood flooring presented itself between the Mexican clay tiles of her living room and a floor that was to be carpeted, she gathered myriad small cans of paint around her, settled on her knees, and painted the old wood in a pattern of trompe l'oeil tiles. She used shades of pale and hot pinks, soft oranges, lavenders, and creamy whites, each square drawn with a subtle suggestion of checks, stripes, slightly mottled solids—none of them quite the same. She took up making floor cloths, painted canvases that, once sealed with multiple coats of varnish, are as durable as linoleum. Her designs were graphically stunning. She used the same technique to create table surfaces for her deck and her new bedroom. She made papier-mâché fruit—pomegranates, lemons, plums, and oranges—and papier mâché vases and bowls to hold the fruit. She finished each piece by wrapping it with surgical gauze—which afforded the fruit surprisingly realistic textures—then painted them in whimsical pastels. Then she gave them all away to people she liked.

There was nothing random or desperate about what she did. Shortly before her death she would write, "It's so lovely to die at home & since I've taken 5 years to die of this I'm so proud to have made myself such a lovely place to do it in."

❖ ❖ ❖

In 1978, on September 26, her fiftieth birthday, Ruth enrolled as a freshman at the University of Minnesota. The campus was industrial-sized, bisected by the Mississippi. Its two parts were connected by the footbridge from which poet John Berryman had leapt to his death six years earlier. Even a grim factory school like the U. of M. was an enormous adventure for Ruth. Since girlhood, she had dreamt of such an opportunity. She toyed with the notion of becoming a Latin scholar, or a student of Greek mythology, but she quickly embraced the study of art.

I remember how she looked during those years. She abandoned cosmetics and took to having seven-dollar hair-shearings at the local SuperCuts franchise. Her men's clothing—work shirts, overalls, her husband's cast-off vests and sweaters—was inevitably touched here and there with bright shades of paint, usually oranges, reds, or purples. Her drugstore reading glasses, faux tortoiseshell, rested perennially at the tip of her nose. She carried her generic cigarettes to class packed in their yellow boxes with black lettering ("CIGA-RETTES") by the carton rather than in individual, cellophane-wrapped packages, as if they were one more component of her artist's tools. Curiously, defying her own natural glamour served to intensify it.

At the time, in my mind's eye, when I thought of my mother in faraway Minnesota, I saw a mostly solitary figure in her house, her husband somewhere in the background. I had little sense of the rich life she was leading, or of the respectful, almost reverential, following she was inspiring among her professors, as well as her fellow students—most of whom were less than half her age.

In some part, she was a standout precisely because of her age. Although older than most of the people around her, she was somehow more innocent in spirit. She asked a lot of questions, even in the large survey classes attended by hundreds of students. They were very good questions, and people who were in those classes still remember her. In her studio art classes, Ruth was far livelier, physically and intellectually, more eager to experiment and take chances, than her younger classmates, say her art professors. She rapidly earned their esteem. That first quarter, she got an early-morning call from one of them. He was sick. Could she please teach the class that day?

Another recalled that the experience of having Ruth in his drawing class was akin to team-teaching. "It was almost like having a translator," the professor said, almost twenty years after my mother's only class with him. "She brought her experience into the class. She was doing the projects along with the students, and talking about the process." My mother always arranged her easel in the back of the room near the door so she could flee into the hall whenever the need for a smoke arose. "Students gravitated to her because she had so much presence," the professor continued, "so there was Ruth's little outpost in back, where she would sit surrounded by people who enjoyed talking to her, and if you wanted to find out something, you could come up front and ask me, or you could go in back and ask Ruth. . . . She was interesting," he mused as he thought about this particular student, now dead. "She was especially supportive of students who were drawing on the spiritual and the emotional—the inner life—to make their art."

The moral code by which my mother lived was apparent to all. Once a classmate appropriated a piece of her work drawn months earlier and presented it as his own In class. When Ruth established her authorship of the piece, he owned up to his mistake and offered to buy it from her after the class, but she simply gave it to him— with her compliments. If he admired the piece that much, she reasoned, he ought to own it free and clear. A reason so little of Ruth's art can be found in any one place today is because she gave so much of it away. Virtually anyone—classmates, teachers, or friends—who expressed honest pleasure in her art was immediately offered whatever piece they had admired. When I was a child, Ruth urged me to do the same with my own possessions: offer them graciously to those who admired them. It was a lot to ask of a child, and I rarely measured up. Still, it was one of those curious precepts by which Ruth herself had always lived.

My mother was the first student to arrive at the art department's warehouselike building each morning at seven-thirty. Wrapped in scarves and a woolen hat and heavy gloves and quilted jackets, she would stride eagerly into the building, even when temperatures ranged as low as twenty degrees below zero. Her first painting instructor, a gay man twelve years her junior named Bill Roode, was the second to arrive. The two would remove themselves to a nearby coffee shop Ruth called the Plastic Palace. Eventually, other students would join them. If there was anyone at the table Ruth found dull or impossibly naive, she would, according to Roode, "tell nose-picking jokes" or whatever she could think of to drive them away, leaving herself surrounded with the crowd she liked.

Among Ruth's oft-visited topics was her daughter's career then under way in distant Manhattan. Sample: "The editor-in-chief of *Women's Wear* is furious with Hillary. He loves it when she pokes fun of rich people, but when she made fun of Jackie O the other day, he leapt from his chair, the veins of his neck bulging. He hollered at her across the newsroom, 'Jackie is off-limits!' " "What did Hillary *do?*" was the response of my mother's rapt audience. "Well, my dears," my mother answered with enormous dignity, "not to worry. She told him to go fuck himself." In truth, I had taken an early lunch and gone home to cry, a fact my mother revealed eventually, but only after teasing her listeners with what I might have said in her best fantasy. My mother desperately wanted me to be brave and powerful—"queen of the world," she would have said. Her friends found her Scheherazade-like revelations about my workaday vicissitudes powerfully addictive soap opera, with the added wonderment of being completely true.

When she chose to take a serious lunch break during her busy college years, Ruth required a civilized restaurant where she could order a double martini or whiskey sour or Irish coffee—something grown up. There were a few bars around the fringes of the campus that offered liquid delicacies of the kind she liked. The eighteen-year-olds in her art classes who admired her particular genius sometimes threw their Big Macs and Whoppers to the wind and followed suit; they had found their oracle, their Aunt Mame. Often, lunch was an exclusive affair between Ruth and her friend Roode, who believed he had stumbled onto a twentieth-century Oscar Wilde in a woman's body.

My mother's friendship with her first painting instructor endured for years. They were drinking partners; they were confidants. They talked about art incessantly and, Roode says, they learned about art from each other. Roode learned about life from Ruth. As he heard more of her history—leavened out "montage style," as he recalls—and watched her art evolve, he found Ruth increasingly evocative of that generation of hard-working, hard-drinking artists who in the Fifties had flung themselves two-fisted into life, casting aside middle-class convention. It was a generation that fascinated Roode, and although Ruth herself had not been part of the De Kooning–Jackson Pollack–Joan Mitchell crowd, in Roode's eye, she was nevertheless in spirit somehow among them.

During those remarkable years, my mother, entirely without my cognizance, was in the process of achieving something that had been just outside her grasp for decades. She was still finding her way that first year in her drawing and painting classes, however. She would have what Roode called her "spells," when she would worry that she should be doing more classical—"classroom" or academic—figure drawing. Roode encouraged her to do what came naturally instead. He worked to inspire in her the confidence to proceed in what was probably the only direction she could go: toward comedy, politics, pathos; to "layer" those things into her work.

"I tried to encourage Ruth to be Ruth," Roode remembered, years afterward. "I was sensitive to the wittiness, but I also tried to encourage the darker side."

"She *could* draw," Roode continued, "but it just wasn't her way of expressing herself. She was interested in everything *but* academic drawing. She thought in a more metaphorical way. She stored up all these images. She had this didactic thing going on—she had these stories that she worked from. They were rich with pathology or political commentary—[the work] was witty and funny, but it had its other side. All those animals became metaphors for people."

❖ ❖ ❖

The closest my mother came to chronicling the days of her life via the printed word were the records she kept of menus she designed and ultimately served to friends and family. She composed them in a fine longhand on scraps of paper, anything would do—index cards,

Ménage à Cinq II & III

pale gray copy paper during the years my stepfather still worked for the newspaper; spare pages torn from her address book. She stored them, in no special order at all, in a Carson Pirie gift box. "Luncheon for Alice Atherton, Friday May 15, 1992," she would begin in her typical fashion. Alice Atherton was a magazine editor friend of mine who had decided to visit Minneapolis for the weekend in the spring of that year. Alice wanted to meet Ruth, and she was trying to comfort me, too. Ruth, in turn, wanted to prove to me that she could put her best foot forward and not be found wanting; she had met so few of my friends from New York. Before she died, she wrote to me, "I *loved* Alice. It felt so pleasing because I felt I had pleased the very difficult to please Ms. Alice Atherton. And you must never show her this because I fear I have misspelled her name." Alice wasn't at all difficult to please, of course; it was me Ruth sought to please.

"Champagne," my mother's menu began. "Scallops in cilantro salsa." The latter was scratched out and replaced with "Graavlox & caviar." The menu continued without further editing: "Roast pork with sumac & cumin (or goat seasoning: sage, paprika & turmeric). Mom's chutney. Florida sweet corn pudding. Sweet potatoes with vermouth. Tomatoes roasted with garlic. Green salad—try for watercress with tabbouleh. Home made buns, butter. Lemon cakes or key lime tarts or key lime napoleons (pie crust, key lime curd & whipped cream.)" Detailed recipes for each component of the meal always followed, as well as a shopping list for the edification of her husband.

Meticulously planned and executed, Ruth's parties were events that hardly anyone left voluntarily. Only by announcing that she was retiring, usually in the early hours of the morning, could she bring an end to these affairs, leaving her guests to rifle through the coat closet's profusion of mufflers and boots long after she had disappeared into her bedroom and fallen asleep, often too exhausted to remove her clothes. After she died, Garrison Keillor wrote to my stepfather that he had never forgotten his first dinner at my mother's house in the early 1970s. At the time, Keillor was a little-known, audacious local radio announcer who went on the air before dawn. My mother had loved listening to him at that hour; she said it was like having a secret lover, one who was dazzlingly funny and knowing. The dinner was the most glamorous evening the young Keillor had ever experienced, he wrote, and had launched in him a hunger for the intimate literary galas he imagined must be under way in Manhattan each night.

During the late 1970s, when I was still in my twenties, I would come home to Minneapolis each year, either at Christmas or during the summer. I was blond, thin, and perhaps the most solvent and fashionably dressed I would ever be. Ruth always had a party for me. I didn't think I deserved a party; worse, I wasn't particularly interested in her friends. Ruth ignored my protestations. Her living room, its twenty five-foot ceiling capped with a ten-foot-square skylight through which sunlight or starlight poured onto the busy scene, might be filled with artists, carpenters, university professors, whatever cleaning lady she was then employing, my five stepsiblings and their spouses or lovers, Ugandan musicians in dreadlocks, used-bookstore owners, gay couples, rich people from Wayzata, the ornithologist and publisher who lived across the street, and anyone else my mother had caught in her sybaritic embrace that year. Most of her friends were younger than I was. There would be canapes and bubbly and great platters of couscous or steamed mussels, or perhaps a roasted baby goat or grilled quail. The constant was my mother, turning up at my side whenever I moved on to meet the next guest. "Isn't she pretty?" my mother would interrupt. "Isn't she *marvelous?*" She was talking about me. I would never again be blessed with an admirer of such caliber and intensity. Yet, in those days, a certain arrogance often characterized my social behavior. My mother didn't seem to notice.

In 1980, I was in town on a rare visit to Minneapolis when Ruth insisted I accompany her to all of her university classes. She made a point of introducing me to her professors and friends. Afterward, she took me to the studio arts department, housed in its own disheveled building close to the riverbank, where she held my hand and walked me from room to room as if in possession of a white tiger, introducing me to her art instructors. They shook my hand with the kind of warmth and familiarity reserved for an old friend. So this was the famous daughter—the journalist from New York. The memory of the day threatens to crush me. I was cloaked with that hateful arrogance. I was bored, and I was embarrassed by Ruth's manic pride. Blind to my discomfort, Ruth brought me next to the loft studio of the man who would build her print press, George Weplo. She was overjoyed that she would now be able to make prints at all hours of the day or night, in her own house, without first seeking permission from anyone. The two talked for more than an hour, exploring myriad possible configurations and options. I behaved morosely, like an American on a tour of Versailles with an Italian-speaking guide. At the time, I saw my mother's enthusiasm for owning her own press as neither more nor less important than any of her other interests, like preparing a French meal or ripping an interior wall out of her house to expand a room.

❖ ❖ ❖

Ruth didn't speak very much about her art then, nor did I speak of it, but its existence was suddenly of critical importance to me when

I returned to Minneapolis that first summer, nearly ten years later. I was only beginning to understand that it was her legacy—to me, to her friends, to anyone who might care to study it. Just weeks after I returned, however, Ruth announced one afternoon in the washed-out brightness of a summer day that she had "cleaned out" her studio.

"What did you do with your art?" I asked, with a casualness that today curdles my stomach. In that same instant, I realized that the art I had come upon some weeks before could have been created by none other than Ruth.

"I threw it out," she said gently, not wishing to make more of what was, she assumed, only a small matter to me.

"Threw it out where?" I asked, a distant alarm ringing in my head.

"I put it in the trash," she responded, staring at me oddly; was I retarded?

"Well, I'll just go remove it from the trash," I answered, becoming excited.

"But darling, the trash has been collected," she said, continuing to stare at me as though mystified and worried; she hated to alarm me.

"Well, at least you still have your plates," I now countered with the dumb certainty of one who cannot yet grasp the bleakness of what has occurred.

"Why, no," she answered, honestly surprised. "I threw those out as well."

"In the trash?" I asked, flabbergasted.

"In the trash," she assured me.

We are all killing one another in small traceless increments, I thought then. In 1984, when she was fifty-five and I was thirty-three, Ruth had sent me seven beautifully executed prints of the etchings she considered to be her best. Her only show, held in a restaurant owned by an architect friend, had just ended. Most of her friends came to the opening and several bought pieces. The show was billed "The Artful Cat Event," since the bulk of the images was of cats. Afterward, Ruth gave much of what remained to the architect and his wife. I had been invited, of course, but had failed to attend. I was in Los Angeles at the time, interviewing a sixteen-year-old named Molly Ringwald for *Rolling Stone*, assiduously recording the teenager's affinity for fried onion rings, Warren Beatty, and the Psychedelic Furs.

The prints were Ruth's Christmas gift to me and she noted in her accompanying letter that, if they failed to arrive by December 25, she hoped that wouldn't make me "cross" or "spoil any amusement they might offer." She assured me she had sent the very best print of each series. One of them, a cat, was called *Do you know where your cat is tonight?*

"I made it after a conversation with you about some god awful party you described," Ruth explained to me. "The only comfort I could give you was, 'Don't take it personally,' which was the original title. . . . I recaptioned it for the show (theme was 'cats' you know)."

I scanned the prints exactly once. They were so . . . *Ruth*, I remember thinking. I never framed them, although I expected I might someday when I had more money. When she and her husband came to visit a few months later, she looked at the place where I had left them after unpacking them—in a stack leaning against the wall, art-side in. She said nothing, but her hurt showed on her face. When I returned to Minneapolis four years later, I brought the unframed prints with me and stored them in her studio—temporarily, I thought—while I looked for an apartment. They were among the art she tossed when she threw everything else away. Perhaps she felt that if I didn't love them as she did, then she didn't want them to be something I would remember her by: She didn't want them encumbering my life. I tried to make the point with her then that she had thrown away something that belonged to me, not her, when she threw those particular prints away. Even as I argued I knew I was wrong. She had given them to me, but I had never properly claimed them.

Ruth began mulling the possibility of selling the press she had commissioned to be made for her even before she destroyed the cache of art in her studio. Before the sale occurred, we sat together at the top of the stairs leading down to her studio, while she wondered out loud if she should part with it. She must have known little else could so powerfully punctuate the end of her career as an artist. The press would garner six thousand dollars.

We spent the six thousand dollars together over the next two years. I was the designated driver, she the designated collector of stuff. I was always confused by the ceiling-high jumble of dusty shapes in the junk and antique stores we frequented; I could make no sense of any of it. She had an incredible eye. She found old chairs and loveseats to upholster, antique mirrors to hang, library-quality reading lamps to rest on her newly acquired side tables. She took to ordering items from catalogs as well—baskets that nested inside one another; tall French garden vases forged from nickel to accommodate bunches of lilacs from her yard; a wildly designed set of dishes she would eventually say she wanted me to have after she died. Occasionally she insisted on purchasing things of no earthly use at all, like a sculpted wooden cat with a secret compartment in which to hide small items. She didn't care about the little compartment; she had nothing to hide there.

I have tortured myself with these memories, my thoughtless crimes. Ruth's teachers and friends who are also artists have sought to comfort me. Artists are unpredictable, they have told me. Artists are famous for black moods during which they destroy their own work. Any among us might be prone to commit surprising, unpredictable acts after receiving a diagnosis of terminal cancer, they insist.

My years of indifference, according to Ruth's friend and teacher Bill Roode, "was partially Ruth's doing. Art was *very* important to Ruth, but she didn't convey that to a lot of people. It was *hard* for her to say that she was an artist. That's something all artists deal with, especially women artists. . . . She also did this thing of giving her art away, and when she did have a show, her most personal work was not in it."

I want to believe these explanations encompass the entirety of Ruth's motives. Yet I'm unable to dispel the terrible suspicion that I alone am to blame for Ruth's great purge. For thirty-eight years, among other omissions, I had failed to perceive that she was more than merely clever; she was an artist. She had always been an artist. Formal training had merely focused her talent. It is my sense now that upon my homecoming she decided to purge her studio precisely to erase her past as an artist, an endeavor in which for years I had evinced only polite interest, and summon a new identity, one I would find more "amusing," as she surely would have said. Indeed, I had recently expressed a sincere fancy for homemade quilts, and she would that very summer embark on a fantastically complex quilt for me, a legacy she had it on good authority—me—would be appreciated, unlike, she mistakenly presumed, her art. Yet if I am guilty of blindness and indifference, I may be guilty of hubris as well.

Roode recalls he was startled by the turn of events in the household of his former student that summer. "She was doing more decorative things—the quilts, the floor cloths—stuff that didn't demand so much of her emotionally," he said. "They all seemed so different from what she had done before. I was shocked. But toward the end she couldn't deal with emotional content. She really didn't want to think that way—the morality plays and the stories in her head. She didn't talk about those things anymore. She wanted to 'make nice,' 'make pretty.' I just knew—I could tell."

Only in the final weeks of her life, and in the years following, did I begin collecting my mother's art, eventually cobbling together my own cache. I was able to find mostly the scraps—the pieces she had overlooked that summer—though I also have a few very beautiful works. Sometimes I wonder if she left them there for me, rolled up in cardboard tubes and tucked behind shelves and appliances, in the secret hope that one day I would find them by mere chance, and think of her. I began, as well, conducting a careful investigation into where other pieces of her art might be found. I have been fortunate to see some of this work, and two of her friends have given me pieces and offered other pieces on loan. Nevertheless, what was lost weighs on me like a ship's anchor. Year after year, the burden pulls on me, as if the anchor were moving along an ocean floor in tortuous slow motion, scraping its impression deep into my spirit.

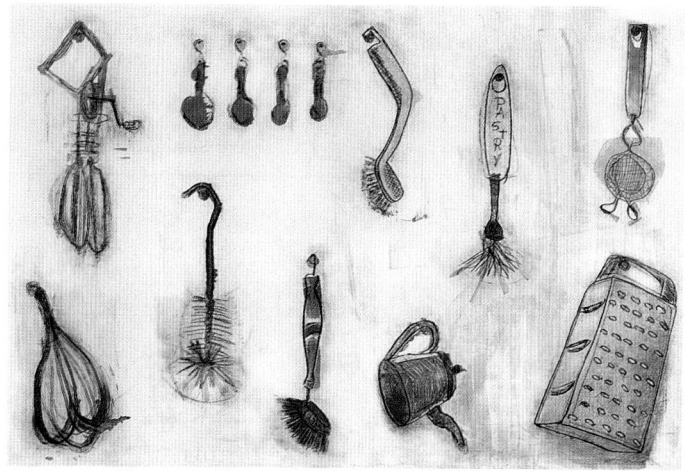

Part Two

I am picking mushrooms in a field that almost seems to be undulating. It is an optical illusion, or the surrealistic embellishment of a snapshot of memory. There are people all around me, bending toward the ground, working the earth with their hands. We are singing "Frere Jacques! Frere Jacques! Dormez vous? Dormez vous?" The verses start at one end of the open space and shimmer in waves of sound to the other. It is dusk. I drop the mushrooms into a ruffled apron tied over my patterned dress. When my apron is full, I carry the mushrooms to an unpainted, peak-roofed shed. Light is stealing through the spaces between the planks, creating a pink-gold luminosity inside. A wooden barrel consumes most of the floor space. A jovial man, his dark hair falling rakishly across his collar, lofts me by my waist to the rim of the barrel. I fling the mushrooms out of my apron into the barrel, but he doesn't put me down. He tosses me high into the air above him, and he shouts with excitement. Just when I quit floating near the eaves and start to come down, he intercepts my descent. I go up again, nearly to the roof. I'm laughing and watching the faces of the other farmers standing in a circle below me now, smiling at me, sharing my delight. A woman protests, but not harshly. She is chiding the man, afraid he might drop me.

Ruth liked to say that she did little more than leave a note on the kitchen table for my father to find one morning. "Gone to Paris. Took the kids," this infamous note was to have stated. But our departure couldn't possibly have been so hasty or surreptitious. Ruth brought Ethan and me to Dayton's for a passport photograph. The photo, sepia-toned now, evokes a *Life* magazine wholesomeness that looks almost fake, like an ad for Ipana toothpaste or Studebaker cars. Ruth wears gold hoop earrings and pale, nubby silk; her smile is eager and happy. I'm sitting on her lap; her young hand, its wrist decorated with a bracelet of white beads, is wrapped around me protectively. I'm dressed in a pleated skirt and matching jacket of gray moire silk and white lace cuffs and collar, and sporting a Dutch boy haircut exactly like the one Ruth wore throughout her childhood. Like my mother, I'm looking directly into the camera, my expression one of innocent delight. Ethan is dressed in a T-shirt and corduroy pants held up with a narrow leather belt. His blond hair, just starting to darken, is sculpted into a tidy crew cut. Clearly more fascinated with the technology of the camera than with anything else, he is leaning against us, his mouth open in a dreamy half-smile. Ruth had just turned twenty-five; I was not yet three; Ethan was nearly six. The year was 1953.

The three of us traveled by train to New York. From there, we boarded a passenger ship to England, finally making our way to Paris. We didn't come home for a year.

Ruth quickly learned the phrase "Avez vous une petite chambre pour moi?" The answer was always "Non," and Ethan and I were the reason. Finally she paid the proprietors of a farm outside Paris a small sum for our room and board. When she discovered we were being fed wine with our meals, she bought the farmers a dairy cow and pleaded with them to give us milk. Other than to say we were treated badly, Ethan refuses to speak of France. In Paris, Ruth met American novelists Frank Yerby and James Baldwin, and other writers and artists in their circle. She became part of that group, and Yerby's lover. It's possible she would have stayed in Paris forever, the boundaries of her life radically altered, were it not for Ethan and me and our problems on that rustic farm. Our mere existence had already razored the edges off the blank page of Ruth's future, and the page was filling up with words.

We needed a new passport picture to leave France, since, as Ruth once told the story, I had ripped the original off the page and eaten it. Yerby arranged for the sitting. The second photograph bears little similarity to the portrait of American middle-class resplendence taken a year earlier. We seem to be refugees. Ruth is wearing an oddly patterned sweater and faded jeans. Her short hair is a mass of neglected curls. Her smile looks dreamier, more melancholic, even if she also seems more beautiful, her features more starkly defined. I am wearing a pair of shabby overalls and a dark T-shirt with a stain on one arm. Tearful and cross, I am clutching at Ruth's thigh with one hand, holding a French-made teddy bear, a farewell present from Yerby, in the other. Another second, and I will bolt out of the camera frame. Ethan looks beyond tears, beyond happiness; he is alone in space, touching no one.

When my mother arrived in Minneapolis with her French-speaking children in tow, my father accepted us into his household, but I don't believe he ever forgave her. It wasn't Ruth's desertion that enraged him; it was her unequivocal clarification of who she was: a woman out of place and time who had dared seek a radical new existence for herself, one beyond his imagining.

Her Parisian foray tortured Ruth for the rest of her life. Like the Victorians in the gondola, she had cut the ropes that bound her, but her children had been hurt in the process.

When my mother lay on her hospital bed that first week I was in Minneapolis in 1989, and we watched the blue poison making its way into her body, Ruth focused hard on my face, suddenly posing a question:

"What do you remember about France?"

Her expression was fierce with worry. Should she die unexpectedly from the toxic effects of that incredible glue, she wanted to be reassured of something first. My mind was flooded for the umpteenth time by the golden light, the boisterous man with the dark hair and powerful hands, the sensation of floating above the upturned faces like some holy child. Like Ethan, I was habitualized to secrecy on certain matters, however, and France particularly. Nor could I be sure the story would soothe or alarm her.

I told her, "Nothing."

"Good," Ruth snapped. Her body relaxed into the bed. I looked at the nurse, but she was staring into the middle distance. My lie must have been as transparent as the molten glass entering my mother's arm, but it was apparent Ruth needed to believe me just then. That was how we exhumed for the first time in a serious manner, then just as suddenly interred forever, the subject of our year lived in France.

❖ ❖ ❖

My father was stationed at Fort Logan outside Denver during the Second World War. A case of astigmatism had saved him from the battlefields of Europe. Ruth's father, George Hines, liked to invite G.I.s for dinner on holidays like Thanksgiving and Christmas, and somehow my father was among them. He dated Betty Hines first, Ruth's elder sister, but then Ruth caught his notice. My mother agreed to marry him when his army stint ended.

Ruth arrived in Minneapolis late one night in December of 1946. Six months before, she had graduated from Englewood High School. "Ropes of the Past Ring the Bells of the Future" was the strangely ominous motto of her graduating class. She carried in her new handbag one hundred dollars in cash, a fortune, and the last beneficence she would ever receive from George Hines. My father's mother, Sarah, loved Ruth from the moment she saw the leggy eighteen-year-old holding a small suitcase step off the train from Denver. Sarah had been an orphan. She recognized loneliness and fear when she saw it, and her heart melted at the sight of my mother. "Ruthie was just a little girl," Sarah often said, recalling their first encounter, "and so *terribly* alone."

My mother alighted from the Denver train onto the Great Northern Station platform, looking up, no doubt, to examine the stately art deco portico fashioned of wrought iron. Likely she didn't see the Mississippi rushing past a few blocks away, but she might have noticed the lights illuminating the Washington Avenue bridge that spanned that wide crossing, and heard the water crashing over St. Anthony Falls a quarter mile north. Although she nurtured fantasies of escape during her first few decades in fly-over-land, as she herself called it, her address to the end would be Minneapolis, a town that always bristled more than it bustled.

At her wedding, she wore a dark suit with broad shoulders and a single button at the waist. Her skirt ended just above her knees; she wore chunky, open-toed high heels of black suede, and her stockings were seamed. Her legs looked sensational. In most of the photographs of the event, she appears happy and sophisticated, but in a few, snapped without her knowledge, she seems uneasy. Soon after the marriage, Ruth relayed in a letter to her little brother, Johnnie, back in Colorado that my father had brought her home to a bedroom with two single beds. My father seemed to view the arrangement as perfectly normal, but Ruth was stung. When he was at school, Ruth wired the beds together with coat hangers. "He married me," she wrote Johnnie. "He's going to sleep with me."

My mother lived with my father and Ethan, and eventually me, in student housing near the University of Minnesota, where my father had enrolled in law school. It was a community of Quonset huts, little more than corrugated metal igloos. Ruth penciled letters to Johnnie on butcher paper or large brown squares she ripped from supermarket bags. She read a dozen books a month, as had been her habit since childhood, and followed world events in the *Minneapolis Tribune*. She earned what she could posing for life-drawing classes at the university. Sometimes she was clothed; sometimes she was nude. She was the subject of a great many Minnesota artists who were at the start of their careers. One student presented her with an oil portrait he had made of her. The painting survives to this day. Ruth is wearing a red scarf tucked into a navy blue sweatshirt, and her hair is trimmed in a short bob, turned under just above her jawline. Her forehead is lined with Mamie Eisenhower bangs. She wears no makeup, no jewelry. Her faraway gaze suggests a melancholy that belies her youth.

One summer, she canvased the neighborhood, carrying Ethan on her hip, soliciting signatures on a petition to save the lives of Julius and Ethel Rosenberg. She was very tan, her pixie-style hair bleached by the sun. She was twenty. She wore shorts that ended just where her legs began, and a sleeveless blouse she didn't bother to tuck in. She wended her way amongst the Quonset huts, outrage and horror rising in her throat whenever she pondered the execution by her government of two intellectuals, the parents of two small boys. When a woman answered the door, she was inevitably turned away; when a man answered, she was usually invited in for a drink.

Days and nights with my father unfolded without change. It was his habit to arrive home after school, seat himself in the one comfortable chair the couple owned—a canvas sling chair—open the newspaper, and read it cover to cover. He did all this without speaking to Ruth. One day, my mother stood in the kitchen and watched her husband's ritual. When he was comfortably settled, she advanced upon him wordlessly with a book of matches and lit the newspaper on fire.

❖ ❖ ❖

When we were all very young, my mother read aloud to my brother, Ethan, and myself from an ancient edition of fairy tales by Hans Christian Andersen. The book was thick, but also very small, perhaps so that the hands of a child could grasp it comfortably. The edges of the jacket fabric were frayed, revealing hints of cardboard; its sepia pages were thin as tissue paper. My brother would lie on his stomach on the floor, his chin resting on his fists, wearing a look of surprise and curiosity that was his typical expression then. Ruth might as well have read us the collected works of Edgar Allan Poe, so terrifying were these cautionary tales, which always seemed to have at their center a female child paying a deathly price for some minor transgression: *The Little Match Girl; The Red Shoes.* I was tormented well into my adulthood by the image of the girl in the red shoes, her feet bleeding, her bones ready to snap, as the red shoes danced her helplessly over the countryside, hither and yon, into infinity. My mother wanted to warn us about the harshness of life. She wanted us to know that our lives might spin out of control someday, that we might be hurt and alone, that such things happened. But Ethan, who was older, got too scared and asked her to stop reading from the book. In the discussion that ensued, we all agreed that these allegories were simply too frightening, they were giving us—even Ruth—nightmares. My mother put the book away.

Ruth herself was not far removed from childhood in those years. We three inhabited a rented bungalow in southeast Minneapolis like wayward orphans, awaiting the major event of our day: the moment when my father would come home from work. He was out of law school at last, and working in a firm downtown. Without him, we were adrift in a sea of spooky fantasies and banal realities. By day, we listened to the trains chugging slowly along the fringes of the neighborhood, their cars brimming with grain from the Pillsbury company's elevators near the Mississippi. We played board games and searched for a children's literature that wouldn't cause us to wake screaming in the night. We finally found solace in Frank Baum and A. A. Milne.

Ruth studied me carefully for signs of superior or even above-average intelligence, but it was Ethan who was clearly the brilliant one. I was barely four, but Ethan and my mother were well acquainted, having already shared a life together that I, little more than half his age at the time, had missed entirely. Ethan's imagination was so powerful and his articulation of his fears so persuasive that my mother began to share them. Ruth, too, lived in secret terror

of the barrel of bears that Ethan insisted was hiding underneath the basement stairs.

Ethan had refused to stop crying for months after his birth; for a while, he grew skinnier rather than fatter. Once, he appeared to have a seizure, but Ruth, who was nineteen at the time, didn't recognize it for what it was until long after it had passed. I can imagine that when she learned she was pregnant with me, she believed she was being offered a second chance. Home from the hospital, she left me briefly alone on the sofa. When she returned to discover Ethan had lifted me into his arms, she didn't see a curious child testing the heft of his new sibling; she saw a jealous child about to

kill his infant sister by dropping her on her head. Ruth struck him, hard. The reflexive action, a millisecond of primal unreason, burned hot as an ember somewhere in her heart well into her middle age. She had caused her son to feel like an outcast.

Our triangle was broken when Ethan started kindergarten at Tuttle Grade School, a three-story brick building with tall, foreboding windows. My mother and I missed him. Ruth made up games to distract us. Pencil in hand, she would emblazon a mark—mysterious but rife with possibilities—on one of the blank yellow legal pads my father occasionally brought home. Then she would hand the notepad and pencil to me. I would embellish her mark and return the pad to her. In this way, we would collaborate for what seemed like hours in a wordless, equitable rhythm of creation: two minds, two hands, one drawing.

Each afternoon, Ruth would announce it was time to nap, and she would lead me or carry me down the hallway to the tiny bedroom I shared with Ethan. She would lie down with me on the bottom half of the trundle bed, my half, and tell me to sleep. It was she who would sleep, however, in long, solemn stretches during which she would not move and barely seemed to breathe. She was gone, silent and alone, away from me and Ethan, away from our miserable bungalow. I lay beside her, snug in the curve of her torso, watching the water stains on the ceiling turn into animal herds or roiling clouds, and waiting for her to wake up. I tried to imagine where she might have gone, in her dreams. On occasion, though she was not even an inch away, the sick fear of abandonment raced through me. Sometimes I got panicky and tried to wake her. She would rouse herself momentarily to ascertain that I was safe, but then she would be gone again, back to the place I couldn't get in. She was twenty-four.

Ruth with Hillary at Cedar Lake, circa 1954

My first-grade teacher, Miss Christianson, demanded that we recount our breakfasts in drill-like fashion each day. Ruth often boiled eggs for my father, but left Ethan and me to dine on whatever we pleased: a tin of pineapple; egg white still in the shell overlooked by my father; applesauce; bread and butter. Miss Christianson was deeply displeased by my accounts. Apprised by me of my teacher's strange obsession, Ruth coached me: *white wine and escargot*. She made me repeat the words again and again until I could utter them as if I knew perfectly well what they meant. "White wine and escargot," I recited one morning at the inquisition. Miss Christianson executed a military pivot and abandoned us in the classroom. My classmates regarded me with heightened interest: Had I discovered something better than Trix? Our teacher telephoned Ruth from the principal's office. "Why aren't you teaching my daughter to read?" Ruth demanded, pleased she had snared the dull-witted Miss Christianson.

Staff from NBC's *Today Show* came to Minneapolis to scout locations for an upcoming week of broadcasts from the nation's vast middle. My father, Ruth, and Ethan were riding bicycles on the path around Lake of the Isles when a producer saw them. I was a passenger in a wire basket attached to the handlebars of my father's bicycle. My father had cut an opening in the basket for my legs and padded the interior with his Army blanket. Once seated, I enjoyed swinging my feet, although it threatened our balance and forced him to pump his legs harder to keep the vehicle upright.

Two small islands, sanctuaries to birds and orange-dappled turtles, were at the center of the man-made lake. Elms towered over the three-mile bike path, creating a natural bower where their branches intersected high in the air. Formidable mansions with porticos, turrets, and Victorian winter gardens lined Lake of the Isles Boulevard, reminding everyone who didn't live in these castles just how rich a few people were in this city. The sight of our family pedaling through this enchanted scene caught the New Yorker's fancy.

It was still dark when we arrived at the lake the next morning. The network had parked its trucks and set bright lights on tripods along the parkway. Men in their shirtsleeves rushed about shouting commands. Ethan, by then an eerily beautiful, somber child, was there with his pet mouse, Mouser, who periodically poked an inquisitive snout from Ethan's breast pocket, then retreated. We were offered steaming black coffee from an enormous silver urn. Ruth held my hand in a steely grip as Dave Garroway, exhibiting his vaguely lascivious smile, chatted with her and my father. Afterward, I was aloft in the wire basket, my legs still for once, because now that we had become actors in a play, I wanted to be good. Ruth and Ethan pedaled steadily along the path behind my father as the sun rose, casting the four of us in silhouette. For a few minutes, with the cameras and floodlights trained on our caravan, everyone stopped shouting. I could hear only the wheels of my father's bicycle rumbling along the path. In this way, nearly two million early-morning TV viewers were assured one summer day in 1956 that all was well in the heartland.

I don't believe Ruth and I were ever closer, I don't believe I was ever happier, than during the early years we lived in the gray clapboard house at 1775 Girard Avenue. The Kenwood neighborhood was filled with houses that had been constructed for railroad barons, founders of grain empires, and merchants who had earned great sums of money at the turn of the century. Our own house was one of the oldest, having been erected in the 1880s, although far from the biggest. It had thirteen-foot ceilings, five bedrooms, and a forty-foot living room with a fireplace. The closets were the size of small rooms. There were sun porches on two floors, a breakfast room, a formal dining room, front and rear staircases, and polished wood floors that creaked and groaned, even when no one was treading on them. Without discussing the matter, Ethan and I knew the place was haunted.

"This is your room, darling," my mother said as we reached the top of the front-hall stairs the day of the move. It was directly across the corridor from the room she and my father had decided would be their bedroom. I was nearly five. I walked into the empty space and was entranced by the wallpaper, a trompe l'oeil design in yellow drawn to look like quilted fabric. The closet had built-in drawers, and attached to each drawer was a metal pull fashioned to resemble a seashell. I reached for the intricately patterned brass knob of the room's door and pulled it toward me to see if there were more marvels behind it. The movers had left the door off its hinges. Amid a rush of air and the sound of wood crashing upon wood, I was suddenly buried under the massive walnut slab. I don't remember whether Ruth cried out. I recall her astonished expression when she raised the door off me and discovered I was unscathed. Not a tear was shed. Instead, we looked at each other with a curious happiness. We were, both of us, still alive; we had been spared the pain of parting.

❖ ❖ ❖

In the Fifties, Ruth did her part for her country. She sought mercy for the Rosenbergs. She sewed scores of beanbags shaped like donkeys to sell at the Democratic Farmer Labor Party's rallies in support of Hubert Humphrey's Senate campaign. She gamely threw DFL fund-raisers at our house on Girard, to which she might invite three hundred people she barely knew. When her marriage to my father ended, her passion for involvement retreated, but her fascination with the political scene was unflagging. In the spring of 1993, four months before she died, Ruth wrote to me, "I have been trying to understand why I can't seem to read *The New York Times* anymore and I discovered it is because the Clinton Administration has become such an embarrassment that the only decent thing to do is to avert one's eyes."

My mother's disappointment with American Presidents reached its apex with the election of Ronald Reagan. She inevitably referred to him as "our calcified head of state." She found the people Reagan chose as his advisers equally distasteful. As her skin began to develop fine lines, Ruth complained that her face was "taking Jeane Kirkpatrick lessons."

Ruth enjoyed national spectacles the way anthropologists might, deeply but without serious emotional engagement. Independence Day was her favorite holiday, one she routinely celebrated with grand Southern meals, Southern whiskey, and as many friends as she could entice to her house at Cedar Lake—many of whom stayed until dawn the next day. There was little Ruth loved more than presiding over an undeniably great party. "It's a kind of vanity, you know," she would admit to me once. She was never patriotic.

"It came to me on July 4, right about noon, that I simply don't love my country," Ruth wrote to me in 1976 after watching the televised entrance into New York Harbor of the tall sailing ships. She knew I had been at the harbor that day, watching from a rooftop in Brooklyn Heights, while Norman Mailer, one rooftop over, performed a full-throated solo rendition of "God Bless America." "I mean," she continued, "I don't *hate* my country—I just feel about my country like I feel about my toothbrush or my sox. If I had been born in London or Paris or New Delhi I can't believe I would love England or France or India, either. I mean, how can you love a

America Standing Tall

COUNTRY? Whole bunch of them TV guys claim to have brought it off but I didn't believe a word of it."

She allowed herself to be lured into a subscription to *The New Republic* once, but reeled with disgust when in her very first issue she was faced with two thousand "pro-life" words by Morton Kondracke. She was outraged that the magazine dared call itself liberal. She considered herself to have been hondled and canceled her subscription with a devastating letter to the editor outlining her reasons, false advertising being the most serious.

When Ruth began making art, her feelings about American politics emerged quite naturally in her images. The most powerful piece of those that survive is her depiction of the Reagan cabinet, a lithograph she created in 1984 and titled *America Standing Tall*. A large rat, its chest puffed with pride, is at the center; an oversize sheriff's badge dangles from his chest. His eyes are those of a remorselessly crafty creature, but one who both deceives and is deceived. He is pompous and ridiculous. He is surrounded by groups of rats, some of them, the most important, rendered in full-bodied splendor, others—the Supreme Court?—drawn as a cluster of pink figures, shoulders and heads only. Nancy, shorter than the President, stands near her husband, her round body drizzled diagonally from head to toe with yellow spots and painted with orange stripes.

At first look, the image seems to be an innocent, if mysterious, cabal of cartoon rodents. On closer inspection the dark side emerges from the dreamy pastels. The energetic communication under way within this powerful group is the most striking aspect of the piece: the winks and nods, the conspiratorial glances, the deeply felt communal satisfaction. Their secrets are safe as long as they keep the sheriff front and center, as long as they hold their own united front.

❖ ❖ ❖

For a little while, Ruth and my father seemed to have found peace with each other in our new house. One night I slipped out of my bed and tiptoed down the front stairs. I had heard a curious sound. Midstairway, I sat down and peered through the stair rails into the living room. My parents sat weeping together like lost children, their shapes illuminated by the glow of a television set, a handful of empty liquor bottles on the coffee table in front of them. Adlai Stevenson was conceding the presidential election to Dwight Eisenhower. It was 1956, and Stevenson's career was over.

Ruth signed her letters "Mrs. CLJ," using my father's initials as her name, as if she was pleased to be a missus, and my father's especially. "I like him," she wrote of her husband of by then ten years, in a Christmas card to her little brother, Johnnie, and his new wife. A few months later, she also wrote, "Dear Johnnie, I am writing this to assure myself that there really is a world with people in it and 1775 Girard Avenue So. is not a desert island. It's 10:30. The chil-

Have I Been Too Long at the Fair?

dren are off to school and [her husband] is in court and the phone does not ring nor does the door bell and the radio is playing sad songs & I'm so lonesome I could die."

She told her brother about the magazines published in 1890 and 1891 that my father had recovered from the attic. "Fascinating things," she wrote. "Rudyard Kipling's latest serial, Mark Twain on Christian Science, Dewey's dispatches from Manila, adds for *rust* proof corsets—much fun."

She explained that for some time she had been embarked on a project, which happened to be removing sixty-year-old lead paint from the pantry cupboards. She had invented a toxic-sounding process to achieve the look she wanted, one that involved many stages and techniques. "I do what I can with paint remover and then I sand," she wrote. "I use the coarsest sandpaper made (the next coarsest grade is a yard of gravel and two barefoot black boys to grind it into the wood) which of course gouges the wood somewhat and then I use an electric sander with a more realistic grade of paper to smooth it and then I apply grey stain, rub in white paint, then 2 coats of sealer and finally the wax. I used 3 gallons of paint remover and it has taken me about 4 months of sporadic effort—during which time I have completely lost interest in the whole matter. . . .

"I've really not learned," she continued, "how to keep this place clean yet—can't cope with a house I can't clean top to bottom in one day—the sheer size of it is appalling—all the windows are nine feet tall—takes a whole day just to wash the windows. . . . It's a beautiful house and we love it but I haven't figured out how to cope with it yet."

Ruth was trying hard to embrace what was. Four decades later, she would write to her daughter, couching the sentence as an aside, as if it were a small matter, "Of course, I know for sure that if I had not been a mother my marriage to your father would have lasted months—not years."

Ruth was compulsively inventive, and I lived under the spell she cast. She came home from cocktail parties and handed me elegant miniature tables for my dollhouse; she had fashioned the little tables from the fine twists of wire that held champagne corks in the bottle. She mixed flour and water and strips of newspaper and draped the entire mess over bent coat hangers, and the results were always remarkable. I was never sure, in fact, what I might encounter upon my return from school during those years. She might be planting a tropical jungle in miniature by lowering a succession of tiny plants to the earth-filled bottom of a twenty-gallon bottle, or she might have commandeered our dining table in service to the creation of papier-mâché objets d'art, or merely fingerpaints. One day, I walked in the house and realized all the upholstery had been removed from the odd bits of furniture we then owned. Ruth was on her knees, the heads of straight pins jutting from between her tightly pursed lips, fitting brand-new fabric to an old chair. How had she learned to do this, I wanted to know, astounded by her display of bravura. Careful of the pins, she answered, "I'm working it out as I go along."

Excitement rose to fever pitch after Ruth somehow managed to persuade my father to buy her a brand-new Singer sewing machine. For an entire winter, Ruth passed the time stitching together matching wool suits and jumpers for the two of us. At her request, I would sit nearby, reading *Winnie the Pooh* aloud. On Saturdays, we rode downtown on the Hennepin Avenue bus, its seats lined with dark green velvet, to Amluxen's fabric emporium. Ruth dressed well for these outings. She held my hand in one of hers; with her free hand, she fingered the wool tweeds and silk and rayon lining fabrics, and studied the pages of pattern books arrayed on burnished library tables. As spring came, we would stroll home in a kind of reverie, often taking Mt. Curve Avenue, a steep, precarious road still paved with cobblestones, passing the sandstone mansions of the Pillsburys and the Daytons, and inhaling the scent of lilacs that were as common as weeds in Kenwood.

Once, when I was six, I managed somehow to drive Ruth to her bedroom in tears, and I heard her say to my father, "I hate that child." The words sent me into a free fall. Her outburst was the first sally in an inconsistent push-and-pull that would, every so often, mar our intimacy. We were madly in love, then we were out of love, then we were in love again. By the time I left childhood, however, it was I who kept pulling away. I was the cruelest lover of the pair. That first time, my father lifted me into his lap and tried to explain why mothers sometimes felt that way. He made me feel loved and calm. Whatever I had done, Ruth quickly forgave me, but those four words, my mother proclaiming her hatred for me, ring in my head even now. Still, regardless of the turmoil that would follow, Ruth bonded me to her with an especially powerful adhesive. Hers was a kind of invincible, knowing love that seemed to spoil me for every other kind. Further, she needed me, I needed her; it was that simple.

On occasion, Ruth would take me to my father's law firm in the Rand Tower on Marquette Avenue. Ruth and I would ride the elevators with the China-red lacquered doors to the mahogany-paneled offices. My father would offer his hand, I would wrap my fingers around just one of his, and we would make our way through the carpeted corridors, stopping to visit each of his associates. Downstairs, he would let me trace with my feet the stars and half-moons set into the terrazzo floors of the art deco lobby. We would linger before the bronze statue of Icarus, a nude, helmeted figure with wings instead of arms, each wing as long as the body. These appendages looked menacing, like enormous scythes, one raised to the sky, one pointing at the earth, but the eyes were noble, almost sorrowful.

Either I would be stolid and unyielding, like my father, or I would be something I didn't know about yet. Nevertheless, before I

went to sleep one night I wrote my mother a note in which I confessed my ardent desire to be like her. I left the note propped against
her bedroom door. I was hoping that if I made my preference clear,
she would be able to help me. It never occurred to me that my father might read the note, too.

When I was four, I began to dream a dream that would revisit me
well into my thirties. In this unchanging drama, my mother and I are
descending a succession of concrete steps deep below the earth.
Thousands upon thousands of people, fleeing some unknown terror,
are descending with us in a kind of martial lockstep. The concrete
shudders violently with each impact; the sound is deafening. I look
up at my willowy mother and discover that the vibrations are causing her head to break loose from her neck. She looks down at me,
but she can no longer speak. Her gaze is sorrowful, apologetic. She
can't help what is happening. You must be brave now, she seems to
be telling me with her eyes. I'm not at all brave. I cry out to the people nearest us, begging them to slow their march. The noise is by

then so thunderous, no one hears me. My own distress inevitably awakens me.

Ruth liked to maintain that I was clairvoyant when I was a child. The only clairvoyance I recall was this: I identified that vital connection, the neck to the head, as the site of the damage that would leave me motherless forty years hence.

❖ ❖ ❖

Ruth and my father argued. My father wanted to see June Cleaver standing in the living room with a feather duster when he left for work each day. In her wildest dreams, Ruth could not possibly re-make herself into the icon he desired.

Frequently their arguments would culminate with my father storming out of the house. He hadn't a prayer of winning a war of words with Ruth; retreat was his only option. Days might pass before he returned. A hotel near Loring Park, an unsavory greensward at the edge of downtown, became his refuge from the chaos of our household. Pink flamingos were a motif in this particular establish-ment, a bit of kitsch Ruth seized upon with a vengeance. More than once I heard her say to him, her voice seething with contempt and hurt, "Go back to your hotel with the pink flamingos!" If he could bear to live in a room with images of flamingos embossed on the mirror, her tone seemed to suggest, he wasn't someone with whom she wished to associate.

In 1959, a ravaged-looking Judy Garland performed live in an hour-long television special, her last. Ruth told me point-blank that she had decided to watch Judy Garland without me. When I pressed for an explanation, she remanded me to my bedroom. Two hours later, my father came home. I heard him enter the room where my mother had said she planned to watch the performance. I heard him shouting, and then he was half-dragging, half-carrying

Ruth down the front stairs. Red lights were spinning on vehicles in the dark outside. Suddenly the house was quiet. When he returned the following morning, my father strode purposefully into my room. He gripped my arms with his hands and squatted on his haunches so that we were face-to-face. "Your mother tried to kill herself last night," he said. "The doctors say that when people succeed, it's because they really want to die. When they fail, it's because they want attention. Your mother was just trying to attract attention to herself. Do you understand?"

I nodded. I was eight.

I went to visit Ruth in the psychiatric wing of Abbott Hospital, which rapidly became known around our house as the loony bin, and later, simply, the bin. An orderly was playing a banjo in the common room, and several patients and their visitors were singing. I was a musician and singer myself then; Ruth had finagled a ukelele for Ethan and me, and we were learning labor union anthems from the 1930s written by Woody Guthrie, Josh White blues songs, and certain ditties Ruth taught us: "I don't care if it rains or freezes, 'long as I've got my plastic Jesus on the dashboard of my car." My mother appeared wistful but not unhappy. The storm clouds that had descended upon her at 1775 Girard and obscured her sight seemed to have broken. She had been airlifted off the desert island. She would not be required to clean Abbott Hospital. The fact that I was refusing to participate in the hootenanny seemed to be her only serious source of discomfort. Her face wore that high-intensity look of adoration; no one else had such a pretty child as she. She wanted me to show off my voice to her fellow depressives. I tried, but when I opened my mouth, no sound came out.

My sense of my mother's fragility had been confirmed utterly. She was not a solid, intractable mass like my father. She was spun sugar. I had always, *always* known, and now everyone else knew, too.

Ruth was well into her forties before she began to offer those around her anecdotes about her childhood, but they were offered for consumption without her usual verve. Ruth was a performer; she didn't seek to please so much as she sought to entertain. It took her decades to find a way to talk about the world of her youth in a fashion that simply wouldn't break the hearts of those who loved her. Even so, her second husband would declare in the final years of her life, "When Ruth talks about her childhood, I cry." He wasn't exaggerating; tears filled his eyes and rolled down his face from under his enormous round spectacles. In thrall to my mother's narrative, he would sit stock-still like a man whose lifeblood was draining away. Ruth, on the other hand, remained dry-eyed. Out of consideration for her audience, she sought to disengage herself from the impotent child at the center of her own stories.

My mother's parents were natives of Missouri and Mississippi. Her father had been given away by his parents, who couldn't afford to feed him, to a Missouri farmer and his wife early in the century. The informal adoption of George Hines could be fairly characterized as a form of child enslavement. He was sheltered on the Missouri farm and was fed in return for his labor. Once, when he was still very small, the farmer's wife let George know that the fluffy white mess in the wooden tub she was stirring was candy. When it was done, she would give him some. The farmwife kept her promise to share her special concoction, but the white stuff turned out to be lye. When he was sixteen, George joined the navy. He was shipped to Europe to fight in the First World War. After a mustard gassing in France, he contracted tuberculosis. Rendered useless to his government and his adoptive parents before he was eighteen, George was dispatched by the military to a veterans hospital in Colorado where a nursing aid named Mabel helped him survive the ulceration of his lungs, though just barely.

Mabel had lived her adolescence in a house built just after the Civil War in Algiers, the Parish of Orleans, on the east side of the Mississippi. Hers was likely the first kindness George had ever known. He asked her to marry him and she accepted. George became a carpenter, and eventually a building contractor who supervised the construction of dozens of houses in and around Denver, specializing in one-story structures with sloping eaves, front porches, and a certain dependable symmetry of design, a style revered today as Craftsman. Three children were born: Betty Jean, Edna Ruth, and John. Something continued to burn inside George, however, and once the notion came to him, as it regularly did, the house would be sold, the family loaded into the Ford, and the journey back to Missouri begun. George found his own ten-acre farm there, lush with walnut and pecan trees and wild strawberries thriving in a carpet of violets. A natural spring kept crocks of butter and cream icy cold. George bought a sweet-tempered horse named Doll, and a Jersey cow, which soon bore a calf. Mabel worked hard to become, as she would recount decades later in a letter to her children, "that good and efficient Wife. Don't think I ever attained the efficiency part of my Wifely role," she added.

Mabel was a small woman prone to depression. She would sit, quiet and withdrawn, for days that sometimes stretched into weeks. In her mid-thirties, she was found to have a brain tumor, although for a long time her doctors suggested her symptoms could be resolved by hysterectomy surgery. George finally spoke up. "I think you're lookin' at the wrong end of that woman," he told Mabel's doctors. The tumor was reputedly the size of a softball. She had been suffering dizzy spells since the age of five, when her father, Meridian, Mississippi's, finest carpenter and most notorious drunk, struck her and caused her head to crash against the corner of a mahogany table. After that, Mabel's mother took her to New Orleans, away from the carpenter.

Mabel sought relief from her painful interior landscape in Christ. In a late-life letter to her eldest child, Betty, Mabel wrote, "So many thoughts crowd into my own heart and weary mind and the burden is so heavy, too feeble to overcome, by me alone. I have laid all the weariness, sinfulness, on the Lamb, Christ the Lord. They fit very well on him, far better than on me. The oppression of sin is terrific, I would have collapsed under the heavy burden. I am free now and so can you be, but it must be with a humble spirit and an honest desire for forgiveness."

It was Mabel's steady drumbeat about sin and her embrace of its oppression that weighed so formidably on Ruth when she was a child. Ruth was unlike her siblings; she was unlike anyone Mabel had ever known, for that matter, and that worried Mabel. She did the only thing she could think of to put her wayward child on a path toward righteousness: She warned her second-born that she was destined for eternal damnation. Johnnie and Betty would be saved. Edna Ruth was six, but already she was bound for an eternity spent in hell.

On her deathbed, when she could no longer speak, my mother wrote about Mabel for the edification of her oncologist, a doctor who made house calls. He was sitting next to her—his shoes off and his knees pulled up—on the empty space usually occupied by her husband. Ruth couldn't be bothered to discuss with him the progress of her cancer, or even her impending death, other than to note matter-of-factly, "Thank you for coming. I think I may be dying." She wrote instead about the brutal nature of religion, about Mabel's one great failing. "It all seem [sic] so garbagey to me—my mother the Christer. Hurting people seems what it is all about. I can be cruel but try not to seek justification for it. People are a lot part bad but when you know that, you look hard to find ways to be good."

Ruth never found the solution to her mother's passion for the Lord, or her own inability to conform to Mabel's specifications. She searched but simply couldn't find within herself the grievous sinfulness Mabel assured her was there. Instead, Mabel's escape into

Lutheranism sent Ruth down an entirely different path. Early on, she demonstrated a potent ability for fantasy. She seemed to require beauty and artistry in her life the way other people require oxygen, and from her earliest years, she was able to see beauty where none existed because she created it in her mind's eye. The gift stayed with her until she died.

Edna Ruth Hines, 1933

Ruth had been the middle child in her own family. Her older sister, Betty, was the recipient of everything good—and everything bad— George Hines could offer. Cruelty begets cruelty, and George had a great deal of cruelty reserved for Betty, his firstborn and apparent obsession. Ruth, at a loss, simply ran for cover. When she was fifty-seven, Ruth surprised me with a tearful, frantic rush of words that described how she had untied Betty's wrists from a rope strung to a ceiling beam, where George had hung the child before leaving one night. Ruth watched at the window for hours until George's car turned into the drive, then returned Betty to her ropes of torture.

"When I had a birthday," Ruth recalled very near the end of her life, "Betty got the pony. But when I was bad, Betty got the beating. Neither George nor Betty liked me very much for it, so I stayed away from both of 'em." She also wrote, "My brother & I decided that my father clearly loved my sister best."

This confusing, poisonous synergy of love and hate, favoritism wherein there can be no doubt a parent loves one child more than another, and the vain hope of pleasing someone who can never be pleased, were the psychic injuries my mother struggled for the rest of her life to erase from her history. When she began making art, however, those memories emerged.

In some of her work, she drew her creatures in a bucolic setting. She left behind an ink sketch of cows grazing in the field, for instance. The bodies of the cows are filled in with pale blue pastel; the grass is a soft yellow; there is no sense of competition or jealousy among these animals. In a lithograph, Ruth engraved a peculiar group of sheep (my brother thinks they are bison) who appear to be quiet, calm creatures, happy in their proximity and genetic connect-edness—in spite of the fact that they are stacked on top of one another like so many soda bottles. Nevertheless, in many of her pieces, as placid as they may seem to the casual observer, there is unmistakable familial pathos. *Sibling Rivalry* was the name of one of her favorite prints. Looking at it, one might see only a series of cows—someone else thought lions—at rest in a field, until one notices the sidelong glances being traded amongst these anxious, tortured beasts.

❖ ❖ ❖

Ruth was my muse as much as she was my mother. I was seven when she began her seductive dialogues with me about the many possibilities life offered. I retreated to my room and wrote a long story about the misadventures of a cat, with illustrations. She bound the pages together with a pale blue ribbon and declared me to be the author of a book. She carried it with her and showed it to other people. "This is Hillary's first book, you know," she would say. As the years passed, she fed me literature: Madeline L'Engle, Rumer Godden, the Brontës, F. Scott Fitzgerald, Jane Austen, William Golding,

John Dos Passos, and, as I was about to embark for prep school, J. D. Salinger.

I kept diaries in grade school, all of them dedicated to Ruth. Her faith in my writerly talent afforded me the hilarious combination of modesty and audacity to note in one of them: "I'm very smart in school except for arithmetics. I am very good in art and singing. I can write lovely stories and I am writing a book which I hope will be published." I also reported that I was ten years old and taking sleeping medicine every night.

Ruth's despair during her marriage to my father, a suffering that she finally couldn't keep under wraps, was something else again. Her pain was my burden, too; her annihilation was my annihilation. We were more than merely close: It was as if our bloodstreams had never been separated. Even then, I was alarmed that there was too much need on both sides. I hadn't a clue what to do about it.

❖ ❖ ❖

Ruth did her bin time and returned to a household in which little had changed outwardly. I was altered, however: I was worried all the time. My grandmother and grandfather, my father's parents, invited me to spend a weekend with them at their lakeside cabin in the North Woods. I went with my grandparents, but in spite of Sarah's gifts of wildflowers and empty snail shells, her breakfasts of waffles and wild raspberries, I couldn't stop talking about Ruth. I was barely able to keep my panic under control, in fact. Mommy was sad; I missed Mommy. No matter how many tree frogs we found on our walks through the virgin landscape or how many loons we counted on the lake at dusk, Sarah couldn't deter me from my single-minded concern. My grandmother teased me afterward about my infantile case of homesickness. But it was so much more serious than Sarah realized. Didn't she know? Ruth could *die*. When I arrived home at last and located Ruth, who was seated comfortably on the patio behind the house, smoking cigarettes, sipping gin, and reading a book, I was dumb with relief.

Ruth was seeing a shrink, Dr. Jepson. Every Wednesday morning that summer she and I would drive to the Fairview Medical Center next to the Southdale shopping mall in the suburb of Edina. I would seat myself on a swivel stool at the drugstore's soda counter and try to make a slice of apple pie last an hour. I wasn't allowed to eat sugary deserts at home. One morning, Ruth came to fetch me from the drugstore, saying she wanted Dr. Jepson to meet me. He turned out to be a small, meticulous man, blond and prim. He looked me over but said nothing. Ruth wore that expression, the one that demanded of him, "Isn't she marvelous?" but she was impatient with me, too. I couldn't think of anything clever to say to this man who was so important to her, and to me, since he was the person whose job it was to keep her alive. I had the same job, of course, but it was unofficial and I kept it to myself. A few months later, Ruth abruptly quit seeing Jepson. She had looked up at him during their session and discovered he was asleep.

❖ ❖ ❖

Our parents explained to Ethan and to me that Ruth was going to go to work when school started that year. She would be gone all day long. I was furious. I climbed on top of the refrigerator and refused to come down. Ruth let me stay there as long as I wanted. She was genuinely amused; she appreciated innocuous forms of deviancy. The next day, I resumed my siege, with Ruth's tacit approval. Pretty soon, I wasn't angry anymore, but I had grown fond of the vantage from atop the tallest appliance in our house. Ruth and I chatted and communed with each other just as always, except that I had a bird's-eye view of the scene. Eventually I got bored with the stunt and forgave Ruth her flight into the workplace. My mother was hired as the catering manager for the Edgewater Inn, a new restaurant by the Mississippi. She took me there for a lunch of thin slices of roast beef and horseradish, although as usual she herself barely ate. She wanted her boss and the rest of the staff to meet me.

My father acquiesced to Ruth's notion of employing a "live-in girl," someone who would take care of Ethan and me and—this was important to my father—help Ruth clean the house. In preparation, Ruth and I swept and dusted the deserted bedroom next to Ethan's. We cut peonies and baby's breath from the garden and put them in a vase next to the bed. I laid out a hairbrush and hand mirror on top of the bureau, returning to reassess their placement every few hours. My anticipation was so high, I announced the imminent arrival of our live-in girl at my third-grade show-and-tell.

Frannie Burt was seventeen. She came to us from a small town in Ohio, the eldest of four daughters. She had enormous blue eyes and an athlete's body. Her father, a baseball coach, had wanted a boy. Ruth immediately identified Frannie as a "ground gripper," high praise from Ruth. Frannie knew about girls my age. She taught me how to braid my own hair, and how to sing in harmony. She knew what words to say to make me go to bed without whimpering, even what words to say to insure that I actually slept. She let me perch on the arm of her chair and tease her hair into wild configurations. She trundled me around the lakes on my father's old bicycle; I sat on the crossbar. We sunned ourselves on the city's beaches, picnicking on Fresca and celery and smoked oysters packed in tins. We giggled hysterically about boys and their strange ways, but we each knew boys were our future.

Frannie was sacred. For a while it seemed that even without knowing we four needed saving, Frannie was going to save us. My father and Ethan treated Frannie with deference. With three females in residence, in fact, the fulcrum of power began to shift away from center.

My father gave in to Ruth's fervent desire to renovate the ancient kitchen. By the terms of a deal that had been struck between the couple, he was paying for Frannie to attend the University of Minnesota—mostly to insure that Frannie would stay with us for a very long time—and one of Frannie's first assignments was to read *War and Peace*. It fell to me to read the book aloud while Frannie and Ruth knocked down walls and ripped out cupboards. After workmen built new walls and installed glass cabinets, Ruth and Frannie painted while I continued to narrate the Russian classic from atop the refrigerator. Ruth was never happier. Speckled from head to toe with fine droplets of white enamel, she smoked endless cartons of Winstons and kept a succession of sweating beer bottles balanced on her ladder's topmost rung. She annotated my rendition of Tolstoy's masterpiece with wry, off-color observations about the lovesick characters. Having read the book as a child, Ruth knew exactly how the tale played out. Ours was a bawdy party that seemed to go on for days, although the two finished the kitchen well before I finished *War and Peace*.

❖ ❖ ❖

In spite of an occasional show of camaraderie, Ruth and my father remained at odds. One evening in late autumn, Ruth baked an eggplant she had stuffed with lamb, tomatoes, and garlic and served me a portion. We two were alone; my father hadn't been home for dinner for quite some time. Ruth was thirty-one, I was ten. She was so inordinately delicate in her manner, she scared me. When I had finished eating, she introduced a new topic: my father. Your father and I have decided to get a divorce, she finally said, Did that mean he wouldn't live with us anymore? I asked, stupefied. Yes, Ruth said.

A friend deterred my parents from their plan, "for the sake of the children," but their will dissolved two years later. After one spectacular fight, their marriage collapsed like an ancient, well-trod stairway crashing into the basement under the pressure of a single footfall.

There were three justifications for divorce in Minnesota in the 1960s: abandonment, adultery, or cruel and inhuman treatment. My father shouldered the role of villain and confessed to the last. When he asked one of his lawyer friends to represent Ruth in the dispute, she was too shellshocked to protest. She just wanted her connection to my father severed, whatever it took. The house at 1775 Girard was sold. Ruth offered not to seek alimony if, in addition to monthly child support, my father would pay the college tuitions of his children, a condition he readily accepted.

My brother and I found reasons to feel disappointed by my father in the decades ahead; that we disappointed him in myriad ways is beyond doubt. Still, unlike many men, he kept the legal commitment he made to us when we were children. He made his child-support payments in a timely fashion. He sent us to expensive schools. His desire for our success was never in question.

More than a year passed before my parents' divorce became final on June 15, 1964. Some of the "Findings of Fact" listed in the official decree were that "defendant did on various occasions during the course of the parties' marriage indicate to plaintiff that he hated her and no longer desired to live with her," and that "defendant was on numerous occasions during the course of the parties' marriage extremely critical of plaintiff in front of other people. That as a direct result of said cruel and inhuman treatment of the plaintiff by defendant, plaintiff was made sick, upset and nervous, and is unable to endure defendant any longer or to live with him."

"Here is my pitifully inadequate guideline to ENDING A MARRIAGE. (Think of it as a movie credit title with little scenes of joy & bliss overlaid—Okay?)" So began Ruth's letter, written eight years after her own divorce to a close friend who had just learned that her husband was leaving her. "A. Realize that 'it's over.' Do not think me cruel—or do think me so if it's therapeutic for you—but however much you may disbelieve that he could have forgotten the shared things that won't be happening anymore—they ain't gonna be happening baby and you must have protection—

"Protection A is they ain't gonna be & Protection B is what do you care? (He doesn't) & C (the most therapeutic of all) is there will be other good things to share with others or some ONE other—perhaps someone not yet discovered. . . .

"The concern I have is for you & the kids (guys always seem to make out) & you must be super strong now (ironically when your ego has to be at its lowest ebb). Oh! honey—I ache for you and a fat lot of good it will do for you. . . . I know that warm, loving, giving ladies, if they don't die of all that unrequited warmth, love & generosity by self pity & self hate (the other side of the coin) survive and prosper.

"Some dos and don'ts that are necessary to survival & prosperity:

"1) DON'T MAKE SCENES

"2) APPEAR TO BE REASONABLE (I know you can't be, but say to yourself 'what would a person who wishes to appear to be reasonable do at this point?')

"3) Don't be in a hurry.

"You can't go back to where it was & darling—after all the hurts—probably not under any conditions. Get free and open up to other options—in that order: free first & open then."

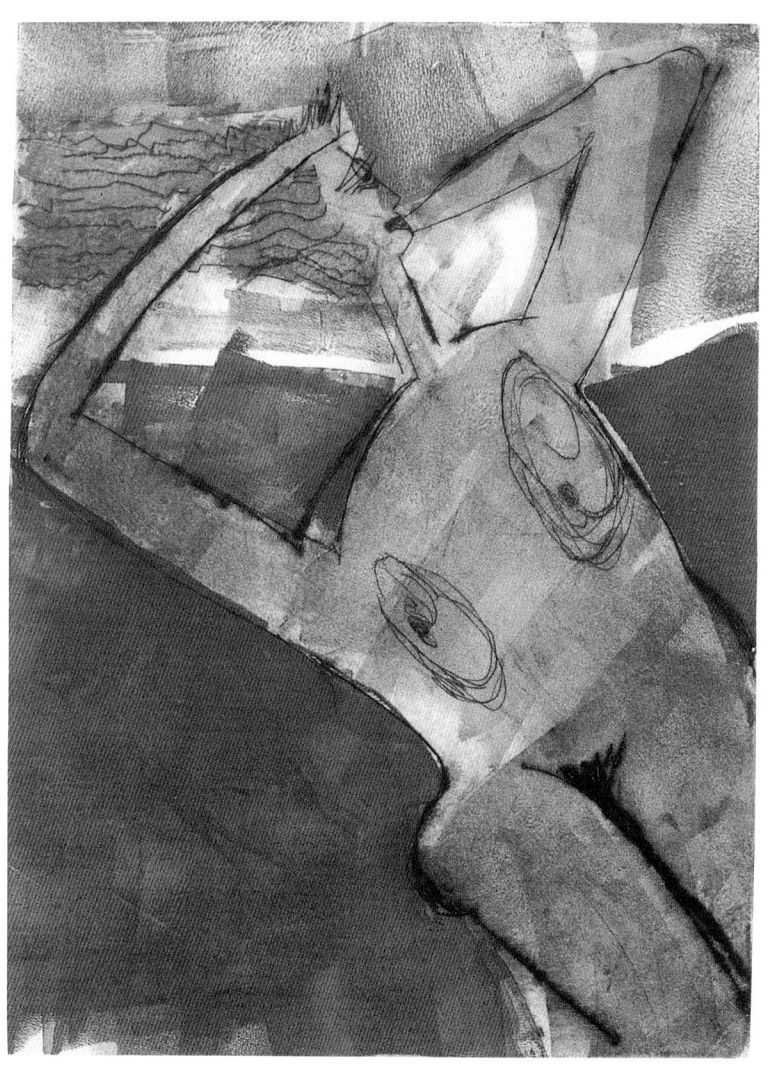

Ruth had a job managing public relations for the local symphony. One of her duties was to pick up visiting performers at the airport and chauffeur them on their press rounds. She owned a red Corvair. When it started, the Corvair got remarkable traction in the snow because its rear-mounted engine weighed the vehicle down in the right place, and because, like a Humvee precursor, it was built extremely low to the ground. On one occasion, Ruth met the American violinist Yehudi Menuhin and the opera singer Beverly Sills, who had arrived on the same flight. When the pair saw the Corvair, a discussion between them escalated into a lively debate over who would sit in the back. The rear seat was a plank about eleven inches deep; it afforded only a few inches of legroom. Menuhin finally clambered into the back, leaving Sills a generous bucket seat in the front next to Ruth, but the musician was understandably distraught that he would be required to stow his violin in the trunk with the spare tire to make room for himself.

Ruth was thirty-two. She wore a black cape with satin ties over her clothes instead of a proper winter coat. In the summer, she wore black linen sheaths and black pumps and pink lipstick. She tanned herself and had blond highlights bleached into her Amelia Earhart hair. She was a striking figure around the symphony, and a famous Russian musician in residence wanted desperately to sleep with her. A wiry, powerful young man, he would come directly from performances to our house in Kenwood. Dressed in his formal white shirt and tuxedo trousers, his black bow tie undone and hanging unevenly around his neck, he would sit on the sofa a good yard from my mother, one leg folded under him. When he spoke, he leaned in her direction, all sexual energy. The air was thick with his misery.

Only after Ruth was dead would I hear the strangely disappointing story from my stepfather: Ruth had finally let the musician have his way, in his house, on a bearskin rug in front of a blazing fireplace, when his wife was out of town. At the moment of his orgasm, the Russian shouted, "*J'arrive!*," a bit of pomposity Ruth simply couldn't forgive.

After the house on Girard was sold, Ruth found us an apartment in a house just a block away. Two interior decorators had transformed the old structure into a triplex. Simon and Reginald lived with their cocker spaniels in lavishly furnished quarters on the first floor; Simon's friend and occasionally his lover, Bob, a six-foot-four-inch, 250-pound blond who was an aspiring opera singer, was already installed in an apartment on the third floor when we moved in. As residents of the second floor, we found ourselves haplessly sandwiched in the middle of an often turbid love triangle. Objects and epithets would be flung up and down the stairwell when this triangle was stressed. We quickly learned not to venture into the stairwell at such times for fear of intercepting a hurled paperweight or book meant for Reginald's skull.

Our rooms were wallpapered in linen. Ruth's bedroom, meant to be a den, had a charming fireplace. A graceful wrought-iron balustrade curved up the stairs and into our apartment. With the child-support payments plus Ruth's and Frannie's salaries—Frannie had dropped out of school to go to work—we could just manage the bills. Indeed, though the process was subtle, Ruth, Ethan, and I were just starting our descent into the predictable economic pattern of a middle-class divorce, in which the husband prospers while the children and first wife end up clinging to whatever floats their way in an effort not to slip into the underclass. In our trio, Ruth was by far the most vulnerable.

Not long after we moved in, the entire house was photographed for a national magazine. When I arrived home from school that particular day, I discovered our furniture and art had been rearranged; someone had even hastily painted two gilt end tables with black lacquer. We were unnerved by the intrusion, but we liked the changes and didn't complain.

❖ ❖ ❖

My father tried hard to sustain his relationship with me. He took me to the symphony on Friday nights. He had acquired a white Corvette with red leather seats; his new law practice was going well. Our standing engagement gradually took on the ritual quality of dating. I put on makeup and stockings and struggled with my hair, trying to force it into a flip at my shoulders. He picked me up at a precise time and returned me exactly three hours later. He was gentlemanly and formal. My own maturation, a process involving not only physical change but emotional and intellectual changes as well, had continued in the years he had been fighting with Ruth and living in the hotel by Loring Park. He had missed the gradual shifts and permutations of thought in his daughter. My transformation from little girl to pert adolescent must have seemed sudden and strange to him. Neither of us really knew how to behave with each other except to be unfailingly polite. In the years ahead, although we occasionally regressed into hostilities, we never got beyond polite. In my early thirties, a television commercial in which a woman strolled a beach with her silver-haired dad, their arms entwined in a comfortable embrace, caused me to feel something close to physical pain.

One summer evening I saw my father's Corvette come to a sharp halt in front of the house we shared with Simon and Reginald. Ruth was gone. My parents took care they would never have to meet. The divorce was final and my father had come to let Ethan and me know he would be marrying his secretary. She had an infant son he planned to adopt. She had come to Minneapolis from South Dakota and was living in Owatana, a distant and dreary suburb of Minneapolis. Ruth immediately dubbed my father's intended "Miss

Owatana." It was hopeless, as far as she was concerned: pink flamingos, Miss Owatana—her former husband simply had no taste or sense of style. She was well out of it.

My father's bride was thin and tall, like Ruth; she had a boy's clipped haircut, like Ruth's. She smoked cigarettes with such desperation her delicate head and broad shoulders seemed permanently enshrouded by a cloud of pale carbon. Her long-fingered hands, their nails chewed to the quick, frequently shook. She was five years older than Ethan, with a waiflike quality. She was shy with us, and we with her. We wished her no ill. In fact, that prescient part of me, an unbidden intelligence that had been extant in childhood but which lately had begun to recede, experienced a kind of dread on her behalf.

As she would confess some years later, Ruth was frightened. My father was getting on with things; he was growing richer, more secure. Her life was moving in the other direction. The Minneapolis symphony was becoming important, and its directors wanted a professional public-relations person who could transport famous visiting artists in a serious car, one that wouldn't deflate the artist's self-esteem prior to his or her performance. Ruth had no money to buy such a vehicle, and the symphony wanted to spend its money in other ways. More worrisome, she had no education beyond high school, no "marketable" skills, as she often said. Ethan and I would be all right, she assumed; we would be educated. Ruth, on the other hand, was experiencing life as a divorced woman like a forced bungee jump.

❖ ❖ ❖

My stepfather, Clayton, began to call upon Ruth in 1964, the summer my father married his secretary. Ruth agreed to the dinner invitations because she was lonely and he was insistent.

He was hardly a stranger. Ruth and her first husband had been friends with Clay and his former wife for a decade. The latter was the proprietor of a toy store catering to people who wanted to buy expensive, European-made baubles for their children. The couple, who had five children, divorced less than a year after Ruth and my father separated for the last time. My stepfather had been intrigued by Ruth for years. Now he was free to pursue her.

After months of platonic dating, he chose to rest his palm on the small of her back while she sat next to him, sipping a martini, at the bar of one of their favorite restaurants. The weight of his hand on her back just at that moment changed everything in an instant. She loved him, plain and simple. She knew it all at once when he touched her that day in that place. Seeking to infect Ethan and me with her enthusiasm, she would tell us, "He has such a beautiful *head*."

Until then, our only competition for our mother's attention had been the books she read compulsively. Clay's burgeoning monopoly on her was something new; he seemed to have her soul in his grip. One day, in a show of unanimity that was new to us, and to her, Ethan and I confronted Ruth. She was our *mother*—why didn't she act like it? Ruth was amazed. She didn't seem to recognize that what we were saying might be true, at least for us. She promised she would do better. We were appeased, and for a while we saw more of her, but then she reverted.

Atlas

In ninth-grade civics class, we were required to report on a career we wanted for ourselves. I was going to be a journalist. Although the original plan, devised some years before, was to be an author of novels, Ruth pointed out that I would have to do something to earn money while I was *becoming* a novelist. It was she who suggested journalism. I worked hard on my report; I even interviewed some newspaper reporters. I had four pages to read, but my presentation came to a premature end when I misspoke in the first paragraph. I notified my classmates that I planned to acquire a "bastard's" degree in journalism. In no time at all, the class was out of control. I, too, struggled for composure, but was finally ordered to sit down.

Early on, the prettiest Kenwood girls had gathered themselves into a clique and unintentionally made everyone else feel hopelessly inferior throughout the ensuing three years of junior high school. I was contemptuous of them and their aspirations to be pom-pom queens and style arbiters. In fact, the prospect of spending yet another three years with this crowd in public high school was loathsome to me. I had caught Ruth's mania: I wanted out of Minneapolis—anywhere would be better. An escape route presented itself with my introduction to Susan Smith, the daughter of a University of Minnesota professor of religion. She was new to the city and to the school. As our friendship deepened, she revealed she would not be attending high school in Minneapolis. She was bound for a boarding school in Massachusetts, the school her sister and brother had attended before they enrolled in Radcliffe and Yale. I had never heard the phrase "prep school" until meeting Susan, but the instant she began to describe these institutions, I felt certain prep school was for me—if only my father would pay for it.

*   *   *

Ethan and I were pretty much on our own in those years. We knew the difference between good behavior and bad, and Ruth clearly believed that, left to our own devices, we would choose goodness. Her judgment on this matter was correct, but it also meant we didn't have any particular curfew; I don't recall there being such a thing as "dinnertime" in our household; we found our own amusements after school and in the evenings; no one rode us about our homework. We were without supervision, and our situation was so widely known throughout the neighborhood that the mothers of most of my friends were wary of letting their children spend time at my house.

Ruth was thirty-five. She had left the symphony and was working for the state's employment agency. Some portion of her salary each month was usually lost to one of the farm boys who had come to the big city from Iowa or North Dakota to find work, only to discover there was no work for them. If they came into Ruth's office and tearfully reported that they had no money to keep their children fed over the weekend, or were about to be evicted, Ruth would open her handbag and give them cash. Her job was grim. She was paid on commission and she rarely had money. On Friday nights, which Clay had unilaterally declared "Independent Activities Night," she toured the expensive downtown bars with her friend John Cash, a stockbroker who had his suits made in London and who always picked up the check.

John was gay; he loved Ruth as much as a friend can love another friend. Without trying, Ruth drew men to the pair and they both flirted. Ruth also dropped in at gay bars with her escort. "Fair's fair, I say," Ruth would assert. Her evenings with John were, in Ruth's parlance of the day, "gassy." Occasionally, tavern owners would ask Ruth for proof she was of drinking age. "I got carded!" she would boast to Frannie and me the next day. But they were also the evenings when she felt the most impotent, the most wounded. If she drank enough, she could make those feelings disappear. For the next several years, Friday nights turned into the hours of the week when Ruth engaged in a purposeful demolition of her conscious mind.

Ruth and I were close then; our bond was not broken, or even weak. I never doubted her love, and she never gave me a moment's reason to do so. Further, she had instilled in me a sure sense that my life *had* to be different from hers, that what had happened to her must not happen to me. We never once talked about marriage or babies; we talked only about the fact that I was going to be a writer, that I needed to acquire practical skills, that I must never count on being supported by someone else. Being pretty wasn't enough, she told me. Beauty was a kind of black hole for a woman, a dangerous trap, she seemed to imply, when it existed in the absence of a profession. *Feminism* was not a word on anyone's lips in those years. This was simply information that Ruth knew to be absolutely true; if she could make her daughter understand nothing else, she had to make her understand this.

By the time I was thirteen, I felt grown up, capable of making my own decisions, capable even of leaving Ruth. The Northfield School for Girls, with its pamphlets advertising little throngs of girls reading in the grass under the shade of leafy sugar maples, all-girl choirs whose participants wore white robes, biology teachers in shorts and tennis shoes pointing out the flora and fauna of Connecticut River tributaries, inspired in me a raging ambition to be part of this idyll.

My father drove me to the school for an interview. I was so overwhelmed by the gravity of the event that I could barely speak to the gentle, gray-haired Miss Bettina Otto, who conducted the interview. I cried afterward, certain my shyness had destroyed my chances. Instead, my long-standing terror of math turned out to be the stumbling block. I had failed ninth-grade algebra at Jefferson Junior High. So had my friend Tyson, Mary McCarthy's niece. Together, we had wished our teacher dead, and we were horrified to learn he had been killed the following summer when a train struck his car at a railroad crossing.

Ruth was convinced from the start that my prospects for admission to this grand institution were poor. She warned me to expect rejection. She was trying to protect me from what she believed was inevitable failure. I had certain gifts, of that she was sure, but I was unlikely to prosper in a rigid intellectual setting. When I was thirteen, I believed her. Still, I pressed on, desperate to avoid the living death of public high school in Minneapolis.

In the spring of my final year of junior high school, the admissions committee at Northfield informed me by letter that I would be welcome in the fall, as long as I took a remedial summer course in algebra. The night before the notice arrived, Ruth again warned me to prepare myself for the eventuality of attending West High, which I was already calling "Waste High." I was probably a fringe candidate for Northfield, she suggested. When we learned of the school's decision, Ruth embraced me and we hugged for a long time, but she made no effort to hide her astonishment.

My grandmother Sarah pleaded with me to stay home. Ruth needed me too much, Sarah said. Ethan was leaving for Berkeley in the fall, and I was Ruth's *baby*. Ruth would not survive the loneliness, Sarah insisted. My heart was hardened. Who in their right mind would forego Northfield for Waste High? Besides, it was her lover's job now to keep Ruth alive.

I was the only student in the summer algebra course taught at Blake School, a boys' private day school where Ethan had attended high school. Each day, for three hours, I sat in a state of white-hot embarrassment struggling to understand algebra. In time, the futility of the exercise was apparent to the instructor and to me. He issued me a C grade sheerly out of compassion; I had tried, harder than most.

I was still thirteen when I left for Massachusetts the following September. My father drove me there in his luxurious black Studebaker. I tried to seem casual on the trip, but a wheel was spinning frantically in my head. Susan Smith was fulfilling a family birthright. I was a rogue, a girl who, even with the finest tutoring, remained impervious to algebra; a girl in flight from a tumultuous past for which she had no vocabulary. I feared my acceptance had been an eleventh-hour decision by the school; I was second or third string, admitted only because someone smarter had dropped out; my purported acceptance had been a clerical error that would quickly be rectified when I showed up on the doorstep of Merrill Keep Hall with my rusty steamer trunk. None of these fears turned out to be true, but their shadows crowded my subconscious for years.

❖ ❖ ❖

Northfield was the great feast I had imagined it to be, but it was one I seemed incapable of enjoying. I lasted two years instead of three, unable to bend to the ways of what felt to me like a convent. Everyone had a nickname; mine was H. Jesus. I was suffering, that was clear to all, and sometimes the suffering was so profound and almost comically sad, it was as if I was suffering on behalf of everyone else, too. "I'm sick of running around for people obeying the rules," I wrote to Ruth after I had been at the school exactly three weeks. I never studied; I socialized instead, distracting my studious dorm mates. Quite predictably, I failed geometry that first year and required tutoring the next. I failed all my Bible courses. I even failed a gym class in folk dancing; I simply never attended.

I soon acquired the identity of bad girl, which fit very well on me. I attended church on Sunday naked but for my trench coat, wearing a folded newspaper on my head, since hats were mandatory, or else I hid in my room. I smoked cigarettes late at night and kept the stubs in a Pepsi can tucked away in a desk drawer. I was a practitioner of the outlawed PDOA—public display of affection—with the boys I dated at the school across the river, Mt. Hermon. For the sadistic purpose of alarming my kindly dorm mother, however, I pretended I was a lesbian while on her turf. My brother's letters from Berkeley, where the Free Speech Movement was in full swing, came addressed to me, Director of Subversive Activities, Merrill Keep Hall.

Every letter from my father contained an admonition to spend less money, to expect less money, or an outright denial of my requests for money. When I look at the letters I exchanged with Ruth during those two years, I realize how much we were, in our own ways, burdened by a lack of money. The first day of school my dorm mother lent me twenty dollars to pay for my books. I had no money to fly home for Thanksgiving and my roommate invited me to her uncle's house in Connecticut. Ruth was working at the AAA Employment Agency in downtown Minneapolis, where she was known, in her words, "as the friggin' office nigger lover," and again earning a salary based on commissions. Over a period of several weeks she managed to save the grand sum of fifty dollars so that I could make that Connecticut trip. My handbag—a red leather envelope with a bamboo latch containing the fifty dollars—was stolen the moment I set it down on the ticket counter at Grand Central. My roommate paid my trainfare to Connecticut. Her aunt and uncle implored me to call my mother and tell her what had happened. They were unable to comprehend that I could not make that call.

Ruth was living alone for the first time in her life. She had a small apartment downtown, minimally furnished but for a nascent art collection. Sometimes, late at night, she would plead with Frannie to visit. After Ruth died, Frannie told me she would find Ruth in her panties and a sweatshirt, nearly out of her mind with loneliness. My mother never let on. "Went out with kindly old John Cash Friday night," she would write to me. "The rest of the week Clay fed me. I seem to be eating rather well these days."

When I was a junior, she wrote, "Clay has been terribly nice to me since his return from Europe but I am sure it's temporary and the honeymoon will soon be over. . . . I suppose I should get on with the rest of my life so I shan't be cracked up when it's 'over.' Right?" Her letters always advised me, "get skinny," or "don't eat," and frequently were accompanied by prescription "diet pills," supplied in due compliance with my own desperate-sounding pleas for the drugs.

In the winter of my second year, I experienced the urge to kill myself; I thought I would take my metal compass, the tool I had acquired to navigate the shoals of geometry, and pierce a vein in my wrist. The bleakness of the moment passed. Near the end of that school year, it was clear to all interested parties I would not be returning to Northfield, no matter how much the shrink I was seeing at the school urged me to come back. In his view, however much I disliked Northfield, it was better than life on the homefront as I had innocently described it to him.

My departure had a lot to do with smoking. Just before school ended that spring, my Pepsi-can ashtray was unearthed during one of my dorm mother's white-glove inspections and I was summoned to the headmaster's office. Dr. Meany allowed as how I would be welcomed back the following year, but I would be grounded until Christmas as punishment for smoking. The tweedy gent and I looked each other dead in the eye: He was proposing a jail sentence I could never endure. The only reason to leave the campus was to go to Mt. Hermon. The boys at our brother school, with their newly shaven faces, their English Leather and Royal Lime scents, their welcoming hands, were what mattered most to me then. I let him know on the spot that I would not be coming back. Northfield had always been too good, too fine a place, for someone like me, anyway. It made sense at the time.

My choice meant I would miss the big dance of the year. Ruth, who referred to the headmaster as the "sniveling Dr. Meany," wrote in consolation, "Sorry you won't have an opportunity to go to the fucking spring formal, lovely daughter, but I suppose both of us will recover from the disappointment, right?" I had recently taken up swearing, and in a comradely gesture, so had she. She signed her letters, "Much love to my beautiful girl child," or simply, "Love mamma," though once she wrote, "I can't even remember how many humps there are in mamma, now."

The shrink was right, of course. Thirty-three years have passed, and I still regularly dream I am back at Northfield being shuttled periodically from room to room in Merrill Keep Hall by my friends like a passenger on some underground railroad. I am living there secretly, unknown to the authorities. It isn't the way I would have preferred, but at least I'm back.

❖ ❖ ❖

Ruth married for the second time late in the spring of 1968. The occasion was momentous for Ruth, coming as it did after a long courtship during which she never, not even for a moment, had been confident of her beloved's love for her. The night she wed, she was confident. She had married, as she would declare countless times in the years ahead to anyone who cared to listen, the love of her life.

I was sixteen and a senior when I began public high school the previous autumn. Ruth and Frannie and I were reunited, living in an apartment in Kenwood, though we were as independent of one another as three people sharing living space could be. Ruth spent her weekends and most of her weeknights with her lover. I, too, was tied to the love of my own young life. I lived for the three o'clock school bell that marked my release from prison. At the sound, I would run through the hallways to the parking lot, where he awaited me in his Volkswagen Beetle. We would race home, smoke a joint, and spend the next three hours in my bed. We were dressed, sitting on the love seat in front of the bay window, sharing a Coke, by the time Ruth came home from work. "Hello, children!" Ruth would call brightly when she saw us.

My boyfriend stayed overnight on weekends; there wasn't a chance in the world that Ruth would be home then, or so we assumed. In the early hours of one Sunday morning, however, we heard Ruth enter the darkened apartment. She walked in the direction of my bedroom. She had raised the subject of marriage with her love that night, and he had replied that she was free to marry anyone she liked. As for himself, he was enjoying the single life. She had folded her clothes and toothbrush into the grocery bag that was her weekend traveling case and left his apartment. My partner, who was six feet, three inches tall and nineteen years old, pulled the covers over his head like a five-year-old with night terrors. Ruth stood over my narrow bed in the blackness. She leaned down until I could smell her cologne and her sweet, boozy fragrance. She kissed my cheek tenderly, leaving her tears on my skin. I didn't move. "Good night, darling," she whispered, as if the words were sacred. "I love you." Then she went to her bedroom and slept.

Ruth would assert her parental authority only occasionally, and always, it seemed to me, at the most inopportune times. Once, I dropped acid on Saturday morning at my boyfriend's house. He lived in one of those Kenwood mansions; his father was a real-estate mogul; his mother had committed suicide when he was in ninth grade. We had known each other, and loved each other, since I was thirteen. We liked our purple Osley LSD so much, we swallowed a second dose an hour later. Through the resulting haze, I heard someone calling me to the phone. I approached the slimy mound of black licorice attached to the wall, unsure which part to speak into. I heard a voice coming at me as if through a five-mile tunnel, demanding I return home immediately to clean my room. Ruth might as well have asked me to orbit the planet using my arms as wings. I dropped the receiver on the floor and spent the next sixteen hours seeking to evade what I imagined was a police manhunt. When I tiptoed into my bedroom, hallucinating wildly, at four A.M., I encountered an unforgettable symbol of Ruth's contempt for my messy ways: She had jammed my leather-covered cigarette lighter into a jar of mayonnaise and pitched the lid-less jar into the center of my unmade bed. Apparently I had finally surpassed Ruth's tolerance for my swinish habit of leaving the mayonnaise jar sitting open and unrefrigerated on the kitchen counter. I slept until noon.

When I emerged from my bedroom, shaky and jangled, Ruth sat facing me, her eyes full of worry and rage. I believe she had finally realized, in what surely must have been a disturbing epiphany, that I was well beyond her control and had been for some time.

I couldn't tell her about the acid trip—I routinely left my marijuana paraphernalia lying all over my room, but even Ruth's laissez-faire parenting had its limits—therefore I could offer no explanation as to why I had been unable to return home and clean my room the day before. Our argument escalated into a surreal battle during which I lofted a large vase filled with roses off a plant stand and pitched it at her head. She ducked, and the vessel exploded on contact with the wall, sending water and vegetation in every direction. We looked at each other for a moment, each of us thinking about what had just happened: I had tried to break a very large piece of pottery against her head. There was no forgiveness in her face and I fled.

Ruth caught up with me on the landing of the exterior stairway that led up to our apartment. She wrapped her hands around my neck and began to shake me; had the weathered wood railing collapsed, we would have fallen two stories onto asphalt. Just then my boyfriend arrived. He took the stairs three at a time until he reached us. Ruth and I were crying. I clung to him for safety, and then Ruth put her arms around us both. "I'm sorry, children," she said. We stood for some time, heads bowed, in a three-way embrace; had anyone seen us, they might have imagined we were praying, which, in a fashion, we were.

In April that year, Ruth announced with a glad heart that she had ended her long affair. She was pulling up her socks and getting on with things. She had that manic quality about her that comes with the relief of ending a relationship that is equal parts torture and pleasure. She was suddenly interested in everything. Her love retreated for three and a half weeks. Then he stepped into Ruth's life again, proposing marriage. She took a few days to think about the invitation.

Ruth's wedding ceremony was one or two minutes in length, conducted in the living room of the couple's new apartment by a judge who was also a friend. Their wedding cake was made of bagel dough, layered with lox, frosted with sour cream, and decorated with poppy seeds. Another friend brought leis of white and lavender orchid blooms and draped them in triplicate around the necks of the newlyweds. The soundtrack from *La Dolce Vita* played on the stereo. Ruth was thirty-nine. She wore a linen suit with gold buttons and a pink and orange–patterned scarf tied at her throat. She was very blond, very thin. In the few snapshots that survive, she is never without champagne and a cigarette. She loved Clay, she loved me, she loved her friends, and now, at last, she truly loved her life. It all showed on her face: Her smile was like a searchlight boring through the dense fog of the world.

I left the wedding after an hour, having dropped acid thirty minutes before my departure according to a plan my boyfriend and I had agreed upon some days before. I took two of the leis with me. The wedding cake had not yet been cut. My boyfriend was waiting outside; my stepfather found him lacking in charm. In the car, I managed to change from my short white dress and push-up bra to my jeans with the paisley fabric sewn into the outside seams and a sleeveless handmade top so loosely knit it exposed my nipples. I wrapped a leather headband around my hair, tying it in a knot at the back. We sped to Dania Hall, a turn-of-the-century labor union hall that, by 1968, was merely a slum and a dance hall for hippies. It was where the beautiful people went, I once told Ruth.

My letters and diaries of the era describe serious depressions. Only a few people seemed to see it: the shrink with the watery blue eyes I used to talk to every few weeks at my boarding school; a few teachers who tried without success to befriend me. Some mornings, I would tell Ruth I simply didn't feel like going to school. "I understand, dear," she would say, in complete sympathy. "I'll write you a note." I attended Waste High four days out of every five; I spent my lunch hours and pep rally time smoking joints behind the football team's equipment locker. My boyfriend and I took amphetamines, big shiny capsules called black widows, and stayed up for days; by the end of the school year, I had to clutch at my skirts to keep them from sliding off my body. The two of us lived like orphans who felt whole and alive only in each other's presence. Sex sealed our connection utterly. A door had only to close, encapsulating us in a room—any room—and we would sink to the floor, his lips on my face, tearing at each other's clothes.

Childish presumptions about being a writer, my eagerness to be very good at *something,* and the intimacy with Ruth I had felt as a little girl—a feeling that was connected up to those dreams—had vanished like the helium from a punctured party balloon. I can't name the hour or day it happened; I simply know that by the time Ruth married, happily this time, I didn't feel eager or hopeful about anything. I was drifting, inhabiting a nation for which my mother would never seek a passport. Those things that had moved me in my childhood were entirely forgotten. I had some sophistic political notions—something about Vietnam, the ruling class, the military-industrial complex, and the white mother country that had spawned it all. I put my trust in Huey Newton, Jimi Hendrix, Chairman Mao, and the Pill. On October 21, 1967, at the Pentagon, I had carried a sign bearing a caricature of Lyndon Johnson, underneath which appeared the words "I'd love to turn you on," as if the greatly hallowed "enlightenment" afforded by a few tokes would inspire a President to radically alter war policies. "How many kids will you kill today?" I had shouted ragefully with the rest of the raggedy civilians.

Ruth, on the other hand, was starting life anew. She loved deeply, and now she was loved in return. She was looking forward to the rest of her new life, and enjoying each minute of her marriage. She had a raw, imperishable optimism about her. She was shot through with pleasure.

A veritable lifetime passed, Ruth was fatally ill, and I stood before her in her living room struggling to make amends that first summer. "I've been a bad daughter," I insisted, not knowing where to begin, or precisely how I had failed her, but just then certain I had done so. Ruth was puzzled. She assured me I had been a wonderful daughter. When it became apparent that little she could say would confer salvation, however, she confessed that she wished I had not left her wedding prematurely. She had held this slight inside her for twenty-one years. In contrast to the monstrous cruelties I suspected I had committed, my early departure from her wedding seemed to me to be the mildest, most forgettable sin of all, a bubble of sea foam riding on a noisy breaker of misdeeds. My mother saw it differently: She had forgiven everything, but the fact that I had deliberately and with premeditation snubbed the cardinal event of her life still hurt.

The day after I graduated high school, I flew to Berkeley to live with Ethan, arriving with the clothes I wore, a copy of *One Flew Over the Cuckoo's Nest*, and what remained after my plane fare of a five-hundred-dollar reward from my father for having actually graduated. I was seventeen. The third night I was there, I sustained a bruising blow to my back when an Alameda County sheriff cornered me in an alley during a riot; the entire town lived under an eight o'clock curfew for much of the rest of that summer. By August, my circumstances radically reduced, I could often be found with the rest of the panhandlers on Telegraph Avenue. A few friends from Northfield, having graduated, drove west that summer on a lark before starting classes at their Ivy League colleges. They tried to find me, but I was lost out there for some time.

I never lived with Ruth again.

Part Three

I was nineteen when I finally shrugged off the boy and psychedelia, and found my one true religion. My ancestors, paternal and maternal—Ruth being an obvious exception—had demonstrated a weakness for messianic seduction in several directions. I, too, was ripe. Like any good religion, this one ushered out my fog of confusion and revealed the world in vivid new colors. The cosmos of human relationships was clarified in an instant, as was my own turmoil. A door swung wide. I stepped through and came out the other side nearly insane with outrage and to-the-death devotion to certain principles. I am referring to feminism. I don't believe more than a few weeks passed between the afternoon when a friend innocently defined for me a brand-new phrase, "male chauvinism," and my acquisition of the can of spray paint I used to write "Women Only" diagonally on the front door of my apartment. The Reverend Moon himself couldn't have worked with greater speed.

I was in the Midwest again, and living dangerously. I tossed a drink in a man's face in a bar because he dared touch the breast of a friend of mine. I was chased around the pool table by bikers eager to split my skull until the bouncer intervened and shoved me out of the establishment with a warning never to return. I bought more spray paint and each morning before dawn slowly worked my way, with like-minded zealots, through the moonscape of Minneapolis in search of sexist billboards. Our message, in three-foot block letters: THIS EXPLOITS WOMEN. In our pockets we carried hard-to-remove Day-Glo stickers lettered with the same phrase, ready to plaster them on absolutely anything, even people. I held consciousness-raising groups in my living room during which an interesting assortment of women talked about their oppression; no matter how seriously we began, we always ended in nearly uncontrollable bouts of laughter. Those sessions had a happy, familiar feel to me: They were just another Friday night in Merrill Keep Hall, except that the consequence for many of the participants was divorce.

I was thrilled when, walking along the street with another woman, two businessmen began soliciting us, backing us into a corner, and my companion suddenly pulled a handgun from her fringed and beaded bag and pointed it at one of their heads. "Say it again!" she told him. She made them swear they would never do that again to another woman and then they retreated on tiptoe, apologizing. It's a war, I remember thinking at the time, a fucking *war*. Soon thereafter, I braided my hair into a honey-colored rope ending several inches below my shoulder blades; using a pair of rusty shears, I sawed the braid off at the nape of my neck.

One day, my father, whom I rarely saw, arrived unannounced at my apartment on the West Bank, the slum student neighborhood on the west side of the Mississippi, with the woman who would be his third wife. My father had found his ideal companion at last: a woman so steadfast, so resolute, her children called her "the Rock." Like my mother, he, too, was now settled for life. The couple tried hard to ignore a poster displayed prominently in the foyer: a photograph of a plaster of Paris penis the size of a mummy, decorated with stars and stripes, jutting out of a trash can. "I would like you to meet my daughter," my father said to his intended in his best formal fashion. I wasn't invited to the wedding; my father notified me after the fact.

I considered the miniskirted, eyelash-batting Gloria Steinem a con artist and an embarrassment to the cause. Betty Friedan was too middle class to stomach. Valerie Solanas, on the other hand, was a genius, her *Scum Manifesto*, poetry. Kate Millet, having produced *Sexual Politics*, her fresh literary analysis of venerated authors like D. H. Lawrence and Henry Miller, was brilliant. Together with my most ardent sister-in-arms, I dreamed of blowing up, in simultaneous splendor, every Playboy Club around the world. Our only stumbling block was devising a means of warning the women without alerting the men. We were flummoxed. "Chicks under the table!"

the two of us used to shout at each other by way of greeting. "Women's Liverashun," as we sometimes called it, was rich with comedy; it was men who were entirely lacking in humor.

"You'll get over this," one of my stepbrothers told me as we sat drinking wine at a sidewalk café in Paris that year, 1969. Ruth and her husband had generously treated us to a trip to Europe; we were repaying them by playing at sulky, ersatz existentialism all over the Continent.

"No, I'll never get over this," I told him.

As things turned out, my stepbrother was correct. I got over it. Eighteen years later, I found myself sitting before "Satan" himself, Hugh Hefner, his grizzled head framed by the nipples on a naked bust of Barbi Benton just behind him, his Pepsi-stoked eyes burning into mine, as he defended for six hours—when I finally ran out of tape—his starring role in the Sexual Revolution for the readers of *Rolling Stone*. The Playboy Clubs had just closed worldwide due to lack of patronage, the Playboy logo was about as low rent as a corporate logo could possibly be, and Hefner was being accused—by other men—of fostering an environment that encouraged the rape and murder of women. I didn't go home and dance on a tabletop. I didn't even call my old friend—by then an attorney—with whom I had plotted the destruction of the Playboy empire, to share some laughs. Public Enemy Number One of yore was just a self-deluded old man. My meeting with him signified little more than the fast-approaching deadline of another magazine article.

When I was nineteen, however, Ruth, on whose behalf Betty Friedan had raised her voice, was bewildered by this tsunami of rage that had me declaring sex was rape and reciting from memory Valerie Solanas's homicidal musings. Her brows would furrow with worry when I began my rants, but she never tried to argue with me. She recognized the elemental truths swirling beneath the wrath. A culturally sanctioned tyranny had been abroad in the land for some time. Moreover, she had suffered from it so much more than I ever would. She had lived "behind the ironing board of life," as actress

Ruby Dee once described it, for fifteen years of marriage to my father. But we diverged in a significant way: She could not comprehend the hard-hearted anger that burned inside me. She rather liked men, she admitted in a quiet, testing-the-waters entreaty one afternoon, as if waiting to see whether I could handle such a confession without throwing her furniture out the windows. Every once in a while, she continued when I failed to react, men had surprised her with acts of kindness or generosity, something unexpected and perfectly timed to ease her life. And that was why she just couldn't hate the way I hated.

Ruth in a hotel in Paris, early 1960s

When I was in my early twenties, many of my contemporaries claimed that feminism had saved their lives. Had they missed out, they believed, they would have gone insane, killed themselves, ended up on the street. I believe I felt similarly at the time, although I think now we all would have found a way to live our lives without becoming bag ladies. In my case, feminism was like a tempest that blew the sand off a long-undisturbed memory. It roiled my recollections of the childhood I had spent with Ruth, the lilac-scented, pre-divorce years on Girard Avenue during which she told me again and again I could be anything I wanted to be for the simple reason that she loved me, and most especially that I was already—though a child—a writer. Feminism returned me to that state of innocence. I discovered that I wanted to do good; I wanted to be a reporter and a debunker. I was, for the first time since those distant enchanted years, full of hope and heart-pounding ambition.

Having dropped out of college once, I now returned fired with purpose. I hated the dull courses I had to take to get where I wanted to be—inside the journalism department at U.C. Berkeley—so I wore blinders, looking neither right nor left, only toward the future that awaited. I had a kind of warrior quality: I spurned men as if they were funhouse goblins set in my way to entice me from my goal. Dressed in jeans and a surplus fatigue jacket from Vietnam bearing the name DeCaro, my hair shorn unbecomingly, I worked my way through nearly two years at the University of Minnesota and then transferred to Berkeley, not as a seventeen-year-old panhandler and rioter who hurled bricks at the windows of the Berkeley branch of the Bank of America, but as a journalist-in-training. I was twenty-one the day I entered a small classroom to take my first journalism course: Newswriting 101. Before the class started, a fellow who was taking the course as a lark intruded on the sacred moment by inviting me to dinner. I brushed him off like a fly that had settled on my sleeve.

All those failures in boarding school, the heartfelt identity of "bad girl," were forgotten. I tunneled my way through the undergraduate journalism courses, and most of the graduate ones. *Harper's* bought the first magazine piece I ventured to write, a class assignment, and I was being published in the *San Francisco Chronicle's* Sunday magazine. I learned at the end of my junior year that I had been inducted into Phi Beta Kappa; assuming some overzealous sorority was trying to rush me, I tossed the letter. My professors called me Hildy. They invited me to speak at the J-school commencement. I wrote a bad check to buy a dress for the occasion; I had nothing but jeans in my closet and almost no money. After my speech, I was honored with a citation naming me the most distinguished student in my graduating class.

Ruth was equal parts thrilled and amazed; I wasn't going to be a Sixties casualty after all. She sent me a massive Random House dictionary as a gift, advising me that I would be able to find once-forbidden words like *cunnilingus* and *fellatio* in it. My father was similarly flabbergasted; he sent me another five hundred dollars, accompanied by a gently worded note informing me that my graduation marked the end of his court-ordered fiscal responsibility to me.

Success, even on this modest level, hardly left me without anxiety, however. In fact, I was still at Berkeley when The Problem began, quite suddenly and like the onset of some specific if obscure order of mental illness. Ruth and I both recognized something was seriously wrong when I called her in a panic one Friday afternoon: Should I go to Magnin's in San Francisco the next day and buy a slip, or should I go to a party? For some reason, these options were mutually exclusive. We discussed my dilemma for two hours, diverted not so much by the decision as by my inability to make it.

Curiously, the more trivial the options, the more paralyzed I became. Ruth tried to help. Like every other Berkeley student, I had a free phone: the toll-free number used by the Committee to Re-elect the President, which was spray-painted on every vacant building and parking lot in town. It was the start of our Mother Watts Line, as Ruth called it. Later, I used toll-free lines at *Women's Wear Daily* and, most especially, *Life* magazine, then a writer's hell-on-earth where I languished in the late 1970s. Settled at last, Ruth emerged as shrink on twenty-four-hour call to a difficult patient. She was infinitely generous in her attentiveness to me. I inhaled every word of comfort she offered and called back the next day for more. It wasn't until my late twenties that I finally admitted to myself my hopeless dependence upon her. ("Hi, my name is Hillary . . ." Chorus of female voices: "Hi, Hillary!" If only there *were* help available for this overweening feeling that to draw breath you must first alert your mother and, second, solicit her encouragement.) While I was still at Berkeley, Ruth worked hard to underline my small triumphs and make light of the failures. "CHERISH IMPROVEMENT," she would write to me emphatically, once she had enumerated specific ways in which I had demonstrated improvement.

After a year of graduate J-school at Columbia, I struggled to find true reporting jobs instead of exalted secretarial or copy assistant positions. I left one initially promising-sounding job after four months, but not before threatening an EEOC lawsuit. I covered federal agencies for a news service in Washington, D.C. I freelanced for magazines. Finally I scored the coveted *Women's Wear* job in New York. "Your letter was a real cliff hanger," Ruth wrote me afterward. "See, I've been saying for months 'She can't miss! I mean, she's done everything right & and all that preparation & those splendid earned credentials & the gifts that underlie the whole thing cannot be ignored & spurned & misused & undervalued for very long.' But, of course, I couldn't say WHEN it would all come right or WHICH paper would first recognize how beautiful you are—just knew it would happen.

"See, honey—in addition to all the above qualities, gifts, credentials, preparations etc you have the *extra* magic quality—you keep your eye on the ball—you fool around a lot & suffer grandly about whether you should buy a petticoat or take an escalator or come home for Christmas or take broadcast journalism but you never fool around about whether you ought to be a success or not."

It wasn't long after that when she noted, at the end of another letter, "I think it's lovely that we are both having the best time of our life so far at the same time."

Ruth was starting to make art then. She was forty-six, I was twenty-five. An enduring bout of pneumonia had kept her out of work for so long she had been fired, to her enormous joy. Her husband suggested she stay home and do as she pleased.

❖ ❖ ❖

Ruth had to take courses in subjects other than art once she entered college, of course, and she was drawn powerfully to Greek mythology. She considered her education to be all of a piece; whatever ideas she was exploring in one class inevitably made their way into the others.

My mother drew and then etched her figures of gods and goddesses in contemporary dress. Her Pasiphaë, in spike heels, a miniskirt, a breast plate Madonna would love, and a ridiculous crown, has a perfect circle of pink blush on each cheek as she stares intently at the bull standing next to her. In order to wreak vengeance upon an enemy, Poseidon has cast a spell upon Pasiphaë, condemning her to fall in love with the beautiful bull and to mate with it, a conjugal pairing that will produce the Minotaur. The sea god, his head usually wreathed in gold and rendered in superhuman perfection, stands—implacable and unrepentant—in profile next to the spellbound Pasiphaë. He, too, wears a crown, from which water rolls down his face and over a middle-aged biker's undignified belly. He is staring harshly at Pasiphaë; revenge is at hand. The bull, seeing the lust and determination in Pasiphaë's eyes, cowers in terror.

Some among Ruth's artist friends consider this panorama to be among her very best efforts.

The work is large, a sophisticated intaglio process undertaken on a sheet of Plexiglas. In a notebook Ruth kept for a brief period while a student, I spotted the phrase "Pasiphaë on the Colorado Plain," around which Ruth had drawn a box. I am uncertain whether she considered the phrase to be the title of the piece, or if it was merely a notation marking her first thoughts on the subject of Pasiphaë and her difficulties. Ruth herself had been around cattle from her earliest childhood, first on the Missouri farm her father owned, and later in Colorado, where she spent most of her first seventeen years. Cows were among her favorite subjects. She drew cows in every humor: angry, placid, grazing contentedly, threatened, worried; often, according to her friend Roode, Ruth's cows were metaphorical stand-ins for women. She had felt the soul-crushing disapprobation of specific men from her earliest days as well.

The time has long since passed, of course, when I might have asked Ruth why she worked so hard to make this print. I remember her telling me about it once, however. I was standing in her kitchen. When I concentrate, I can see her mouth moving, her body turning this way and that, her eyes bright and eager as she tried to convey to me her fascination for the subject matter; I can even hear her laughter. I am unable to recall a word she said.

Recently, I found a letter she wrote to me when I was a college student at Berkeley that suggests she had been moved by the literature of human and animal love at an early age. She was responding to my complaint that I seemed unable to fully erase my adolescent love, the boy from Kenwood, from my thoughts; that I compared all men to him and found them wanting. "I have suspected for some time that your lack of interest in men is more complicated than a consecration to the liberation of women," she wrote. "Now—you need a lover—and the more room you make in your head for new qualities to love in other men, the less space that phantom will take up and the nearer you will come to a life that fills *all* your needs."

She offered several more theories, the last of which she called "THE INAPPROPRIATE LOVE OBJECT theory." This theory, she continued, "is drawn from a beautiful story by Faulkner about a simple minded rural orphan who falls in love with a neighboring farmer's cow. He was super naive—never having had mother or father or a close relationship with another human & he took a fancy to this cow—a fancy that grew into one of the most beautiful loves in history. One is touched by the flame of his ardor and the delicacy of his perceptions of his love—his patience, kindness, tact, and generosity are marvelous to hear of but as I recall both the boy & the heifer came to a bad end.

Love, Mother."

❖ ❖ ❖

I was twenty-five, a reporter for *W* and *Women's Wear Daily,* and I was interviewing people I admired like Gore Vidal, Irwin Shaw, and Truman Capote. I was interviewing, as well, people of momentary anthropological interest: clothes designers; self-important Park Avenue matrons—the women Tom Wolfe would in due time characterize as "social X-rays"—and rich Texans striving to be just like them. My editors were surprised, then enchanted, by my ear for the ridiculous, and encouraged the arch point of view, often skirting the cruel, that I employed when I wrote about the ultrarich. My prose read like something written with a dangerously sharp quill pen instead of a Smith-Corona.

I had been schooled to cover breaking news events, and average people who had suffered Job-like catastrophes. I had written competently about migrant workers washed away in floods; welfare recipients on New York's Upper West Side who routinely blew their checks at the Broadway Bingo Hall; a bridegroom who electrocuted himself with an electric shoe buffer moments before his wedding; the Roller Derby; the index of economic indicators; toxic waste, OPEC. I had the *stomach* for journalism. I had no problem asking a mother for the high-school yearbook photo of her fatally injured son—if that's what my editors wanted. I did whatever was required: I maneuvered like a battering ram, or I donned kid gloves. I subscribed fully to Jessica Mitford's paramount rule: Graduate your questions from kind to cruel. I rarely asked a question to which I didn't already know the answer.

I believed it was necessary to perform not just averagely but brilliantly. The stress was enormous. I wasn't remotely distracted by the desires crowding the minds of other women my age. Marriage, motherhood, a house of my own, the accrual of money—worldly enchantments with the power to afford pleasure or comfort paled before my desire to get that story. A friend from Columbia, attempting to characterize my particular reporting style, once summarized: "Imagine a pit bull with a notebook." Recently I found a letter Ruth sent me during my pit bull days: "I love your idea of going through Ralph Nader's garbage," she wrote supportively. "If he is what he claims to be, of course, there won't be any."

I was using journalism the way other people use religion or alcohol or heroin, as a means to keep from slipping below the waterline into some inchoate pain for which no medicine was available. I couldn't even name the force lapping at my ankles, threatening to drown me; it was simply there by then, most of the time. The byline, the cover story—these were the flimsy triumphs that shot me through with happiness, again and again, but their soothing effect was always short-lived. One might guess I was an egomaniac, but I think in truth my ego was barely there.

Little I had written garnered me more attention than my stories about the rich and famous for *Women's Wear*. Sheerly by coincidence of employment, I had tapped into a rising fascination with celebrity and money. "I *read* you," people sometimes said to me, startled expressions on their faces, when I introduced myself at social gatherings. In person I was so—well—*demure*. That "white-gloved presentation," which a shrink once put a name to, then accused me of hiding behind, was a professional hazard. People *unburdened* themselves to me. One of my professors at Columbia described me as a lamb with innocent-looking eyes that people simply fell into; he pitied them. Sometimes I sensed my subjects were suspicious: I couldn't possibly be old enough to be doing what I was doing—I looked too young to occupy a bar stool. Richard Darman, an Assistant Secretary of Commerce at the time, chortled through an entire interview with me, shaking his head, repeating every so often, "This isn't for *real* is it?" Their most serious miscalculation by far: They assumed I could be counted on to be compassionate.

Ruth was astonished. After reading my interviews in *W*, she would inquire, "Do you *know* how funny you are?" Or "Did you do this on purpose or did it just sort of . . . *emerge?*" Her implication that my prose was anything less than studiously executed or had arisen from a source outside of me ignited harsh reprisals from me. Looking back, however, I think Ruth was on to something. The phrasing, the worldview, the wit—they were her own as much as or more than they were mine. I was part chronicler, part channeler.

Ruth began collecting the pictures of me snapped by the photographers with whom I worked. Sometimes they were candid shots of me; sometimes they included me and my subject. She attached them with pushpins to the rough-hewn cedar walls of her designated smoking room. When I first saw the photographs crowded together in a kind of happy profusion, I was startled: The collage looked like a shrine. I worried over the matter for some time: Did she love me more than I loved her?

This was the place where Ruth sat for hours at a time drinking gin neat and smoking cigarettes, reading cookbooks like novels—from start to finish—then plotting enormously complex menus. It was the place where she tuned in each day to giggle at the soap opera she had renamed *The Young and the Shiftless*. She studied the trailer-trash diction with the absorption of a professional linguist. This was also the room in which she entertained friends, who inevitably arrayed themselves around her like devotees in the presence of their guru, sated by my mother's extravagant meals, sipping scotch or cordials, listening for the jokes, the observations. Once I overheard her discussing me in this room with a friend in a manner that suggested she considered me to be a phenomenon of nature with miraculous if enigmatic talents.

"Valerie J. is rich and beautiful and lives in New York," Ruth eventually would write in a clever, knowing essay about me called "A Case Study: The Mime Killer." It was a revenge fantasy she fashioned after I described being assaulted by a mime on Seventh Avenue in front of an audience of men basking themselves in the sun on the Exxon building plaza. "Tomorrow, with premeditation and in cold blood," Ruth continued, "Valerie J. is going to off a clown. . . . Not, mind you, that Valerie was brought up to be a murderess. Valerie wasn't even brought up to be rich and beautiful and live in New York. She was brought up to be dull and married and live in the Midwest."

A mere twenty-two years separated the year of my birth from that of Ruth's. I had wondered, at the pinnacle of my feminist rage, why Ruth hadn't prepared me for a life of oppression, and thus, in addition to being angry at half of humanity, I was angry at her specifically. In time, however, I realized she had prepared me. In fact, she had tried to *save* me from life behind the ironing board. Indeed, as the Seventies wore on, she frequently referred to me, with obvious pride, as a "pioneer." I wasn't married to a brute, unemployed, and living in the suburbs somewhere with three children under the age of five; I was writing for national magazines in New York City. Unlike the white and black divisions fostered by my use of drugs, which sometimes left us barely speaking to each other in my adolescence, feminism was little more than a hand inserted between our shoulders that nudged us apart for a short while, but left no lasting scars on our relationship.

Today I realize that her art suggests how deeply preoccupied my mother was with women—not just with what they looked like, but with how they faced the world, how they felt about themselves, and how they survived.

I was stunned in the late Seventies to discover that Ruth had produced one of the most powerful feminist images I had ever seen. She had used a large canvas, four feet by six feet. Using wide, powerful brush strokes, she had painted a group of women in outline. The piece was like a comic version of a corporate photo; the figures wore dresses in bright hues, they were redheaded, blond, dark-haired. They stood together closely, shoulder to shoulder; there was no doubt these women liked one another and took pleasure in their comradeship. The piece could have been a gallery of secretaries or dental hygienists or an all-female law firm. It was a cheerful, lively portrait, but for one unsettling fact: The women were faceless.

When I admired the piece, Ruth offered it to me, of course. I wanted it, but couldn't imagine how I would transport it back to New York, and once I got home, I was soon distracted and forgot about the painting. Ruth displayed the piece in her house for a year or two, then she cut the canvas out of the frame and destroyed it, saving only the frame.

Human sexuality, animal sexuality, and the strange mix of inequities and abundance that may be implicit in either forum, were subjects Ruth seemed drawn to, if the work that survives is any indication. The notes she kept in a small, blank-paged book I gave her as a gift one year, all of them relating to her art in progress that year, suggests she was working on etchings of horses, knights on horses, birds, cats, rats, rabbits, and, of course, cows. Sometimes they were slap-happy, wigged-out animals engaged in frantic sex. She labored over compositions she collectively called her "Bird Bangs." In each version, three or four birds are piled upon one another in a perverse attempt at mating with a bird at the bottom. She also produced *Ménage à Quatre*, in which four cats are similarly engaged, but the cats aren't necessarily enjoying their menage as much as the birds are enjoying theirs. One cat sandwiched in the middle is crying; the cat on the bottom looks not just physically but emotionally squashed.

"The animals became characters in her morality play," her friend Roode recalled. Her bird prints, and the cat print, are about power, about literal pecking orders, every bit as much as they are visual-verbal puns, he noted. Implicit in all human interplay, of course, is a struggle for power, and the winner comes out on top.

Ruth worried a lot about rhythm and motion inside the limited, two-dimensional world of the page as well. She wanted her images to make the paper throb, and perhaps that is another reason she opted to depict such avid carnality. The gang-banging that went on in some of her work was hardly her sole effort to create excitement and movement, however. The work described in one particular series of notes can no longer be found, but Ruth wrote about it, "Birds must go rapidly," illustrating with arrows the horizontal direction in which the birds were to move; "knights (already in place) in reverse direction," she continued, with more arrows. "Rats—make them little & down at the edge." Her hasty, casual sketch of this composition in her notebook is so lively it looks like an original orchestral score, with the composer's directions written above certain passages— "space—space," instead of "pizzicato."

❖ ❖ ❖

In 1976, shortly after my twenty-sixth birthday, I went to Blue Hill, Maine, a notebook stowed in my handbag. I was driving up the Maine coast in a rental car, too fast, on assignment for *W*. Per usual, my official mission was to locate a few of the richest inhabitants of the state, interview them, and write about them as if they were interesting. I had a secret plan, however, which I had told only to Ruth. I stepped into the Blue Hill Pharmacy and said hello to the druggist. I asked him if he could tell me where E. B. White lived.

"He won't give you an interview," the man said, as if he had been expecting me. I hadn't even mentioned that I was a reporter; my trench coat must have given me away.

"I would like to ask him myself," I said. He examined me carefully from his raised platform behind the counter, taking his time.

"Keep going on the road you're on," he said finally. "You'll see a big house with a picket fence by the ocean. Can't miss it."

I pushed on. In five minutes, I was there. I slowed down but suddenly lost my nerve and continued along the road. Ten minutes later, I turned around, newly determined, and headed back. When I was at the house again, my foot refused to depress the brake pedal. I wouldn't drop in on a friend unannounced; the notion of disturbing E. B. White in this manner was beginning to seem grotesque. Pretty soon, I was in Blue Hill again. I set off for White's house once more, but passed it twice. The day was slipping away. I returned to town and found the sole public telephone in a booth at the corner of a small park. Ruth was on the line in an instant. We had never faced this dilemma before; when it came to tracking quarry, I was fearless.

"Honey, try again," she said. There was a war raging in my head. "Darling, you're a reporter—this is what you *do*."

I considered the truth of her statement. I described the whole scene for her: Blue Hill, the choppy, slate-colored ocean, White's unremarkable house and shingled barn next to the sea.

"Go back *now*, dear," she urged me.

I called my mother three hours later from Blue Hill. As if sighting an orphan in search of food scraps, White had invited me in without asking my name. "Come in! Come in out of the cold!" he had insisted. I stepped into the generous kitchen about which he had written, "You can wash a dog in my kitchen without any trouble except from the dog." He pulled a chair away from the table for me to sit on, and told me to warm myself by the wood-burning stove. When I told him I was a reporter for *Women's Wear Daily*, he laughed with honest amusement.

"Really?" he asked. I assured him it was true, with the expectation of being shown the door. Instead, White shook his head goodnaturedly; stranger things had happened.

"Tea?" he said, already filling a kettle with water. In a minute, he had poured the tea into delicate matching cups, set them in saucers on a tray, and invited me into his study at the front of the house. The room was wallpapered with antique maps of the Maine coast. An unkempt Westy named Jones, a deeply disturbed dog, by White's account, sat at our feet. I had prepared twelve pages of questions for the essayist, but I never thought to pull them from my bag.

Ruth was ecstatic upon hearing the news. "Genius girl!" she exulted. I wanted to be with her, settled in her kitchen, which had its own wood-burning stove, watching her cook, sipping the champagne she surely would have offered me.

My editors in New York would never know the beneficence they were receiving on a daily basis from a housewife in Minneapolis. They thought I was kidding when I told them I had interviewed the writer. White had refused interview requests for years. A day later when I turned in the story, they decided to feature White on the cover of *W*.

❖ ❖ ❖

Two years later, the phone rang one evening and Ruth was at the other end speaking in a frightened voice about her Latin midterm, scheduled for the following morning. She was certain she was going to fail the test. Surely her college-savvy daughter would know what to do. I could offer no help on the Latin midterm, which Ruth indeed went on to fail. I was able to tell her with some certainty, however, that as a determined middle-aged woman who knew exactly why she was in college—to study art—she held an enormous advantage over the eighteen-year-olds, half of whom typically drop out in the first year as I had done less than a decade before, the other half of whom haven't a clue why they are even enrolled.

It felt odd, this sudden role reversal. I enjoyed it in a kind of condescending way; I joked about my mother and her Latin midterm with friends at work the next day. I don't think I understood how momentous her foray into formal education was for Ruth. It took only a quarter or two for Ruth to discover I was right about the eighteen-year-olds, however. From that point on, she handled her courses confidently and just as she pleased, turning in papers that were half-prose and half-illustration, or written in the form of letters to an anonymous recipient. She experimented with voices, sometimes employing the diction of an innocent, wide-eyed yokel from, say, Missouri ("Some dude who just fell off the 'tater truck," as she would have said), other times adopting a stylish, literary patter that could have been excerpted from *The New York Review of Books*. I have often wondered if Ruth might have become a writer instead of an artist at some point during her years in college had she not feared upsetting my shaky confidence with an appearance of competitiveness.

In 1979, when she was fifty-one, she took a course called Women's Physiology and found it to be so lame she soon began referring to it as her course in menstruation. In one paper, she fashioned a false account of the editor of a euphemistic 1854 tract, *The Young Woman's Book of Health*. She wrote:

> When author William Alcott set out for the printer's carrying the manuscript that became his popular manual, several illustrated case histories were left behind . . . Historians speculate that the absent-minded author, who was known to suffer from acute obscuraphobia (the irrational fear of going blind), frequently went about his daily affairs with eyes closed, presumably to ready himself for what he feared was the soon-to-come day when his sight would fail him for all time.

Ruth produced the lost documents: Alcott's case study of Mary Louise X. "Mrs. X brought the child to my office because, as a good mother, she was tormented by the fear that her daughter might become precocious," Ruth's Edwardian author began. "Fully aware of the peril to young girls of that dread condition, I examined Mary Louise with some care and, to the mother's great relief, I was able to find no evidence that anything was amiss with Miss X." Ruth offered Alcott's accompanying sketch. "Fig. 11, Mary Louise X at age 13 years 2 mos.," depicted a flat-chested, innocent if mystified-looking young girl.

"Alas, all our hopes for Miss X's good health were dashed a short two months later," Ruth's author continued. In the accompanying "Fig. 12, Mary Louise X at age 13 yrs. 4 mos.," the girl had sprouted breasts. "Miss X herself seemed unconcerned at her predicament. She paced restlessly about the office, now crying, now laughing, occasionally muttering dark curses directed at her mother, and taking the Lord's name in vain, as in her frequently repeated phrase, 'Oh, Mother, for Christ's sake!' and such like."

In "Fig. 13, Mary Louis X at age 13 yrs. 6 mos.," the girl had full-alert breasts and she was slumped to the floor, masturbating wildly. "I could give poor Mrs. X. no consolation," Ruth's Alcott wrote in his case notes. "(Let me remind the young practitioner that to raise false hopes in a situation with such a dismal prognosis is cruel indeed.) My only comfort in the dreadful case of Mary Louise X is that dear Mrs. X, being somewhat astigmatic, never fully perceived the true extent of her daughter's degraded condition (see fig. 13)." Ruth noted that Mary Louis X was "remittanced to Paris at the age of 20. Nothing is known of her life thereafter."

Of course, Ruth conjured an older sister, the good sister Blanche, who was loved unreservedly by her mother. Mrs. X "took pride and comfort in the perfect flowering of her older daughter Blanche," Ruth wrote. She followed up with a photograph of Blanche, who turned out to be a preadolescent child wearing a tiara and holding a jeweled scepter. Ruth's caption:

Mrs. Harold Tidwell (nee Blanche X) presides at tea in her lovely home on the occasion of her fiftieth birthday.

"I love your drawings," the teacher wrote on Ruth's paper, and awarded her an A-.

Another time, in another course, one of her professors wrote on one of Ruth's papers, "Not quite what I had in mind, but what's here is very good. B+."

Fig. 11. Mary Louise X at Age 13 yrs. 2 mos.   Fig 12. Mary Louise X at Age 13 yrs. 4 mos.

Fig 13. Mary Louise X at Age 13 yrs. 6 mos.

117

Unlike me, Ruth made her points about sexism without defacing property or brawling with strangers in saloons. Although she may have tried to summon the kind of outrage I had once evinced, she clearly didn't feel it. "Two Pretty Good Ideas About Why Men Seem to Be a Bit Better Off Than Are Women in American Society," was how she titled a paper for a course called Women's History. She accused Daniel Boorstein of contributing to the "cultural smog that obscures the potential of women in American society" with his two volumes, *The Landmark History of the American People,* in which Ruth had discovered just eight women in the index of fifteen hundred listings. She tempered that observation with comic illustrations, however, using Pasiphaë and Poseidon as her models to illustrate Boorstein's boorishness.

In one drawing, *A Landmark History of the American People,* Ruth wrote the names of Dorothea Dix and Jane Addams on each of Pasiphaë's legs; on Pasipahe's skirt hem appear the words "Lady on the Train," in homage to the Viscountess Avonmore. The Viscountess was among the eight women cited by Boorstein; she had complained about a lack of privacy on early-American trains. Poseidon's portly torso, in contrast, is a mass of perhaps two hundred names, starting with Marquis De Chastellux and including Robert E. Lee, Paul Revere, and Kit Carson.

A second drawing, *Some Stars of the Silver Screen,* features Pasiphaë wearing little medals on her cowgirl's skirt: widow, missionary, nurse, schoolteacher, steno. In Pasiphaë's crown Ruth drew the word *Wife.* She gave Pasiphaë an armband which reads, in large letters, "HOOKER"; hanging like sequins from Pasiphaë's hem are the letters "H-O-O-F-E-R." Poseidon, in contrast, is covered with medals: Tribal Chief, Secretary of State, Mogul, Artist, Gigolo, City Slicker, Abe Lincoln, J. Edgar Hoover, Spy, Athlete, Gangster, Huck Finn, Handy Man, Murderer, Priest, Tsar, Liar, FDR, Ace Reporter, Heel, Rat, Chairman-O-the-Board, Oxford Don, Plumber, Castaway, First Baseman, Father.

"Pretty well written!" her professor noted. "A-."

I start school next Monday," Ruth wrote to me on September 20, 1978. I was living at Eighty-first and Madison, kitty-corner from the Frank E. Campbell funeral home and across the street from P.S. 6, where the grade schoolers arrived and departed in stretch limos. The notion that Ronald Reagan could achieve the presidency was unimaginable, and John Lennon was living on the other side of the park, composing songs in his kitchen about his infant son. I was still reeling from a month spent with Halston at his atelier overlooking St. Patrick's on Fifth Avenue and Studio 54 for a *Life* assignment. Ruth was soon to be fifty; I was almost twenty-eight.

"I'm taking a painting class from H– —my last I fear," she wrote, "since the credit distribution system prohibits specializing in even one discipline, let alone one professor.

> I have a drawing class from F–, the young man you thought nice but dull—remember, he lectured us in the hall about handball or weightlifting or baseball or something neither of us had the slightest interest in?
>
> I've also got a "printmaking-intaglio" class from an old guy named Malcolm Meyers. He chews tobacco & paints animals with clothes on. Someone once asked him why he puts clothes on his animals. He answered "Can't stand all that HAIR!" Malcolm also holds critiques where the student lays his work out on the floor—& in appraising the work he walks all over it. He suggested I take his class & I said O.K. But let him know that I had heard about his critiques & said, "If you put one boot on my work, you son of a bitch, I'll cut your *balls* off!" He replied that he couldn't understand *that* attitude. Walked all over his own. "Seasons 'em, you know."

I am told by other students that printmaking is a very technical business—something like a course in Toaster Repair—and though I have been invited to learn that skill by thousands of match books and, approaching my 50th year, I can say that I have never *once* been even tempted—still a guy who knows his own tolerance for hair & likes a nicely seasoned print can't be *all* bad. You may hear from me about this later—I'm kind of nervous about the technology.

I am also toying with the idea of taking an English comp. class this fall. Gotta take one sometime and I have an awkward 3 hr. gap as my schedule now stands—and I could slip it in pretty easy—couldn't get a class card but I figure I could mau mau my way in. The trouble is that would give me 20 credits & that's a brave & perhaps foolhardy number. What I figure though is that I can draw something for F–, paint it for H– & print it for Malcolm. Then get thru the comp. class by pretending to be writing letters. Let me know what you think.

I don't think I can make Phi Beta Kappa—shit—I don't think I can spell it. Doesn't look right. . . . [But] I've gotten many more As than Bs, & no Cs, & I intend to get a lot more As—now that I know the way.

Well darling, that's all I can think of now.

Love, Mother

Protestations aside, Ruth was drawn to complex technology, to clearly ordered systems, to successively complicated stages of creation. Her natural attraction to the marriage of art and technology was evident in the process she invented on Girard Avenue to remove generations of paint and then stain the wood of the pantry cupboards. It was evident in the imaginative way she went about remaking the small, turn-of-the-century lake cabin she and her second husband acquired not long after their marriage. Her house, in fact, was among her most interesting works of art and it was always in progress. Her love of complexity, of process, was apparent when she began making quilts, at my request, in the last years of her life. She gave away the secret of her attraction only weeks before she died. Writing in her curious new organic language, as if her English was recently acquired, she encouraged me to take up quilting: "One of the nice things about quilting is that when things are troubling if you can get into the patchey rhythms of quilting it just smoothes out under your fingers. Just lay out how you would have your quilting going—it is easeful."

Little could have been more easeful to Ruth than the infinite permutations of printmaking. In retrospect, it is unsurprising that her initial encounter with Professor Malcolm Meyers and the rudiments of etching images onto copper or zinc plates—only the first of many steps in the process—would raise her sights and inspire her highest ambitions. The options available to the printmaker were endless. In between the idea and the finished art lay not just conventions to be followed but possibilities for ingenuity and experiment at every point. No two prints could ever be the same, and that was the beauty part, as far as Ruth was concerned; that was the art of printmaking.

When she gave me a set of her prints in 1984, she explained her principled, signature technique—albeit in layman's shorthand so as not to bore me: "If you care, the rule I've made for myself is that if I can't get it on the plate, it doesn't belong in the print," she wrote. "Lots of very fine printmakers hand color a print after the plate has been printed but for me the game is to get it all thru the press so I ink & wipe the plate & then apply a thin layer of oil paint (usually with a roller) over the ink. The press sucks the ink up thru the color to give the appearance of its being on top of the color."

When the tobacco-chewing Malcom Meyers actually did critique her prints by first placing them on the floor, my mother sat quietly by accounts, even when he used the tip of his tennis shoe to point out worthy aspects of her composition. I am guessing Ruth was deeply pleased. I'll bet she wanted her prints seasoned, too.

Ruth had moved past her fantasies of a life lived in New York by then. Once, in the late Seventies, I took a vacation in Italy. I offered my vacant apartment to Ruth and her husband. My stepfather was a writer and he used the time to conduct interviews and sample restaurants. When I returned, they had gone, but I found two or three long letters Ruth had left behind for me describing their adventures. Ruth had enjoyed herself, but for an evening spent with a couple of New Yorkers of the worst kind: snobs. She simply wasn't prepared for that particular gift life in the City often brings.

"Just got back from a most GAWD awful evening with Jerzy Kosinski & his 'great good friend' KiKi or Kee Kee or however you spell such a name," she wrote.

An English lady who is, I guess, a wife-mistress figure in his life. I thought Kosinski liked Clay & thought it would be a friendly evening. It was, instead, like a four hour phone call from Al Milgrom of the U. of M. film society. Dull ego stuff from the writer & Super dull stuff from the mistress and poor dull old me expected to be grateful for a chance to be in the presence of great persons. Something to tell the girls at bridge or golf or whatever dull little persons such as myself amuse themselves with back in Indianapolis or wherever it is we all come from. That's a super YETCH kind of casting—and I resent being "cast"—ignored is O.K.—pushed around is even all right but CAST I just gut resent. Especially when I've been misled about the nature of the event. Ah! Well—we all pay our dues. Except I cry "foul" when I didn't ask to join this particular club. Or perhaps it's "fowl" I cry. My perceptions get blurred by screaming rage. I mean, I'm capable of being dull but it's a badge I would like the privilege of earning—is that asking too much?

By the time the 1980s were under way, Ruth was fully at peace with her residency in the Midwest. In fact, during one of my rare visits to Minneapolis in those years, she pointed out to me in a voice that held not braggadocio exactly but was certainly heartfelt, "I rather like my life here."

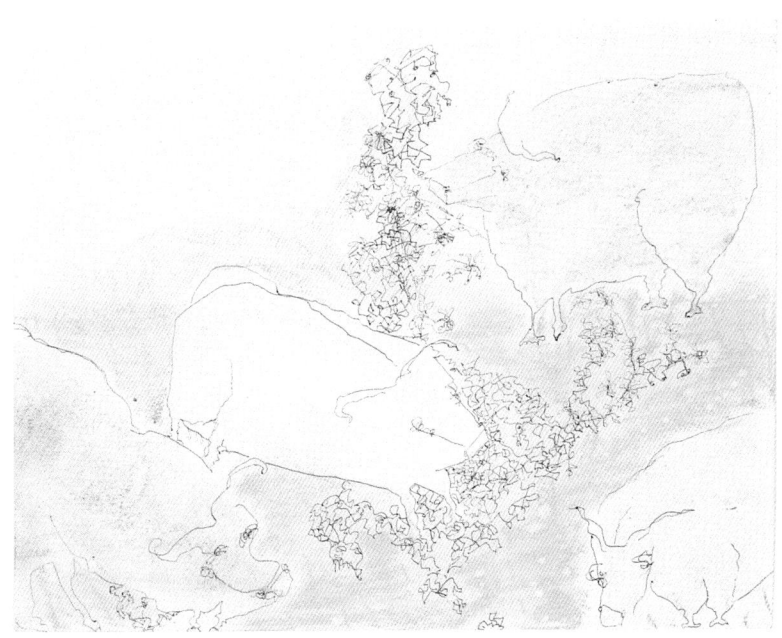

The greatest mystery is neither how cancer begins nor how it can be cured; the greatest mystery is why, among people with identical risk factors, some fall ill and others do not. Millions of people drink and smoke, and the epidemiological link between drinking and smoking and esophageal cancer is a powerful one—better established even than the link between smoking and lung cancer. Yet only a few actually get the disease. In the years leading up to my mother's death, I was obsessed with these scientific linkages. There is another mystery, however, even greater, and that is why some people embark upon a path with a powerful likelihood of killing them, though they appear to love life.

Ruth took up smoking in her fifteenth year. It was wartime. She had a job running the elevator in the Ford office building in Denver, where her uncle George Kobalt was working. She was supposed to be sixteen to run the cage, and she looked at least that old. George, who was her mother's younger brother by twelve years, was thirty-four. He wore manly blue and white seersucker suits, and although Ruth had known him all her life, she suddenly desperately wanted him to notice her.

She loved the way smoking made her feel sophisticated and desirable. She loved the light, sensual weight of the cigarette on her lip, the satisfying burn in the lungs when she inhaled deeply, the languid, unpredictable shapes of the rising smoke when she exhaled. She liked it when men offered to light the fresh cigarette she held effortlessly between her index and middle finger, how the action brought her closer to the man without seeming overtly flirtatious on her part. Every aspect of the ritual delighted her. She particularly liked the way she could tamp any impulse to eat merely by lighting up.

When I was fourteen, and I had just failed the grapefruit diet because Ethan—seventeen and thin as a rail—had viciously devoured five Twinkies right in front of me, Ruth addressed me with a tenderness of voice some mothers might employ to explain the rudiments of sex to their daughters. "Here, darling," she said, offering me one of her Winstons. "This will help, I promise. One puff, and you won't think about food for hours."

By that time, Ruth had taken up drinking. In my adolescence, on Independent Activities Night, I occasionally found Ruth alone and drunk in a despairing, semiconscious way that suggested she was near suicide. These sorrowful episodes seemed to be exclusive events, however, spurred by the unusual circumstances of her courtship, and they ended when she married. I was at Berkeley before I began to think seriously about Ruth's drinking. By then I was distinctly aware that she drank heavily and steadily, that booze was a fundamental requirement for her, like food and sleep.

I knew nothing about epidemiology in those years, or about the especially toxic synergy of drinking and smoking. I simply intuited that my mother had hit upon a deadly combination that would probably kill her. Standing close to her, I could hear the little wheeze in her lungs when she inhaled. The sound, barely perceptible, always scared me. She had a smoker's chronic cough; every few years the cough evolved into bronchitis, and occasionally pneumonia. At least once, when I was at Berkeley, the pneumonia became pleurisy. I noticed, too, how her eyes got increasingly dreamy and unfocused as day became night, until—not wishing to derail the festivities—she would quietly turn in and fall unconscious the moment she lay down. I would feel jolts of helpless rage toward Ruth for pursuing such a deadly course, and sorry for myself that my mother seemed so bent on self-destruction.

As I aged, I wanted to know who my mother was when she was fully sober. I dreamt of reconciliation with that person. More powerfully, I was worried in the fashion to which I had become accustomed in childhood: I was going to lose her, and I needed her. I tried to make myself more comfortable simply by staying away, as one might distance oneself from an impending natural disaster, but I was never peaceful. Ethan, too, fled. We just couldn't stand around and watch.

Ruth failed to espouse drinking to me as she once had espoused smoking. In 1972, when I was twenty-one, she sent me a letter in which she wrote, "The lady who told you to avoid excessive drinking for your whole life long did you a service beyond any price. Drinking is expensive, inconvenient, rots your brain, shortens your life, ruins your skin & makes you fat. How relieved I would be if someone told me I couldn't drink anymore. The discipline involved will be easier for you since you have not acquired a serious appetite for booze. I drank probably less than you do now until 10-12 years ago—so you see what a relatively short period of time is involved in making an alcoholic. . . . We are dieting now so I'm not drinking—perhaps we can make it permanent."

There was never any permanence to my mother's efforts to stop drinking. Her husband might stop in tandem with her for a while, to drop a few pounds, but they both took it up again soon enough.

Once, in the late seventies, Ruth was hospitalized with cirrhosis. I heard about it from a stepsibling, long after the fact. Later, a year after she enrolled in college, Ruth checked herself into a drug and alcohol recovery program in a hospital in St. Paul. She called to let me know about it three days later, by which time she was home again. Her voice shook as she told me the hospital staff had, upon her arrival, confiscated the myriad books she had thoughtfully packed in her suitcase and given her Bible tracts to read instead; had awakened her at odd times during the night by shining a flashlight in her face to ascertain whether she was sneaking a hit of gin or whiskey; had paired her with a bellicose sixteen-year-old heroin addict for a roommate. Ruth said the daytime discussion groups were comprised primarily of elderly homeless men picked up in nightly sweeps of the city's alleyways and high school–aged drug addicts who were also petty thieves.

My heart broke as she described these scenes to me. I had to agree: Ruth could not possibly survive in such a setting, yet I felt that for the first time in our lives she had presented me with an opening for frank discussion. I urged her to search for a kinder alternative. She had the right idea, I told her; she just needed to find an institution with a little humanity, an establishment with the imagination and flexibility to accommodate a woman like herself. In truth, I doubt there was one—not in Minnesota, not at that time. Had there been, it wouldn't have mattered. No matter how vigorous my pleas, Ruth was forever hardened against the huge business of addiction treatment for which Minnesota was increasingly famous. As far as she was concerned, she had delivered up her soul to strangers who had turned out to be even more censorious and obtuse than her mother, Mabel—and discovered the treatment was more debasing than the addiction. Now that she knew the alternative, she preferred to drink. As suddenly as our dialogue began, it ended. She would brook no further discussion of the subject.

When I returned to Minneapolis in 1989 and discovered the degree to which alcohol framed her days, I was distraught in a new way. Alcohol cut a corridor between us. She had, for most of my adult life, existed just slightly out of my reach. It occurred to me that she would remain just out of reach to the end: As her disease progressed, I imagined, she would move directly from bourbon to morphine.

In my early thirties, I sometimes sat in desolate church basements on the East Side of Manhattan, the weeknight domain of twelve-step habitués. In those rooms that seemed to shudder periodically with the indelible memories of ruined childhoods and breathtaking cruelties, I listened to the stories recounted by "adult children" of alcoholics. I sat quietly, feeling fraudulent, even voyeuristic. I had nothing to contribute. I had never been beaten, starved, raped, or made to live in a shed in the backyard. Ruth had never set out to hurt me. I was dubious that the word *alcoholic*—given its powerful cultural associations with degradation, destitution, belligerence, and the like—could be applied fairly to Ruth. The twelve-steppers would debate me on this point with extreme vehemence. Yet drinking rarely if ever seemed to stop my mother from doing what she wanted to do. By the time she remarried, she was a tranquil, steady drinker, never a "binge" drinker. Whether the habit blunted her growth as an artist I cannot say; certainly, she drank less and worried about her drinking more when she was studying art. When she quit making art, in the late 1980s, she began drinking more, but by then she also knew she had a fatal cancer.

Few of her friends of decades' duration would have dreamed of coupling the word *alcoholic* with her name. Ruth was Ruth; to them, she was always the same: brilliant host and raconteur, someone who, as one of her admirers exclaimed to me years after her death, "seemed to create art wherever she *looked*." I was the strangely reserved daughter, a complete mystery, no doubt, to those who knew my mother but who saw me only on the rare holiday. Had I been conceived during an eclipse? In contrast to my exuberant mother, I felt like an invisible moderator, the interlocutor standing just offstage, looking around the room from face to face in quiet puzzlement, wondering why her friends couldn't see just how Ruth was being destroyed.

Now I find myself wondering if drinking quelled a sadness that might have destroyed her even faster than the booze; I wonder, too, if it allowed her to *survive* as long as she did. Alcohol was her medicine—self-prescribed, of course, but medicine nonetheless, the only Prozac available to her generation. In the final years of her life, she required a shot of bourbon before moving on to brush her teeth in the morning.

The professionals would say Ruth was ill, she had a "disease," she needed help. After sampling that help, Ruth declared her aversion to it. Knowing my mother as I know her now, especially through her art, I realize she could never have admitted she was powerless over anything, nor could she have submitted to some mysterious "higher power," certainly not after Mabel's rapacious Bible-thumping. Ruth made her own decisions; she lived as she pleased and tried not to harm anyone else in the process. A "cure" for her drinking was simply not at hand, nor was it particularly desired by the patient.

The synergy took a long time to work—decades. There were years available to us during which we could have given each other joy and demonstrated our goodwill, years during which we would have had time to struggle with our development as mother and daughter, and ultimately with our mutual development as human beings. Instead, I chose to focus on those things that I felt certain would harm Ruth, those appetites she had that seemed to me to represent a kind of determined march to the grave. It was hard to back down from death's challenge; I was able to relinquish the fight to keep Ruth alive only in the final hours of her life. I wish I had recognized at some point early in my own life that my quarrel with Ruth over her choice to smoke and to drink needed to be abandoned as well. Ruth's life, as well as her death, belonged to her alone.

Even now, however, when I stumble across a line in one of my grade-school diaries, "I made breakfast for everyone this morning (scrambled eggs) because Mommy had a hangover," the old feelings are upon me in an instant.

The night Ruth's body was carried out of her house, I reached for a half-empty bottle of Old Crow Kentucky bourbon from under the kitchen sink and took it home, along with her notebooks. I keep it with me in the morbid way a child might save the very gun with which a parent committed suicide. It has more meaning to me than the small brass box holding her ashes. I am flooded with memories and emotion when I happen upon it at the back of the broom closet, or on a shelf in the garage, or wherever it reasserts itself at odd moments when I am searching for something else.

There was an intersection where Ruth and I met, toe to toe, in the realm of illness. Years afterward, I can write it down in shorthand, the dynamics of that meeting, pared down and obvious as they seem to me now. I can and will write it in a simple, declarative style—even if it makes this particular mother and daughter seem monstrous, even if it wasn't necessarily like that at the time—for the sake of clarity. There were undercurrents: things never said, or said very late in the game. There were actions taken that suggested a profound absence of caring, when in fact the caring was so deep we simply tried to pretend certain dire developments were fictions.

I was thirty-five, she fifty-seven, when in the same twelve-month period we learned her life had been suddenly circumscribed, punctuated, and that my life as we had both known it appeared to be over as well. Medicine offers slim advantage. Neither of us required doctors to tell us these things. Doctors offered confirmation, they put names to our illnesses. The tactile reality of our experiences, the implications of our particular diseases, were ours to fathom and to bear alone.

For me, the fable of the red shoes had come true at last. I was no longer a child, of course, but I suddenly felt as though I had been wearing those shoes my entire adult life. My feet broke like glass one day in March of 1986. The man I was seeing drove me from his home in Los Angeles to Santa Barbara to meet his father that day. I felt feverish and shaky as we motored along the quiet inland route. He covered me with his leather jacket. Barely able to lift my head, I shut my eyes and inhaled the scent of oranges ripening in the groves. I wondered if I would marry this man. Another voice, quiet and definitive, was patiently explaining that the red shoes had extracted their toll, that my feet would never be mended, that marriage and motherhood were out of the question now.

The father was as funny and generous as the son; we liked each other on sight. We ate lunch in a restaurant on the beach. I was dizzy and fevered, and I excused myself and walked to the bathroom. There, I stood staring at my face, searching for some radical alteration in appearance that would explain my symptoms, but I saw nothing unusual. I lost my balance and fell to the floor, losing consciousness for some moments. When I awoke I was remarkably weak for someone who typically ran three miles every day. We had to leave Santa Barbara, too soon. It is thirteen years later as I write this and I am still ill. I won't pretend to know what fatal illness is like, but I have become expert on chronic illness.

When I called Ruth to tell her about this curious development—long before I could claim expertise in the subject—she seemed detached. She could have authored lengthy monographs about the internecine office politics of every magazine or newspaper I had worked for. She knew almost everything that could be known about my life. She had always seen me clearly. I might as well have relayed this novel tale to her in Swahili.

"Perhaps you have simply worn yourself out," she said initially, "and you need to rest."

I was bedridden and couldn't care for myself. The man I was seeing asked me to live with him; he believed I would recover, and when I did, we would marry. He was a handsome, witty actor who was thus reduced to a nursemaid. He helped me walk from his bed to the bathroom, helped me bathe and wash my hair. He built me a small wooden shelf on which to place my computer as I sat propped up in bed, but it turned out I had become massively stupid and was unable to compose sentences that tracked. We played Crazy Eights sometimes in the late afternoons, though he was forced to play my hand as well as his own. After six months, editors quit calling. He would rest his large hand in the space between my neck and shoulder, seeking to comfort me. His hand would stay there, neither heavy nor light, as though my body was simply a part of his body.

Eventually a doctor called to say that my recovery, should I have one, was likely two or more years away. He could do nothing more; he had other patients, other problems. I called Ruth then, crazy with panic. It was all crashing, I told her. A few days later, I received a package from Minneapolis containing two sets of crisp Brooks Brothers pajamas, prettily tied with a grosgrain ribbon. It seemed a farcical, denigrating gift. I called my mother to advise her that her action was entirely inappropriate. "You seemed to indicate you would be spending a lot of time in bed," she responded. We didn't speak much after that; whenever I tried to talk about my illness, she would change the subject. "So, aside from all that, what have you been doing?" she would inquire. I was getting the same from friends; I hadn't expected it from Ruth.

When she called six months later to tell me she had found a white spot inside her cheek, and that she was afraid it was cancer, her voice was small. She sounded terrified, like a child who has just seen the foot of a corpse in the woods and rushed home to tell her mother. "Cancer? Impossible," was my preposterous response. When the cancer diagnosis was official, I sent her a gallon of aloe vera juice to drink at the suggestion of the nutritionist I was paying $180 a week to cure me.

A week later, Frannie called to say Ruth could die; she just wanted to be sure I understood that. Ruth had a way of downplaying these things, she added. When the call ended, I lay on the sofa, my knees pulled up to my chin, my eyes squeezed shut until I was floating in blackness. I so much didn't want to cry. I had tried to slip through the gate, deaf and dumb, all innocence. Frannie wasn't going to let me.

"Ducks," my actor said to me one morning a year later, seating himself on the bed where I lay, "you haven't left the apartment in forty-five days." He delivered this news with a neutral smile; he had some interesting information to impart. With his help, I dressed and we set out to walk around the block. I took perhaps forty steps, sat

Ménage à Cinq I

down on the sidewalk for a while, then asked for his help to get back to bed. I turned inward after that, unable to focus on him any longer; my concerns lay elsewhere.

I discovered I had nothing inside myself—no religious faith, no stoic, philosophical underpinnings, not even a single New Age platitude—to draw upon. I was entirely without grace. I might have been nineteen all over again: The unrelenting chronicity of the disease was just a metaphorical stand-in for sexism. It stopped you in dead in your tracks; it ruined your chances of success in any forum; it was extravagantly unfair.

He gave up eventually, as anyone would. It was Ruth who insisted that I gather my belongings and leave. The disease was incomprehensible; the part where the man stops loving you—that she understood to her core. "Darling," she whispered to me from her living room fifteen hundred miles away, both of us in tears, when I phoned her, *you can't survive this.*" He left me sitting on a collection of suitcases and boxes on the curb at LAX and accelerated zestfully without looking back. I was my problem now.

❖ ❖ ❖

Sometime in 1986 my mother had sent me a letter that ended by saying she had the nagging sense that she should be in her studio making prints. "I keep trying to talk myself down to the basement to resume my printmaking activity but seem to have lost confidence, energy, gift or all three. Maybe this afternoon—then on the other hand—maybe not," she wrote. She also wrote that her mother, Mabel, was ill. She had asked her uncle George what she might do for Mabel and he had "suggested that I authorize him to let [Mabel] know that I had been born again—turned at last to my lord & savior Jesus Christ. I have scruples. I'm near to sixty and my head is near as calcified as our dear head of state, but I never lied to an old lady in my life & I ain't going to take it up now."

At some point, Ruth recovered her drive, because in July of 1987, shortly before she would learn she had a small tumor at the base of her tongue, she wrote, "Life in Minneapolis continues at its usual furious pace. . . . I managed to bust my press last week. In an exciting 2/10ths of a second & with one extremely false move I sheared the mother right off the mount. Old George Weplo, the machinist who built the thing, assured me that I could run a semi-truck over it & not damage it but, not having a semi at hand, I just made that cute little move & Whap! Brought it right off. Don't let anybody tell you that your mother is not mechanical."

When her symptoms began to trouble her, and she began to have her earliest encounters with cancer doctors, she didn't write about making art anymore. She wrote instead about doctors: "Went to the throat guy yesterday. He says my condition is 'worrisome'— something they learn in med school, no doubt—the word choice, I mean. God knows what they learn about the condition. In any case, I am to go into hospital for a biopsy on Monday afternoon. Full bullshit general anesthetic affair. Can't do much but fret till then. I mean, I love locals—lovely high—one time a proctologist put a 40-foot electronic snake up my ass—I mean with laser beam on the end to snip out some silly growth—and I remember the whole thing fondly because they pumped gallons of valium into my terrified old bod before & during." Nevertheless, she had a painting project under way, one suitable to the depressing situation in which she had suddenly found herself. She wrote that she was preparing a stencil for her husband, one he would employ to paint a message on their garage door declaring the space a tow-away zone. They were trying to ward off beach traffic.

"I think he ought to soften the threatening effect with some hospitable addendum like—

Gives   Good
Really   Head," she added.

"I've got part of the stencil cut, but by the time I get to the Gives Really Good Head I will have run out of garage door & energy."

By December 17 of that year, she had been diagnosed with cancer. She underwent surgery soon after. She assured me I needn't come home for the event—it was a small matter, she explained— but alerted me that she would bear a serious scar on her neck and that I must not to be alarmed when I next saw her. I sent her several silk scarves patterned with the kind of strong, graphic images I knew she favored—squares, stripes, houndstooth checks; no hearts or cabbage roses, nothing cloying or sentimental.

Just before Christmas, she sent me the gift of a cured ham and a small wheel of Swiss cheese. She talked a lot about food in the letter, proposing all sorts of interesting meals I could cobble together with her present.

"As you can tell from the foregoing," she explained, "I am interested in the social, economic & religious uses of food. I am thinking of doing a piece called Icon in the Pantry, Charismatic Centerpieces & Born Again Pastry Cooks I Have Known. The reason is that I am starved out of my mind, eating nothing & mainlining codeine. If you can't eat it then talk about it, cook it, fondle it, drive yourself mad with lust for broiled chicken & french fries, curries, pies—just write lists of stuff you have eaten or plan to eat. . . . Meantime, they say I should be able to join the eating faction of my fellow man in a week to 10 days. Perhaps I'll write again in a couple of weeks when I'm sane again."

❖ ❖ ❖

The nature of our relationship was symbiotic from the beginning. Our mutual need, the sense that we were, if not a single organism, then at least dependent on each other for survival, was particularly vivid throughout my childhood. Especially then, our intimacy, her devotion, left me feeling powerful and unique. To be sure, that symbiosis was disturbed by Ruth's difficult five-year courtship by her second husband. I was sometimes petulant during those adolescent years, frankly jealous of her lover. The occasional friend and shrink has suggested to me that that period amounted to her second abandonment of me, the first being at the farm outside Paris. From my perspective as a sentient adult, however, I seem incapable of summoning the *specific* rage some have suggested I should feel. Instead, I am defensive on Ruth's behalf. Out of a sense of duty to Ethan and to me, she endured fifteen years of my father's disfavor. She had the right to seek love and security in her lifetime, just as I have always had the right.

Nevertheless, in my early thirties, when my health was still vibrant, I was researching some problems in those church basements where the adult children congregated. I was trying to connect some dots. So far, nothing was coming clear, though I had some scrambled notions pulsing through my head that Ruth might be to blame.

I believed I was failing life in critical ways. I did not have a husband. I was not loved. I was a mature woman yet I was childless. In my twenties, Ruth kept raising her "INAPPROPRIATE LOVE OBJECT" theory to me to explain these failures. But she had encouraged me for two years while I carried on a relationship with a rich, flamboyant married man twenty-five years my senior. When I found someone else who actually liked me—even if he was years younger than I, lived in Los Angeles, spent most of his spare time lifting weights in a gym, and drove a Camaro with surfboard attached—Ruth had suggested, in all seriousness, an alternative: "Why don't you get a parakeet?"

Her reaction to my despair over failed relationships, each devastation exponentially worse than the one before, seemed far too casual by the time I was approaching thirty-five. I began to feel Ruth was simply averting her eyes— "the only decent thing to do," as she would have said. I think now she had run out of things to say; she was as disappointed and mystified as I. Nevertheless, she had drunk fifths of whiskey from the bottle and beat her head against the wall when such things happened to her, and it was I who took care of her, though still a child. When that icy, deadly pendulum swung in my direction, Ruth increasingly behaved as if I must forget the wounding in an instant and be gay like her. Life was a banquet and I need only move to the next course. She seemed to have lost touch with what it felt like—the diminishment, the disbelief.

I began to experience bouts of rage toward Ruth, periods when I simply would not call her, after having called daily for years and years; periods when I refused to check in, refused to give her the opportunity to advise or sympathize, or even listen. Once during this period, I came for a visit; I noticed she had removed all the photographs of me from the wall. Looking at them now probably caused

137

her more pain than pleasure. I was breaking off the affair. I was in the process of abandoning her.

I had a list, some of it real, some of it imagined. I blamed her for my ancient failure at Northfield; she had undermined my confidence. I convinced myself that Ruth had unconsciously warned me off men, instilled distrust, with the result that I was too suspicious to feel relaxed in a relationship with one.

Ruth was the brightest star in her own milieu, but on the rare occasions when she orbited around to what was presumably my little region of the cosmos, accompanied by her husband, I made small effort to introduce her to friends or share my life with her in the way I had shared it for years on the telephone. When I was at Berkeley, she spent two weeks in San Francisco and demanded to be introduced to the dean of the journalism department; I acquiesced, but I sensed the man was flustered by our appearance in his office. Later, when I was working at *Women's Wear*, Ruth visited New York and made her desire known immediately: She wanted to meet the newspaper's editor—the one who held Jackie O in such high esteem—as well as all the other equally vivid and unusual characters, my colleagues, whom I had been describing to her on a daily basis. My mother's request mortified me; I could not recall having seen anyone else at the paper troop through the newsroom with parents in tow. I was too insecure to break new ground. I denied her request roundly, and she was visibly hurt.

In the very early 1980s, I was seeing a man, a renown journalist and dedicated bachelor fifteen years my senior whose books had been required reading at Berkeley. I thought he was brilliant when I was twenty-one; my opinion remained unchanged at thirty-one. I was either infatuated or in love; I'm not sure I ever knew the difference. I was scared of him, too. He liked but certainly didn't love me. I was unsure why he kept me in his life, or how it all would end. I simply knew it would end. I was on the phone with Ruth about this particular man on a regular basis. "Does it seem to you that you deliberately *choose* men who are destined to reject you?" Ruth had inquired politely of me some years before. She had suggested I did so to protect my autonomy, my career. In my early thirties, however, I had those things and longed for more.

Ruth and her husband came to New York in the last days of my tortured liaison with this gray eminence. Ruth was expecting to meet him, to have dinner or drinks—anything. As her stay of four days wore on, she was clearly stunned that this meeting was apparently not to take place. He had expressed no interest in meeting my mother, however, and I hadn't the courage to insist, or even ask, that he do so. In my limited imagination, I couldn't believe he and Ruth would ever find common ground. I was worried, too, that Ruth would blow my cover—my finely tuned (if ineffective) performance as the consummate geisha. Hovering over everything, of course, was the drinking. I couldn't risk jeopardizing that white-gloved presentation, and as I have noted, Ruth never wore white gloves. In hindsight, I believe his manner, which seemed to announce, "I'm the smartest person in the room," wherever he went, would have dispersed in every direction when countenanced by Ruth's spirited seduction.

I recall standing in my mother's hotel room as she and her husband packed their bags, struggling to fit their "traveling booze" into various nooks and crannies, in a rush to leave. Ruth seemed shaken; she wouldn't look at me. I wanted everything to be warm and cozy, hugs and kisses all around. It wasn't that way. A sickening, nauseating sensation of guilt and self-loathing was rising in me, making my hands shake. I had finally clarified things without having to speak a word: Ruth wasn't part of my real life; she was a phantom on the phone.

It is likely here that I cross paths with all the other adult children. It wasn't just the man, it was my entire life. The unending worry I felt was a kind of alarm system with a blinking red light and a hair trigger. The siren could sound at any minute, announcing the spiraling loss of control over events, a result that would leave me vaporized. The great joke, of course, was my belief that after thirty-some turbulent years, I had got my life nearly under control; I believed such a thing was possible.

When I invited Ruth to New York one day before she was told she was soon to die, it was because the anger simply wasn't there anymore, nor was the mask. Three years of illness had chastened me. The foundering of the ship was causing everything on deck to shift wildly. The illusion of control was gone. My mother, our connection, our love—*those* were important. I was suddenly eager to show her off. She was the brains behind the operation, after all, and that was just my operation—what about *hers?* Who else did I know who had a mother quite like mine? There were a whole lot of sweet little old ladies out there, and then there was Ruth. I was also disconcerted by the fatigue and uncertainty in her voice. I think I realized that afternoon that the years of playing the put-upon child, the self-indulgence, had to end at once. It was time to let my mother know how much she mattered, to let her into my life as the flesh-and-blood woman who had raised me, gin and sorrow and bawdiness and searing honesty and all. The byline in the latest "hot" magazine, or the rich boyfriends and their Park Avenue clubs, were not the things that were going to make me whole. Forgiveness and especially acceptance—of myself, of my mother, of our humanity, of the reality of our past, and of our suffering—was going to make me whole.

Ruth used to counsel me when I was a child, "Be *aware* of your effect on the people around you." I found it a demanding task. Her illness opened a new universe for me, one in which every word and gesture is observed and has meaning, where subtle and overt actions spread broadly from individual to individual, and thence to the communal. Anyone can inflict harm on anyone else—by a glance, by the emphasis placed on a word in a sentence, by cavalier, unthinking responses to inquiries, by not speaking when it would be better to speak, by speaking when it would be better not to speak. By the time Ruth's death was a given, I was persuaded that murder is possible without raising a hand.

When my mother called to let me know that she would be unable to pay me a solo visit in New York, the grief I felt was soon matched by crushing guilt. I worried that my withdrawal of affection, my anger, had somehow hastened or even launched her illness. I believed all the years of struggle to achieve that gilded, happy life I thought might be out there had been badly used. I suspected I might have found that rich life had I remained within the boundaries of her calming influence. Most especially, I mourned the wasted, unconscious time I could have shared with her. When I returned to Minneapolis to see Ruth that first summer, I was seeking to reclaim something I felt I had foolishly mislaid: I was trying to recover that safe place, that lover's intimacy we once shared, before it was lost for all time.

The fragile, unaccountable rhythm of life, the ebb and flow of emotions and events that draw us toward, and just as suddenly cast us away from, one another, had afforded me a second chance. I reached for it with the frantic determination of one who is drowning. I was relieved more than I was grateful. I am older now, more worldly-wise, and I am often struck with wonder at the benevolence life offered me that summer.

I was in the middle of writing a book when I left New York. In Minneapolis, I took an apartment downtown where I did little else but sleep and work on the manuscript. In the late afternoons, I would drive to my mother's house, sit in her bedroom and talk for an hour or two, walk her dog, then talk with her a bit more until she shooed me home again by dark. Being near her, listening to her, I would feel my heart slow, my body relax. I never wanted to leave. "Finish your book," she would say at the door, "I feel some urgency about this." The book was about an emerging disease, the one from which I suffered. The year before, government bureaucrats had destroyed any possibility of a concerted research effort by naming it after one of its mildest symptoms, chronic fatigue, and by declaring it a syndrome instead of a disease. I was worrying this development, exploring the curious workings of science and medicine. My mother wanted to hold my invention in her hands, nicely bound and dressed up in a shiny jacket, before she died.

I worked at night. When the orange glow of the sun invaded my seventeenth-floor apartment, I turned the computer off. Sometimes I left my apartment at six A.M. to go the farmer's market to buy fresh asparagus or flowers for Ruth. I frequently slept all day, the hours during which I felt most ill and found it most difficult to write.

Little is more wearing than trying to change what cannot be altered. I could not save Ruth, nor could I make myself well. I was in control of just one thing: the book. In an effort to keep my mind clear on these matters, I often made lists—column A, column B—and left them lying around. To survive the years ahead, I would be required to fashion a new existence, one in which Ruth would not be a participant, one commensurate with my diminished abilities. Perhaps it is among the many reasons I looked upon my mother's demise with such terror: Who would help me in this difficult endeavor if not Ruth?

❖ ❖ ❖

In those final years of Ruth's life, I occasionally drove by the house on Girard. Visiting the architecturally whimsical structure made me feel unearthly. It was as if I, too, had joined the ancestral parade of ghosts who haunted the place, who couldn't leave it and their memories behind. Yet I needed to satisfy myself that the house was still there, that it was not simply part of a dream or something imagined; that my history and Ruth's history, entwined and separate, were equally true and real. The house, utterly unchanged atop its little hill, provided me with evidence, even if the sight of it caused my heart to flutter, my palms to sweat.

Eventually I was introduced to a friend of the owner. Without thinking the matter through, I blurted out: Could I possibly bring my mother there? We had loved the house, and hadn't been inside since 1962. My request was granted and an afternoon was set aside. Ruth seemed as eager as I.

We were welcomed by a woman in her late thirties. She lived there by herself, an undertaking I privately considered terribly brave. She urged us to take our time; she would be sitting on the patio out back. Ruth and I stood together in the front hall marveling at the beauty of the place. Every detail remained unchanged: the stairway newel, the circular, cut-glass window at the landing, the beautifully carved molding that framed the doors and windows. We stepped into the living room and were startled by its dimensions and glistening wood flooring. The windows were still nine feet tall. The kitchen Ruth had designed was perfectly intact; even the glass cabinetry was in place. As we moved through the rooms of the first floor, we exchanged incredulous glances, each thinking the same thought: How remarkable it was that we once had lived here.

By the time we made our way up the front stairway and began our tour of the bedrooms, however, a heaviness of spirit settled on us both. We looked inside Ethan's room and remembered his little boy's figure, playing on the floor with his mice and his chameleons, his Monopoly board spread with messy heaps of toy money. We walked quickly through the room where Ruth and my father had shared their loveless marriage bed; Ruth's face was slack. We entered my bedroom last. The yellow wallpaper was gone, of course, but the great walnut door with its ornate brass fixtures looked just as it had in 1955. I opened the closet door. I had to know: Would the seashell drawer pulls be in place? I dropped to my knees on the closet floor; the drawer pulls were exactly as I had first seen them thirty-seven years before. I was suddenly extravagantly happy. "Mom—look!" I said, almost shouting. When I turned to look at Ruth, she was standing in a far corner, her arms clutching her handbag to her chest like a child might hold a stuffed toy. She had been watching me. Her face was distorted by tears; she couldn't speak. I believe it was the only time I saw Ruth cry in the years before she died.

I am sorry now I brought Ruth back to the old gray Victorian so soon before her death. Ruth hadn't wanted to think about the years we spent there, years that began so auspiciously and ended so badly—her lonely marriage over, her children's childhoods lived out—before she was thirty. As her friend Roode recognized long before I did, Ruth was actively avoiding all that. She was working hard to face her death without regret, without bitterness.

It was during my third summer in Minneapolis, when it was apparent from her symptoms that her life was drawing to a close, that I believe Ruth and I were happiest with each other, when that sense of sharing bloodstreams had finally returned. We began to merge our pronouns in a way that suggested the difficulty we were having differentiating ourselves from each other. I might say, "I loved that book," when I meant to say, "Ruth loved that book." She might say, "I'm going to the store," when she meant, "Hillary is going to the store." We often said "we" when we meant "I." It was embarrassing; people looked at us oddly, yet we were unable to stop. Our strange, inclusive grammar was beyond our control. If one were to draw the phenomenon, one might sketch two figures, her outline and mine; the lines would intersect at every curve.

Just months before she died, Ruth began designing a quilt, one filled with hundreds of tiny squares in fabrics of at least fifty patterns and hues. We laid the larger fabric blocks comprised of the tiny one-inch squares on her bed, taking several hours to decide exactly how these blocks should be sewn together. When we finished, I discovered there was one little square that bothered me. Moments later, Ruth turned to me: There was a piece of fabric in this quilt she didn't like. I pointed to the square that was troubling me. Her eyes smoldered with pleasure. It was the same one-inch square she objected to. I immediately pulled the block off the bed and substituted another one. Just as quickly, Ruth put the original block back. She insisted we keep the tiny patch of fabric in the quilt in memoriam to our shared sensibility.

Just as I was tempted to accept my mother's silent admission—thank you for your concern, but it appears I will not be dying after all—Ruth began speaking in a husky, labored fashion. She was increasingly short of breath. She ate less and less; she couldn't always hide her wince of pain when she swallowed solid food. From the moment she woke until she returned to bed at night, she kept herself hydrated with small tumblers of hot water and bargain-basement bourbon, the only substance that went down without hurting.

In August, one of Ruth's doctors at Abbott hospital ordered a CT scan and sent Ruth to a thoracic surgeon at the same institution. The surgeon recommended surgery to remove a rib; the bone looked slightly abnormal, he said. Following that surgery, a nurse gave the patient Dilaudid, a form of synthetic morphine in use since the 1920s, to control the surgical pain. The drugs, however, sent the patient into respiratory arrest.

Ruth called me just before she was administered the near-fatal Dilaudid. She was already confused and agitated, cardinal signs of Dilaudid poisoning. "Get your cute little bod down here *right now*," she said. "I want to tickle and pinch you and show you off. *Right now!*" My stepfather was sitting by her but had fallen asleep. I showered; I made a short call; I had trouble finding a place to park. When I walked into Ruth's room, she looked stone-faced. Her skin was an odd color, too. She appeared to me like a cigar store Indian someone had stuffed awkwardly between the sheets. My heart was pounding—I had never seen anyone immediately following surgery—could this possibly be normal?

Minutes later, her face was gray and her fingertips were blackening, symptomatic of cyanosis—the loss of blood oxygenation. I discovered she was not breathing. I ran to the nursing station. As staff began to pour into Ruth's room, someone shoved me into the corridor. A code was issued. I watched from the doorway. They plunged a plastic tube down her throat to "bag" her, and a doctor rushed in to administer Narcan, the drug well known to ER staff as the treatment of choice for barbiturate overdoses. Soon I heard Ruth screaming from somewhere deep in her gut. "Help! Help! H–E–L–P!" I pushed my way back into the room, and when she saw my face amongst the myriad white-coated goons surrounding her, she reached out for me. I held her, and the hospital staff backed off for a moment. When they removed the plastic tube from her throat, she gagged. At its end, a large knot of bloody tissue hung precariously. There were clots of blood in Ruth's mouth as well. Everyone present was startled. "What's *that?*" a young nurse gasped when she saw the bloody lump of tissue.

I sat with Ruth for the next eighteen hours. She was attached to a machine that monitored the rising and falling of her chest; the machine beeped noisily whenever she stopped breathing, which occurred every time she shut her eyes. When the beeping began, I would touch her shoulder, call her name, until she opened her eyes again and resumed breathing. Nurses were forced to administer additional Narcan at intervals during the night. Sometimes she stared at me in the darkened room, her eyes blank and affectless. I wasn't certain what she was thinking. Later, she told me: "I wanted out—I wanted to die."

The nurse who had injected the Dilaudid stood next to Ruth and apologized before leaving her shift. The surgeon returned early in the morning. Apparently the staff got to him before I did. He showed me to a private room, where he harangued me, exhibiting what seemed like forced outrage at my accusations of malpractice. He suggested that Ruth's breathing difficulties might be due to emphysema. The rib he removed had turned out to be perfectly normal, he added.

Ruth never really bounced back from the removal of her rib and the ensuing respiratory arrest. She was depressed and withdrawn for several weeks. After an internal investigation, hospital administrators denied the overdose. Instead, they wrote in a letter to my mother, Ruth had suffered an "idiosyncratic" reaction to the painkiller. "Obviously," they continued, "this reaction has been very unpleasant for you and your family." Nevertheless, they concluded, "there is no evidence . . . this complication . . . [was] in any way related to, or the result of, mismanagement or malpractice."

Ruth's breathing was now even more labored, and she was weaker. The damage to her throat caused by the emergency intubation insured she was never again able to eat solid food. When she tried to speak after the surgery, she often coughed, an event that inevitably left her doubled over and almost entirely without breath.

By late fall, it was increasingly apparent to me that Ruth expected to expire on her own without further assistance from the medical profession. She summoned unknown reserves of energy in order to give a succession of small dinner parties and lunches for her closest friends. She herself could not eat; she moved the food around on her plate, distracting her guests' attention with conversation. Her good cheer left them clueless: She was saying good-bye. They said good-bye in return and departed her house in high spirits without realizing they would never see her again. That was precisely how Ruth wanted it.

Ruth gave her best and most serious effort to what she surely knew was the final Christmas of her life. "Christmas Eve 92," her formal menu began. "Graavlox with dill mayonnaise. Chopped liver canapes. Cream of butternut squash soup. Sourdough bread. Oven broiled rack of lamb (oven on broil, 12 minutes). Roasted potatoes, carrots, onions & garlic cloves (Watercress & Greek olives to garnish plates). Chilled fruit compote. Lemon coconut cake. Coffee. Stilton cheese, Port & Brandy." She asked one of her housekeepers, a young man named Alan, to serve the courses so that she could remain seated throughout the meal, insuring that she would have enough breath to talk. Wearing a tuxedo, Alan performed his duties impeccably; Ruth's guests never knew the real reason for his presence that evening.

148

She prepared this meal for the friends she loved best, the widow of a newspaper columnist she had known for three decades, and the widow's two sons, one of them, David, a highly regarded journalist in Washington and a contemporary of mine. David's wild, cynical diatribes about journalism in the capital, his especially hilarious accounts of interviews with "non compos mentis" U.S. Senators, delighted everyone, but none more so than my mother. She responded to his magnetic sexuality, his physical bigness, his precocious mind. She had enormous compassion for the difficulties he had faced in his life. Whenever she stood near David, she touched him, tenderly—massaging his shoulders, smoothing his hair—and he would stop talking, close his eyes, and lean his head back slightly in quiet appreciation. Just weeks before she died, she would begin writing, as if composing a poem, "David and Hillary—David and Hillary to the White House."

David had been struggling intermittently with heroin addiction since he was sixteen, and the problem was hard upon him again. Before her death, I confided David's drug problems to Ruth. No doubt she was hurt David hadn't told her himself. "It's curious that he chooses to tell you—he knows you are even less likely than his mother to be understanding," she commented. "He might as well look for sympathy from those assholes at Hazelden." At the party Ruth's husband gave in her honor after her death, while friends reminisced about Ruth in the living room, David would quietly work his way through Ruth's bedroom cupboards, looking for drugs. He found an enormous cache—enough drugs to keep him home from his job covering the Pentagon and thoroughly strung out for five days. Ruth would have understood completely.

In the evenings during the early days of that winter, my mother would stand in front of her fireplace warming her back, sipping brown booze and hot water, speaking in brief phrases between sharp intakes of air. She talked mostly about the book I was writing. She talked about how the book would make me rich, about how its publication would allow me to buy a house and furnish it with things I loved. I was borne aloft in her fantasies.

In February, when I was unable to bear any longer her struggle for breath, her chronic cough that on occasion threatened to turn her inside out, I called the county hospital's pulmonary clinic and made an appointment for her. It was all I knew to do. Yet the action was like toppling the first in a miles-long stretch of delicately stacked dominoes. My mother was thrust, from that moment, into a final round of medical misfortune from which her only relief would be death. "Hillary got tired of watching me try to die on my own," was how Ruth wanly explained my action in a letter to her brother some months later.

She was signed up for surgery in no time at all; the senior docs at the county hospital knew an emergency case when they saw one. I brought them Ruth's radiology scan of the previous summer. Upon my questioning, the surgeon told me the scan had been misread: A sizable malignancy had been present, just where it would be expected, in Ruth's esophagus; her rib, the one that had been removed, looked normal.

Seven years had passed since my mother's original cancer diagnosis. She understood very well by then that I was ill, and I understood very well that she was dying. The night before the surgery, my stepfather, my mother, and I had a quiet dinner together. We ate soup; Ruth managed two or three teaspoons before she resumed drinking bourbon. We three were gentle with one another. We all knew it was ending. We spoke about nothing in particular—was the soup ready? Had I put the wineglasses on the table? Was there any French bread in the freezer? Had the dog been walked?

Afterward, Ruth and I sat together in her living room. I needed to tell her something.

"When you called me to tell me you were afraid you had cancer," I said finally, "and I brushed it off as if it was nothing—I didn't want to believe it could be true. I was angry because I was sick, too, and you didn't seem to understand. I've been ashamed for so long. Can you forgive me?" She looked at me not as a mother might look upon a daughter, with the complex brew of power and submission and struggle implied in such a relationship; she looked at me as one looks at a beloved fellow human, one on equal footing with oneself. "I am sorry for the way I responded to the news of your illness," she said in her newly husky, breathless voice, her eyes unwavering, her eyebrows stern with the importance she attached to her message. "I thought that if we just ignored it, if we could keep you from *dwelling* on it, it would simply go away. I *didn't* understand, and I would like you to forgive me."

I went home after that. They were the last sentences Ruth ever spoke to me.

Part Four

Ruth is in the cancer ward of the county medical center, her body slack against the starched sheets of a slippery hospital mattress. A surgical incision has been made in her throat and a plastic tube has been inserted there. During the procedure, surgeons discovered that several malignant tumors had virtually replaced the walls of her esophagus. The tumors were also pressing on her vocal chords, nearly paralyzing them, which explains why, in the months leading up to the surgery, she could speak only in a husky, labored rasp. Now she discovers to her dismay that she cannot speak at all; she simply cannot pull enough air into her lungs to force sound out.

A tall, broad-shouldered man, an oncologist, appears in her room. He is impossibly attractive; he looks like a movie star playing a doctor. Scores of doctors have entered, then departed from, her life over the last several years, and for now he is just another one—someone to be regarded with caution, someone with license to cause physical pain with his hands and induce the fearsome, punishing specter of death with his words; someone with accountability to no one, least of all his patients. She waits to see how this one will employ his powers, although she no longer seems as curious as she has been on such occasions in the past. The surgeons have already conveyed the worst to her: She is absolutely going to die this time; no question about it.

The oncologist assures her that her death need not be filled with terror and pain. If she desires it, he says, he will place himself in charge of her case, he will care for her to the end. Ruth's face remains impassive as he tells her these things; she gazes at him as if he were an art professor, perhaps, explaining an interesting new printmaking technique. For a doctor, he seems unusually intelligent. He is more than merely confident of the facts, he seems to understand every nuance of their import. A life, that of a fellow human being, is coming to an end. He respects the gravity of the event, as well as the absolute mysteries of the process. Over time, the oncologist will prove himself to be so unlike every other doctor, Ruth will muse, "I wonder if he is a doctor at all. Perhaps he is one of those terribly clever Canadians who never went to medical school." She will smile her elfin half-smile thinking about the possibility that, in her dying, she has magically slipped below the radar of the medical profession and is now being attended by a shaman.

Her daughter is in the room; Ruth finds it hard to look at her. Her husband is there, too. His expression is uncomprehending, stunned, except that he begins to cry, his round, heavy face suddenly crumpled like a piece of paper someone has balled up, then cast aside. Ruth turns to him, her look one of profound sympathy. "Darling," she says, drawing on some just-discovered strength, like a woman who finds the muscle to lift a tractor off her crushed child, "we've known for a very long time I have cancer." They are the first words she has been able to manage with this new device in her throat; they are the last as well.

The oncologist turns to a box of Kleenex near him, plucks a tissue from it, and hands the tissue to the weeping husband.

He offers Ruth a course of experimental chemotherapy, although he notes the outcome is uncertain and the side effects are guaranteed to be unpleasant. When she looks at him and shakes her head no, he registers quiet relief, even admiration. Silence ensues. The daughter stares at the walls, the frayed laces of her running shoes, the pattern on the linoleum floor. She feels—what is it?— something so familiar, age-old, like hunger or sleepiness. It is fury. She wants her mother to try the new chemicals. The husband's face is slack and reddened now; he stares at his wife, she stares back. The doctor waits, a young Burt Lancaster, stethoscope draped around his neck like a theatrical prop. His large, relaxed frame, seated in a chair inches from the bedside of his new patient, seems to communicate he has nowhere to go, no other engagements. Elsewhere, phantoms are moving about in a dream world where nothing has significance. Here, in this small room lit by fluorescent lights and furnished with orange plastic chairs, four people feel themselves to be at the center of the universe.

"Kid," Ruth's husband says to her finally in a choked voice, "you've got guts."

That night, writing in ballpoint pen on a yellow legal pad, she directs her husband to bring art supplies and fresh flowers when he returns the next day. She is specific to an excruciating degree about what the flowers should look like. It is the first time in several years she has expressed the desire to make art. She delivers her request without amendments, as if the years in between making art and not making art had never happened. When he arrives the next day, she writes to him, "Pull that cart over here & put just the vase of white tulips on it. Lead pencil & bristol board." To her daughter she writes, as if the project will involve them both, "We will sit the Vase on that table & position it in that end of the room & draw it from over here. We will make several outline drawings of the flowers from the same perspective every day as they are buds (day I) fully opened (day II & III) then as they lose their petals. I've always thought that it would be an amusing series to do. And outline drawings are nice & very easy to do. Just a series of pictures of tulips as they progress & age."

She tells her husband he might as well go home; she sends her daughter away as well.

❖ ❖ ❖

Ruth has been in the county hospital for three days. Her ability to breathe has been unenhanced by the surgical procedure. She feels pain everywhere. Her lungs are producing a bloody phlegm that must be washed from the inner canula of the tracheostomy tube once or twice an hour; if not, she begins to suffocate.

For several months before this surgery, she had been unable to swallow solid food. She had subsisted entirely on bourbon mixed with hot water, and cocoa made from melted milk chocolate mixed with whipping cream, with bourbon usually added. Now her throat is so pinched from tumors that she can no longer swallow liquid. It is too late by several days to send a tube down her nose to her stomach; cancer has taken over midway. Soon the woman will be given a feeding tube, a "peg," that will lead from an incision in her abdomen directly into her small bowel.

The neck surgery has rendered her mute. Even breathing is "chancy," she complains. She writes to her daughter, "Airway much diminished & growing ever smaller. I could not imagine anything this bad. The breathing was to be the big reward—all worth while & it has not, so far, worked out that way. I used to get short of breath when I, say, loaded the fireplace. Not when I was reading. . . . I hate it here. I'm going mad. I can't read, I can't talk, can't sleep. Everybody who passes has a right to hurt me. I am losing my mind and none of it works! It's all AWFUL."

Pain is all around. Her daughter has set up camp in her hospital room. Daily, the younger woman attempts to defend her mother from the probes and queries of medical students eager for their first look at what is now being called throat cancer at the top of Ruth's medical chart. One afternoon, a fresh-faced group of male doctors in training hover excitedly around her bed. Peering over her reading glasses, the patient assesses them charitably and then writes to them, "I would love to chat, but I'm not up to my Tallulah Bankhead imitation." They stare at her uncomfortably; they have never heard of the actress.

The resident in charge of this group prepares to send a snake-like probe with a light attached down the fresh wound in Ruth's throat. Ignoring the directive that sterile procedure be followed for this patient, he begins without first donning sterile gloves. Infection is not a pressing issue for him; perhaps he considers the woman to be a corpse already. When the daughter asks him to wash his hands and put on gloves, he responds that there is no need. The students shift on their feet and turn their gaze to the window, studying the outlines of buildings. Without speaking, the daughter pushes her way through their semicircle and plants herself between the resident and her mother. The resident washes and dons gloves with the enthusiasm of a child who has been caught stealing and must now return the goods.

Ruth's husband has renamed the daughter Fights With Doctors. Mostly he seems dazed, as if in a trance.

Since the confirmation of her mother's hopeless condition, the daughter has fallen into a trance of her own. She has become like unsculpted granite: dense, immovable, graceless. With only minor permutations in the script, everything is happening just as she had known for decades it would happen. Anger and terror swathe her in a kind of aura. Like an epileptic hurtling toward a seizure, she has the sense that she is about to spin wildly out of control, committing some spectacular act of violence.

On the fourth day, when the doctor who is to implant the feeding tube enters Ruth's room to examine her, she writes, "If we did nothing more, how long would I last?"

The doctor ignores the query.

❖ ❖ ❖

Ruth is being sustained on sugared water delivered intravenously. A feeding peg has been surgically installed, but it's not working. Yet another surgery with a new, fancier peg has been scheduled.

Early one morning, three days after the second peg is installed, a nurse attempting to inject a quantity of medicine too quickly into the tube ends up rupturing the contraption. Ruth is suddenly pitched into such extreme pain, particularly in her chest and shoulders, that a resident interprets the symptom as a heart attack. He transfers her from the oncology ward to the cardiac intensive care unit. There, in accordance with the unit's inexplicable protocol, nurses and doctors lift Ruth from the gurney and place her in a fabric sling to be weighed like an animal hauled in from the wild. She is incapable of uttering a sound during this procedure, but her head, unsupported, falls back, its weight pulling on her damaged neck. Her eyes squeeze shut, tears run down her cheeks, and her teeth are bared in a silent scream. She is given heparin, a blood thinner, and morphine. No one in the cardiac unit seems to possess even rudimentary knowledge pertaining to the care of a tracheostomy patient, especially one with throat cancer. She is in too much pain to issue directions to the staff via the written word. Two hours later, a pulmonary specialist visiting the unit determines the problem lies with the feeding tube, not Ruth's heart. He orders a surgical resident to reinstall the tube.

A Doogie Howser look-alike appears; he is the surgical resident. After an initial examination, he departs and Ruth remains in the cardiac unit for the next eleven hours, her stomach unattended. By then, the resident who misdiagnosed a heart attack suggests that Ruth is in grave danger of peritonitis because of her exposed abdominal wound. He notes that she may soon require major surgery to prevent death from infection. The daughter pleads with the acting chief of the cardiac unit, another young resident, to call the surgeon back, but he refuses. The surgeon is too busy in the trauma unit to deal with her mother, he says. Triage is occurring, and the terminal-cancer patient with a ruptured feeding peg has failed to make the cut.

The daughter asks the cardiac chief to halt the heparin drip, pointing out that Ruth could bleed to death during surgery for peritonitis. He refuses. "My mother has cancer—she is *not* having a heart attack," the daughter asserts, but the cardiac resident is unimpressed by the lay assessment. The daughter finds a pay phone, calls the oncologist at home—it's Saturday night—and begs for assistance. He promises to call the surgeon out of the trauma unit immediately.

The younger woman hovers over her mother, trying to determine which of the many lines and needles might be leaking heparin into her mother's blood. Ruth is ashen and still, her eyes focused on the ceiling; thick dark liquid is oozing from a hole in her abdomen. The daughter puts on latex gloves and readies a sterile gauze bandage. Just as she is preparing to pull the heparin drip from a vein in her mother's ankle, Doogie Howser appears. He seems chastened; he's been on the phone with the oncologist.

Bare-handed, Howser examines the mass of limp vinyl tubing extruding from Ruth's stomach and grimaces. He begins pulling up the metal guards on either side of the bed in preparation for moving her to the surgical wing of the hospital. He's breathing heavily. An entire day has passed since the nurse ruptured the device. He listens to the daughter's plea that the heparin be stopped, but when he tells the cardiac unit chief that the daughter "has a point," the cardiac doctor again refuses to stop the drip.

There is no time to argue. Howser wheels the bed with Ruth in it through the ward's swinging doors, trailed by a nurse and the daughter, who are pushing steel poles from which swing clear plastic bags filled with drugs. The cardiac doctor snags the daughter's arm, saying, "I want to talk to you!" The oncologist has called him, too. The daughter wrenches her arm from his unfriendly grip and offers a terse, almost casual, "Fuck off." Nurses hover in the background, startled not so much by the words as by the fact that a patient's relative has addressed them to a doctor. "Who gave you permission to call Dr. R–?" he demands. His hands are formed into fists, his feet are spread wide in a fighter's stance. The daughter keeps one hand on her mother's cold bare toes and stays in step with the fast-moving entourage, but she is ready to brawl should the opportunity present itself. The doctor stares murderously, but some unseen force is holding him down, as if his Nikes are attached to the floor with superglue.

Lying in a tangle of bed sheets and intravenous lines, Ruth wears an oddly distant expression. Inside the ascending elevator, she stares at her daughter and the others without affect. The younger woman recognizes the look: Her mother just wants it to end; she wants out of this, right now.

❖ ❖ ❖

Ruth has been in the hospital for twelve days—days during which she has been nourished with nothing but fluids. New crises arise with stunning regularity. There are minor incidents as well. One afternoon the intravenous water drip becomes dislodged and the site on her wrist begins to bleed profusely. She is mute, and the nurses don't respond to the light outside her hospital room door. She takes a page of her notepad and crushes it into a ball; summoning her strength, she pitches it into the hallway. A passing janitor picks up the ball and tosses it back into the room, taking particular care to aim his missile at the patient. Her daughter arrives to find the floor and bed sheets dappled with blood. The daughter summons a nurse, who explains that the rest of the staff is at dinner.

On the thirteenth day, a new tribe of students in Dockers and white coats enter the patient's room. Their leader, another resident, announces that Ruth will now require a blood transfusion; she has become dangerously anemic. A nurse takes the daughter aside and warns that if the blood is not matched perfectly, her mother, already terribly weakened, could die from infection. The daughter suggests to her mother that she leave the hospital before the boys kill her; the two get no argument from Ruth's husband.

She walked in for her surgery fourteen days before, but now she departs the hospital in a wheelchair, fifteen pounds lighter, wearing her Dayton's bargain fur coat over a hospital gown, demonstrating the loveliness of her long shapely legs for the nurses, who cheer her on with shouts and applause. She can think of no other way to thank them. After all, voiceless now, she is unable to regale them with

161

bawdy jokes. The head nurse snaps a Polaroid of Ruth waving good-bye and lifting a beautifully pointed set of toes high in the air. She will be dead soon, like so many others who have been on their corridor, and they want something to remember her by.

"Your mother is quite a woman," a nurse says to the daughter as Ruth exits.

"You should have known her when she could talk," the daughter replies.

The hospital's final bill is $26,500, or, as Ruth later calculates, $81.79 per minute.

❖ ❖ ❖

Ruth returns to her home next to Cedar Lake at last. She begins to cry when her small dog runs from her in terror after hearing the raspy, almost mechanical sound of her breath escaping from a tube in her throat, and no doubt after catching the smell of the hospital that surely clings to her skin. As far as the little dog is concerned, this isn't the being he adored; this is some hair-raising impostor. She can offer no words of comfort to her formerly devoted Yorkie. She crosses a very private Rubicon then; her dog's previously unimaginable defection is the most brutal of all eventualities. She suddenly discovers, too, that shedding tears generates nearly intolerable pain in her face and neck. Nothing, not even the prospect of her own death, moves her to tears again.

The dog spends his days sitting on Ruth's favorite shawl on a daybed in the library just outside her bedroom door, massively depressed. Anyone who tries to move either him or the shawl is met with bared incisors and a growl remarkably low for such a small creature. At night, he hides deep in her clothes closet, watchful and silent as a mouse in the space between her shoes and the wall, the only sound in those hours the sibilant hum of the oxygen pump and her labored breathing.

For the first few nights, Ruth sleeps sitting up in a pink arm-chair at the foot of her bed. Fear of suffocation renders her unwilling to lie down. She can barely breathe in an upright position; the idea of becoming horizontal is terrifying. She keeps a hand mirror near her side at all times. She spends hours each day studying the reflection of the wound in her throat and drawing a series of small pencil sketches of her new self, the self that is mute and breathes through a metal tube held in place with cotton ties knotted at her nape. The drawings reveal a face of indeterminate gender with hair clipped in the style of a convict. The eyes are like those of a Holo-caust victim, the sockets dark and recessed, the eyes wide and lacking any definable emotion except horror. When she is done with a sketch, she crumples it into a ball, tosses it aside, then begins anew. She wants to get this just right.

She writes that she will accept no visits from well-wishers. Her disfigurement will only serve to shock her friends. In addition, she cannot imagine how she will entertain them without her voice. "The fastest lip in the West," as her husband likes to call her, has been permanently silenced.

❖ ❖ ❖

Ruth is furious about the results of her surgery at the county hospital. Above all, she feels betrayed. "I guess I'm pissed—perma-nently. Without speech, I feel myself to be diminished almost to the point of vanishing.

"I think the doctors would have liked me to tell them to consult their pals, and 'Yes, yes, nice Dr. Men, whip up a big pot of chemo & we will just go to work & traumatize that old tumor off the planet.'

& I said, actually I just want to be as easy as medicine can make me. I've had all the treatments I care to have. I think they had expected a more gung ho response. Patient comfort is not high priority with these doctors."

Her daughter assays some pale attempt to appease her, but Ruth's next words are "Shut up & clean my room."

It was her daughter, after all, who introduced her to this latest set of scoundrels.

Three weeks after the operation, during her first post-surgery clinic visit, Ruth is very specific in her comments to the surgeon who performed the operation that rendered her mute. "Three weeks today," she writes, her pen slashing away at her legal pad. "Function—miserably inadequate. 1) insufficient air, 2) no hope of speech with present set up, 3) not a satisfactory resolution to my original problem. All is worse, not better, than before. Clearly we need a NEW approach."

There is no other approach.

On the way home, she writes, "Why are they so reluctant to admit failure & look for something that *WILL* work?"

❖ ❖ ❖

Ruth has been home from the hospital for four weeks. She expresses no rage over the fact that she is fated to die, but she is enormously angry about the deplorable manner in which she believes she is going to die. She writes that she feels so deprived of breath, it is as if she is being held prisoner in a car trunk.

"I just WANT TO BREATHE AND SPEAK," she writes to her daughter. "I would *never* have agreed to this—just went ahead & starved. I am sure you can see it's a matter of a week or a month or two to pneumonia & strangulation—a death more violent and more to be dreaded than starving. I feel terrible, after all your valiant efforts, having to point this out to you, but it seems to me to be my case.

"A person cannot live for very long with an air-deprived, chancy delivery system. Unless [the doctors] can think of something soon, I feel it's all up to me. And a yucky end it is, too. I wanted to be Camille & starve!

"Where are physics and sci fi when I need them?" she adds. "God knows I've slept through enough boring sci fi movies. I've paid my dues. Put your minds to it, special effects folks."

She classifies the noisy malfunctioning machine that is supposed to moisturize the oxygen she receives at her throat as a "Fucking El Amateur Piece of Equipment." For the edification of her daughter, she adds, "That's F.E.A.P.E., pronounced 'feepee.'"

She calls the nursing efforts of her daughter and husband "T.L.D.C.," for Tender Loving Dork Care, but she has made it clear she wants never to return to a hospital.

❖ ❖ ❖

Ruth had become my captive. I hadn't applied for the position of captor, but she was fairly helpless by then, and stuck with me. Not surprisingly, she resented this turn of events. "I fear I have sorely disappointed Hillary," she wrote to her husband one day. "Instead of being sweetly dependant, I have been sleepy and grumpy."

Moreover, for the first time in her life, there was no possibility of a drink. She had stopped smoking, effortlessly, the day she was told she had cancer in 1987. Booze was another matter. She was simultaneously dying of cancer and withdrawing from decades of drink, surely an unspeakable torture. The much longed-for sober mom turned out to be irascible. Ruth found my companionship sorely wanting as well.

"I was born into the hands of one member of the Moral Majority," she wrote to her husband early on. "I think it's unfair, dying as I am in need of drink as much as anything, to have to leave this vale of tears driven out by a maiden lady who goes mad at the mention of pot or drink."

I can't remember what I did or said to precipitate this language, but Ruth could read my mind. Though I had never voiced my thoughts, she understood that I blamed her illness on booze. "I like to think I have been a loving & supportive mother," she wrote to me during this period. "I can't bear the picture that you dredge up from your heart of hearts of a mean destructive drunk. I can't survive that. And you shouldn't put up with it either." I had never thought Ruth mean or destructive, nor had I ever accused her of such things. Those distinctions between drinking in a self-destructive manner and being a destructive drunk had apparently never been properly clarified.

She taunted me. To her husband she wrote, "Want to try a little methadone? I got lots & I'm willing to share. Junkies love it. Relax, Hillary, he just said NO—a little something he picked up from Nancy Reagan." Another time, she wrote to me, "You haven't congratulated me on my amazing recovery from alcoholism—confirms my theory that I was a drinker by choice—not compulsion. When I no longer have a choice, I am easy. No problem. Alcoholics don't make a choice. I chose to drink."

When I page through her notebooks from this period, I find comments like "I'm not in PAIN!!!! I am in AGGRAVATION!!!!!" and "You are going to drive me to suicide." In short, the hospice her husband and I had tried to arrange, affording her a peaceful death at home, unharmed by careless nurses and student doctors, was less than peaceful.

To fully displace our grief, however, Ruth and I required a topic less opaque, less weighted by history, less painful, than the matter of her drinking. We rapidly discovered something about which we could argue endlessly, hour by hour. the number of calories that would be administered each day through the feeding tube in her stomach. Her doctors had prescribed eight cans of a creamy product called Attain. Ruth insisted she would have four. She wrote that she did not want to gain weight, that she did not want to get fat, that never, in her whole life, had she eaten so many calories in a single day.

Her oncologist told us: "This is the last thing you two should be arguing about now." I couldn't seem to let it rest, however. I couldn't let the wisdom of these words override the terror I felt when I thought about my mother dying. I had watched Ruth starve for months—watched her sustain herself with bourbon and chocolate, a regime that resulted in a loss of thirty pounds—before finally bringing her to the county hospital, and then I watched her starve for two weeks in the hospital. I sometimes felt I had watched my mother starve all her life. Whatever might prolong Ruth's life was what I wanted to do, so the struggle continued.

"Weighing 200 pounds does not guarantee eternal life," she wrote to me. Another day, she pointed out, "I weigh 145—hope you are happy now—monstrous child." In response to an inquiry, I told her the doctors were getting their advice from a hospital nutritionist. "Who is this nutritionist?" she demanded to know, and without waiting for a reply, continued, "The nutritionist is a chart from the insurance company. In addition to being a mute and having to worry about whether my next breath will actually get drawn, I don't see why, without the pleasure of the snap of a soda cracker, I should have to feel as if I had just stuffed myself with the heaviest 9 course meal in the history of eating. Why can't you give on this one tiny thing?"

Later that day, she wrote, "Okay, if you are going to sulk, I'll ingest the slop as often as you want to give it to me." But the conflict endured for several more days.

At last Ruth wrote to me, "You are drained and brittle and you are unable to appreciate or contribute to the sweet moments that drop into our laps or are within our grasp from time to time." I studied the words on the page and reluctantly recognized them to be true. I backed down. But Ruth herself was living in a kind of bee swarm of rage. It was increasingly apparent to her that her condition was likely to worsen rather than improve, although she studied herself for signs of better health each day. She let her anger loose upon me, who she knew would not leave her, rather than her husband, about whom she was less certain—although unnecessarily so.

"I'm finding stuff out all the time honey," she wrote one day. "I've never died before, damn it. Give me a chance to get *good* at it. Don't hold me to every position I may have taken early on in this process." And, another time, "I'm not dying to spite you. Give me a break!"

One morning, I came upon a note from my mother to my stepfather, thanking him for being a "co-conspirator" in their scheme to fake the number of cans of Attain she had; they were pouring the substance down the drain, then leaving the empty cans in the wastebasket for me to count when I arrived early each day. When her husband erred and gave her an extra can, she wrote to him, "You were my loyal co-deceiver when we phonied up Attain several mornings in a row. If anybody is entitled to slip me an extra Attain it's you, dear." Outside the range of her hearing, my stepfather addressed me as "Nurse Ratchet." Ruth was unaware of the particulars, only that her husband and I were barely speaking.

Once during those early weeks, when her husband inquired how she was feeling, Ruth wrote, "Up & down and much coughing & anxiety all around. I've been snarling at Hillary & by & large it has not been good."

Weeks passed before Ruth's anger began to wane. Finally she wrote, "I think this whole thing has been so hard for me to accept because NOW—there is simply no denying it—I am very ill indeed—and it will get worse, not better, from here. The notion of being unwell & changes to be for worse & no improvements—is a difficult one to adjust to. I'm not sure how to do it."

I always wondered," Ruth writes to a friend, "during those years when my illness was worrisome and inconvenient but rather easily bearable, what the last part of it was going to be like & why doctors just looked at the floor, or shrugged & said 'it varies' or whatever, whenever they were asked. They simply did not know or did not wish to describe the course of the last phase (or phases—no doubt there is more to come). Well my dear, now that I am in one of them—those mysterious last phases—I can understand the medics' resistance. Nobody wants to be boring and if anybody had tried to describe the amazing variety of boring events that can be packed into—say—twenty-four hours of the ongoing adventures of the advanced cancer patient—well—it just gives a whole new dimension to the concept of drear. . . .

"I will just gloss over the high points of my life here—not try to make a 'typical' day. Actually, if you take the same elements & sort of re-compose them—imagine days as a series of still lifes—the events & elements of each day remain the same: same setting, same cast, same events, but the elements vary in importance (size and position in picture) color (bright-dull, warm-cool, light-dark) speed (fast-slow, rhythmic-erratic) etc. . . . ."

Ruth has accepted her mute status and the fact of her tracheostomy. Signaling her resignation on these matters, she writes to her daughter, "One might have thought that if God chose to make me mute, he might have thought to endow me with a late life gift of spelling. Have you found me any good Helen Keller jokes?" She also writes, "There are none so deaf as those who will not read—I think an appropriate motto for persons in my situation." Band Aid–like patches that release synthetic morphine into the skin, and an anti-anxiety drug called Ativan, have gone a long way toward easing the woman's mind. But she remains actively involved in the minute-by-minute details of her care. She draws a sketch of a nude woman each day, a figure greatly more rotund than herself yet nevertheless evocative of her own body, and marks the places where the patches are to be placed. With her daughter, she calculates which should come off, and when, as well as where and when additional patches should be applied.

By the time May arrives, Ruth is more placid about her situation. She writes, "There are times in this whole enterprise when I feel loved & looked after & a rather lovely tranquil euphoria kind of settles in. It's very nice in its way. Unexpected and a kind of bonus—like we're doing what we are supposed to do & doing it rather well. Satisfaction? I don't know a word for it exactly. But it's nice & has to do with how we feel about ourselves & each other.

"A treasuring of the now, perhaps—Happy moments in an unexpected situation."

Ruth was more peaceful, yet I continued to suffer periods of black, helpless anger qualitatively reminiscent of my adolescence and feminist years. None of this needed to happen, I kept thinking; Ruth should have had twenty more years, and I wanted twenty more years of her. My mother felt this fury. She explained to me then that she chose not to live with anger, that she harbored no blame, and that she took full responsibility for all that had happened to her in her life. Doubtless, she had always hoped I would come to do the same, but now she was dying, and I was still exhibiting that crippling rage she had first encountered decades before, except the target was even more diffuse and the solutions further from our grasp.

"Much as I need you and love you and want you in my life," she wrote to me, "I can't allow you to judge the people & events that are the fabric of my life by the same set of rules that you judge the people and events that make up your own life."

I will try to explain to you once more that: I am responsible for every bottle of booze and pack of cigarettes that I drank or smoked. It was I who let your father bully and harass me. I believed that since I had chosen to marry him, in some way I deserved what followed. I thought— and to a certain extent still think—that people seek out a fate, circumstance, whatever you call it—that they can manage. Seemed like I was obligated to keep trying to make it work. . . .

I do not accept that I am some poor forlorn lump of protoplasm who has been abused by Parents & Husbands—completely without justification. It is my life and I have lived it. I made decisions—in some cases very bad decisions indeed. I have behaved in terribly bad ways. I have been imprudent, mean minded—every mistake possible in human relationships has been made by ME. And a couple with animals on which I do not care to dwell herein. But I am also a nice lady—I've done a few smart things. . . . I like to think I have been a loving & supportive mother. . . . I guess I feel I did better than my mother did, because the guidance I offered was presented as my own—not the reasoned judgement of some Body of Wise Persons (like shrinks) or rule of righteousness handed down by God & the bible. Of course, I had compensatory failures of great magnitude—there are a million *areas* in which to go wrong (as well as ways within each area) in bringing up kids. . . .

I did what I could. I do think that's fair to say. I don't think your father or I ever said, "Ha! This will really get to Ethan and Hillary"—& I know that I did a # of things that I felt obliged to do for your good rather than my own. I know for sure that if I had not been a mother my marriage to your father would have lasted months—not years. I also did a lot of stuff without trying to estimate its impact on you & Ethan.

Her pen stopped finally, and she sat motionless for a little while.

"Please," she continued at last, "let's try to do a little less reality & allow each other the fantasies that get us through life."

One might say reading was Ruth's vocation. She had started early in life, discovering that books offered swift escape into whatever reality the words established; she could remain there, safely involved, as long as the book lasted. Reading became a compulsion; I don't believe my mother was ever *not* reading a book; being bookless made her uneasy. After she died, Ethan wrote, "Being around Ruth meant reading insatiably. We ate small writers for lunch and survived whole seasons on Steinbeck and Hardy. It was clearly a search. We were exploring a frontier of human experience. . . . Every character's life could be reduced to a single crux of decision and we looked for that kind of simple resolution in our own life. . . . I often think how Ruth used to read as though the secrets of the universe were in books."

In her final years, she scoured the *New York Times* book section every Sunday, drawing up a list for her husband to take to the library the following day. At one of our estate sale outings, Ruth bought a 1917 edition of the Harvard classics—those fifty-some titles thought to represent the intellectual backbone of Western civilization. She discovered to her delight that the pages remained bound together; she burrowed methodically into each of the volumes, a table knife in one hand. "Where's my reading knife?" she would ask, padding around the house, peering over her reading glasses.

Her tastes were catholic. She read Proust and Flaubert and the two Henrys, James and Miller. She read the trendies like Scott Turow and Michael Crichton. Her assessments of the latter were pointed. "You gotta figure Turow thought he was writing a movie," she wrote in a note to her husband about Turow's latest thriller, "but I did not get the feeling, as we both did with *Jurassic Park*—and *The Client*, to some extent—that the guy from the studio was in the room."

Ruth was intimately involved with my book. She had edited everything I had ever written for publication. She was a fine editor, and a funny one. She brought her own brand of lightheartedness to the controversial subject matter, suggesting titles like, "Bang the Docs Slowly," and "A Maze of No Grace." Particularly after her tracheostomy, but before morphine pulled her irretrievably into its unearthly realm of wild imaginings, she worked hard to help me reclaim control of the twelve hundred pages I had already written. At night when I was in my apartment writing, she would sit in her bedroom penning page upon page to me about the story I was telling and the people in it, worrying the nuances of every characterization and the details I was or was not including to buttress my case.

"I've been reading a piece in the *New Yorker*," she wrote one time. "The writer is doing that dead pan 'just the facts, ma'am' style of the Reporter At Large, but, every so often, without any notice, he will do a 'now listen up' kind of aside. That's what kind of reporting you have been doing, but I think, every now and again, you could do

a kind of aside—See, gentle reader, already we see signs that Dr. S–
is a shit. Which is why we should take care to put in all the *good*
stuff about the guy. So that we can highlight the really *bad* stuff and
hope the reader can add. I would like a particularly appealing patient, or perhaps Dr. K–,who I thought was a lively guy—I don't
think you should cut him off *at all*—who *likes* patients, and juxta-
pose him with hardhearted Dr. S–, who clearly loathes them. . . ."

Often, she conceptualized my book as if it were painted art instead of journalism.

"I want a picture of events taking place on a canvas," she wrote
another time. "Sort of a mural with three interacting spheres: the
patients, the doctors, the establishment."

One note, written I don't know when, went this way: "I know it
seems rude of me to push you on this book business but I feel it's
crucial to our survival. Your head is more complicated than is mine
and your work is more difficult than anything I ever dreamed of trying. But I am not blind and you & I are not strangers. TRUST me
(and trust yourself)."

My mother and I knew by then that she would never live to see
the jacketed, bound version. Yet she recognized, as did I, that her
peaceful death, and my peaceful life, depended in some part upon
our unwavering faith in its promise. My unfinished first book had
become, in a sense, our private religion. It was our ladder into the
uncharted future, and the altar upon which we quietly laid our sac-
rifices and our love for each other. Completed, it would stand as the
lasting monument to our bond.

More simply, the book belonged to Ruth as much as to me, and
therefore its completion would signify not just my success in life but
her own. After all, I was nothing if not my mother's creation.

Although cancer surgery constrained her from uttering a sound during the last seven months of her life, I was rarely aware that my mother was not speaking to me. Deprived of voice, she pressed on in her eloquent diction by means of ballpoint pens and legal pads. She sat upright in her pink chair in her bedroom hour after hour, writing, reading, sketching, dozing. Ruth had no guile, no secret side, and consequently she had but one voice, no matter how she chose to communicate. In effect, her written word was indistinguishable in tone from her speaking voice; we chatted, just as always. In spite of her dire prognosis, her missives tended to be as fanciful and witty as anything she might have said at any other point in her life. One day I gave her a small bell to keep by her side so that she could call me wherever I might be in her house. "Bring my bell, book and can-dle—on second thought, scratch the candle," she wrote to me that day. We watched a video of *Badlands* another night. "If I ever have another baby," she wrote to me, "I know one thing—I sure ain't gonna name it Charlie Starkweather—you gotta know a kid with a name like that is not gonna come to a happy end."

Eventually my mother filled scores and scores of legal pads, and each time she came to the end of one, I discreetly stashed it in a pa-per shopping bag kept hidden from her view. To have betrayed my reverence for her every utterance, or more accurately, for every scratch of her busy pen, would have been to admit freely between ourselves that she was dying, and that we could not do, not for a very long time: Her impulse toward fantasy was too powerful; we avoided the fact of our parting, of her impending death, until her fi-nal weeks. Sometimes I pulled these notepads, soggy and tattered, from the wastebasket while she was showering. A few times, I dug through the trash cans in the alleyway while she slept, since my stepfather's penchant was to toss the legal pads whenever he had the opportunity. In my view, these were my mother's final precious words, and I considered them my bulwark against that portion of my life remaining when there would be no more words—no more sympathy, wry observation, or encouragement—from the lips of Ruth Jones to her only daughter.

One day, near the end, she wrote to me, sadly, "I wish we had saved more. It's all fading away so fast." I told her then that I had saved as many of her notebooks as I could. She smiled. "Good for you," she wrote. "Let Ethan and your stepfather read what won't hurt—just go to Kinkos with a little time & some money. You keep it. They will want to see it, and maybe even sweet grandsons like Nate."

As Ruth deteriorated, her care became exponentially complicated and demanding. A hospice nurse would visit each day, but for the remaining twenty-three hours, we were on our own. The time came when I moved into my mother's house, supplanting her husband. Clay was nearly seventy; his hands weren't steady enough to deal with Ruth's medical regimens. Her margin of life was narrow; if the tube in her throat became occluded or dislodged, a steady hand was required to clean it and replace it in a matter of moments. Acknowledging his clumsiness, Clay spent his nights on the living room sofa and I took his place next to my mother, but once he threatened to move to the Lakeland if I did not leave the premises. The house he had shared for twenty-five years with his wife was now a hospice, and at my mother's insistence, I was in charge. I said nothing to him, but thought merely, Good riddance.

By then I had foisted my own guilt about my mother's illness upon him. At odd moments, when he seemed not to be cognizant of my presence, I would look at his face and find myself thinking, You killed her. Perhaps he looked at me on occasion and thought the same. Neither of us was entirely rational by then. In fact, as Ruth's death approached, her husband and I were adversaries who barely spoke, who expended enormous energy merely suppressing our rage toward each other in order to perpetuate a false calm in Ruth's presence. Naturally, Ruth saw through our efforts. "Things seem very bleak to me," she wrote. "Our little home made health care has come apart & I do not read either of you clearly. We need to re-think our situation. There are always alternatives. I wish to flee from all of you and I know of no graceful way to do it." Ruth didn't really want to die; that became abundantly clear. She just wanted us to "shape up."

I rented a computer so that I could continue working on my book. I set it up outside my mother's room in her library. Ruth, tortured by the thought that her illness might interfere in any way with my progress, was deeply comforted by the appearance of the machine. "Hillary is having a computer delivered here this afternoon," she wrote with staunch assurance to her husband before the computer arrived. "We are going to get her out of the nursing business and back into book writing. I'm just sick with worry about her book." There might be at most two consecutive hours a day when I found time to write, however, and when I sat at the keyboard, my exhaustion, the complexity of the task, and the piercing awareness that Ruth was in the process of dying in the next room left me in a defeated stupor. Still, I posited myself before the computer as often as possible; the sight of me attentive to the glowing screen, the sound of my fingers on the keys, made Ruth so happy.

At night, Ruth and I lay together on her bed, our hands clasped together exactly as they had been when I was a small child and she was a young woman.

"Will you be here in the morning?" she would ask each night.

"Yes, always," I would answer.

Then she would sleep.

Shamans act as mediators between the visible world and the world of the spirits. By the time she met Brian Rank, who was then head of the oncology department at the Hennepin County Medical Center, a shaman was what Ruth needed. The doctor's untrumpeted appearance in her hospital room would turn out to be the one bit of good fortune Ruth would have in all the years of her illness. It may even have been the best luck of her life. Ruth had to struggle for everything else, but Brian Rank came to her unbidden, like a swash-buckling hero in a romance novel, except that romance was not then, and never would be, on either party's mind.

That isn't to say others weren't swooning. Even Ruth's husband confessed without shame that he was in love with the man; the arrow struck the moment Rank had plucked a tissue from its box and offered it to him. The faces of the hospice nurses who visited Ruth's house flushed pink whenever the doctor's name was mentioned. We lived for crumbs of information about him—where he grew up (in southeast Minneapolis—he had even gone to Tuttle school); how old he was (exactly my age); where he attended medical school (the University of Minnesota); what did his parents do? (they were college professors); did he have a girlfriend? (he was a husband and a father). Rank's seeming physical perfection, in combination with his sophistication—not just in the realm of medicine but in the realm of human suffering—probably hindered in small, annoying ways his effective functioning in the county's enormous, crisis-ridden hospital, which catered primarily to indigents and city employees. The last time I saw him, three years after Ruth's death, I discovered a significant portion of his face was covered with a graying beard; I wondered if he had allowed his whiskers to prosper in order to quell the unrequited passion that must have surged at him from all sides as he made his rounds.

Our biggest surprise was his willingness to visit his patients where they lived. He explained it to us once: He had wearied of seeing his deathly ill patients coming for their clinic appointments in wheelchairs, in a state of collapse, having arrived by ambulance. The system struck him as obscene. He made house calls on cancer patients in the slums of Minneapolis; he made house calls on cancer patients who were city council members. The first time Rank called to say he was on his way to see Ruth, I hung up the phone, breathless. My mother was seated in her pink chair in a robe. "I'm sorry," I told her abruptly, "but I've just got to wash my hair." Clay, too, was stirred. He stashed the busybody Yorkie in the dog's crate, then changed his shirt, put on a red bow tie, and set about vacuuming.

Ruth had seen enough doctors by then. She needed Rank to help her die. Rank helped her with that, and he helped her manage me: her grieving child who was battling nature to keep her alive. That first time, he sat with the three of us in the living room, his eyes primarily on Ruth. In retrospect, I am sure he vastly preferred to be alone with his patients; he had important information to impart, and the presence of others sometimes impeded a straightforward exchange. Nevertheless, he was deliberate and thoughtful when he spoke: He never said anything that would cause injury to anyone present; he never said anything that was untrue.

Together, he and Ruth established that she would die at home. "If they will have me, I'll die here," Ruth said in a reference to me and her husband. We all agreed that Ruth would stay home, that her husband and I would create a hospice for her, though we did not even utter the actual word for many months, I believe, because it implied Ruth would be leaving us no matter what we did. Later, in private, Rank told my mother the mourning period for survivors is shorter when someone dies at home rather than in a hospital. "Poor babies," my mother had written in reply after thinking about Rank's comment.

"Are you going to be in a position to give me things that will shorten (or not prolong—whatever is the appropriate term) those last painful days, weeks, hours, whatever, or must I expect to choke to death or try to drown myself?" she asked. He assured her that she would neither choke to death nor would she drown, and that he had many drugs in his arsenal to make her final days easier.

"I don't have any picture of the end," she wrote to him. "I try not to think of it. I am not experiencing great pain at this point. I have cancer. I expect to be uncomfortable, but when things get unreasonable how much gasping, lingering, am I in for, or conversely, may I be spared?"

Again he reassured her: She would neither gasp nor be uncomfortable. She would be spared all that.

Their relationship became increasingly strong after that visit. She wanted to believe him, and as her opportunities to observe him increased, she did believe him. "My ace oncologist has promised to lead us, step by step, through what has to be done. So I get to go on being feckless as all get out," she wrote to one of her visiting nurses.

It was a revelation for me to observe my frequently acerbic, always irreverent mother during her interactions with Rank. The doctor was perhaps the only person in her life to whom she offered no sarcasm, no edge. One day, Rank loped up the stairs to my mother's bedroom. She was standing in the doorway in her J. Crew cotton bathrobe awaiting him. "Hello, Ruth," he said, and then he enveloped her in a spontaneous embrace that lasted several seconds. It seemed the most natural thing in the world. By then, Ruth considered him to be a part of her family, part of the circle of people she trusted and loved. "There is nothing I would say to either of you that I would not say to both of you," she wrote to me and to Rank one day.

❖ ❖ ❖

My mother hadn't seen me naked for decades. Perhaps the last time she saw my breasts had been when she took me to Dayton's to help me buy my first bra. I had been caring for her body for several months, secretly marveling at how beautiful a sixty-four-year-old woman's body could be, when late one night I stepped out of the shower, dried myself, and walked into her bedroom stark naked in search of pajamas. I had thought she was asleep, but she was upright in bed, reading. She lifted her eyes from her book and stared boldly at me. I suppose I laughed a little—threw up my arms as if to say, "Here I am, in case you were wondering!" But Ruth continued staring, studying me. I realized she was visually exploring my body just as she had assessed other nude bodies for years in life-drawing classes; her distanced, academic interest was second nature by then. I wasn't her daughter at that moment, I was her subject, a challenge that demanded her full concentration.

When she had taken a long, careful look, she began to write:

"Your body looks really cute without any clothes on. I think men would find you in lovely proportion. Breasts to waist to hips to thighs seem pleasingly proportioned, without clothes on."

I complained of being fat, and assured her no sane man would desire me in my current state.

"Well now—" she wrote, "but if somebody you like makes an offer, you needn't fear rejection on the grounds that you are fat."

Her comment came to me like a little gift bound up in pretty ribbons. I found myself wondering, too, just how I might fare as one of her subjects given her finely honed powers of interpretation.

❖ ❖ ❖

I enter her bedroom wearing jeans and a faded purple T-shirt. My constant presence has been leading her thoughts back and back to her own mother, who died alone six months before, at the age of eighty-nine.

"You look very pretty today," she writes as a greeting. "Lavender

182

Good Guys Got Heart

was my mother's favorite color but I never could find just the right shade for her. I fear I was a great disappointment to my mother."

I lie on my mother's bed, curling up next to her, and suggest that perhaps she wasn't as great a disappointment as she fears.

"I *know* I was a great disappointment," Ruth writes. "She explained it to me, in great detail, a matter to which she had given much thought. My mother felt free to talk endlessly about the child she had wished for. But it never occurred to me to think—hey, 2 can play at this game. So, darling, Let's say I'm having a party—and I intend to be the guest of honor—it's a christening party—I am the babe. Now what is the time? (If you could have been born in any century, of any sex, any situation)—"

"Edith Wharton's New York?" I offer.

Ruth frowns.

"I think her young beautiful women are quite pathetic—but the men are so inane to put up with that system. How about Willa Cather. Wasn't she close in age to Wharton?"

I am uneasy. I'm not sure how this game is played or even what it is about. Is my mother seeking to refashion the person who is her daughter, is she trying to invent a different mother, or is she striving to rewrite her own life?

When I hesitate, Ruth begins writing again, taking an entirely new tack. "Perhaps I could make a pot of tea & we could exchange girlish confidences. I'll be Jessica Tandy. Who do you wanna be?"

Ruth is being playful, trying to change the relationship—if only for the day—into a friendship where both of us will be on equal footing, but I find myself too tired to keep up. I feel inadequate, depressed.

"Kathy Bates?" I say, then immediately wish I could take it back.

"Lovely Idea," Ruth writes. "Then, I'll tell you—what I've been working up to all day —ever so gently, Kathy, who your real father is. Do you remember Mr. Borgnine, the gentleman who used to call on Sundays? You called him Uncle Ernie? Well, my dear, Yes! Yes! If I'm Jessica Tandy, and you're Kathy Bates, your real father is E. Borgnine."

❖ ❖ ❖

Oh, you guys—I just want to scrunch down in that pain & turn into like whipped cream or something. All soft & fluffy."

Ruth has been home from the hospital for three months. She is running a low-grade fever and suffering bouts of extreme pain. "The pain is in my ears. Feel like I'm circling an island in a motor boat that keeps slapping the waves. Wham! Wham! Wham!" she writes.

The first episode began one morning about a month after her homecoming, quite suddenly. Her face registered distress and she signaled me and her husband with her hand.

"I don't think I'VE BEEN ASLEEP," she wrote in an utterly unfamiliar script that shrunk telescopically with each word. Then she printed in the tiniest of block letters: "WRITING LOOK FUNNY DONT IT."

She stopped writing. Her eyes widened, her pen and notepad slid off her lap, and she sat still, staring ahead as if in a hypnotic trance.

For the next several minutes, we hovered over her, helpless.

At last the pain subsided. She wrote, "I feel very dumb. But it seems to be getting better. I was just trying to sit very still but the pain just got worse & worse. Throbbing pain in ears. I hope you will never know it. I believe it is worse than childbirth."

The latest incident precipitates a trip to the county medical center to see the surgeon who installed the trache. A nurse ferries Ruth, who is seated in a wheelchair, into the doctor's examining room. Twenty minutes later, the nurse wheels her back to the waiting room. Her husband and I are waiting for her. She studies our worried faces, then takes pen and notepad in hand.

"BAD NEWS," she writes to us, her expression deadpan. We stare at her notepad anxiously, waiting to see what comes next. "I HAVE CANCER."

Part Five

June has arrived. Ruth has been living with a metal tube in her throat, erratic, often incapacitating pain, and breathing difficulties for four months. I have recently moved into her house and am with her twenty-four hours a day. Her husband is suffering, she writes to me. "This whole business has been going on since March. And poor Clay, with the general all night frivolities of Edna Ruth's Down Home Slumber Party, is beginning to show signs of sleep deprivation. . . ."

We have long discussions about what, if anything, can be done to improve her breathing and the pain she feels in her mouth, ears, and throat. "It's like the pain you get on airplanes sometimes. . . . The pain is so bad I can't think," she writes. At the suggestion of the surgeon who installed the tracheostomy tube, Ruth makes yet another difficult trip back to the county hospital, this time to explore solutions to her breathing problem. The surgeon thinks a longer tube might be in order; perhaps the cancer is threading its way around the original tube, shrinking the airway.

She waits in her wheelchair outside the clinic, alternately reading *The Portrait of a Lady*, slicing the pages apart with a butter knife, and studying the women and their small children and infants in the pediatrics clinic nearby. She seems peaceful, happy to be out of her house and in the world again. She stares for some time at a regal-looking black woman holding a tiny child in her lap. "That baby's mother is *such* a handsome woman," she notes. "All beautifully designed planes—like a cubist painting." She looks at her husband and me, but we can't seem to share in her delight. "You are both looking so pale and shaky," she observes.

The wait continues, her pain medication is wearing off. I wheel her to the oncology department, where a nurse injects her with a large dose of Dilaudid. We return to the clinic. At last Ruth's name is called. Accompanied by her husband and myself, she is ushered into a small room. A young man in a white coat steps inside, followed by a woman, a G.P. from a small town in Minnesota who has come to see how medicine is practiced in the big city. I ask why Ruth's ear, nose, and throat surgeon is not present. The young man, Dr. Ferorrelli, tells me he is an ENT resident, and that he has been authorized to install a longer trache tube. It is a routine procedure, he adds. My mother and I exchange uneasy glances.

Ferorrelli lays out several tubes on a tray but discovers they are all mislabeled as to size. Confusion sets in as he tries to determine by visual examination their varying lengths. It becomes obvious within moments that this procedure will be guided by guesswork. Ruth looks frightened; my hands start to sweat. The resident asks the country doctor at his side, "Which is longer?," holding two tubes aloft. "I can't tell."

"Do you ever experience difficulty breathing?" he eventually asks Ruth offhandedly, not looking at her. He seems unaware she cannot speak. Ruth looks at me; now we're both frightened.

In time Ferorrelli turns to the patient, and without warning removes the metal tube in her throat, leaving a bloody wound exposed. He picks up one of the new tubes, hesitates, then picks another. He tears open its cellophane packaging and proceeds to insert it into the opening. Ruth's eyes open wide. She cannot breathe. Ferorrelli waits—too long—then pulls the tube out, a puzzled expression on his youthful face. He has dislodged or broken something deep in Ruth's throat—a portion of tumor; some unstable tissue; a blood vessel; it is uncertain. She tries to inhale. Her face darkens nearly to purple, and she coughs. Blood spews from the wound. The substance sprays across the room, hitting me in the face and mottling Ferorrelli's white coat. I pull my chair near my mother until we are a foot apart. "Mom—you can do this—cough it out," I say. But Ruth's eyes remain large and frightened; she can't cough because she can't breathe. "You can do this," I say again. Suddenly, Ruth coughs, and there is more blood—on the walls, on the floor, on the coats of both doctors. The practitioners simply back away. I grab squares of gauze from a nearby shelf and hold them gently to my mother's chest; blood is running down her clothes. I turn to my stepfather, who is sitting near the door in a state of stupefaction. "Call the oncology department!" I yell. "Get Rank down here, right now!"

He can't move. I grab the phone on the wall and dial the number I know by heart. "It's an emergency—get someone here *now!*" I shout into the phone. Ferrorelli and the rural doctor continue to cower against a far wall. With each weak cough Ruth expels more blood until her clothes and my hair are dripping with it.

"You are going to be okay, Mom. It's okay," I say again and again. Our eyes are locked intently on each other. Ruth is listening, trying to concentrate on what I am telling her, but she is suffocating. She expects she is shortly to die in this small room, with her daughter just inches away, covered in her blood, and two doctors in white coats standing motionless and apart, like observers at a human sacrifice. She is terrified. An oncologist arrives, one the patient has never seen before. Her own oncologist, the Burt Lancaster stand-in, is not in the hospital. Unexpectedly, the new doctor behaves just like the other two; she stands against a far wall.

The room has become an abattoir. A curious nurse opens the door, eyes the scene, then shuts it quickly. Voices and footsteps are heard outside; the staff is preparing for a death. With what seems like the last fraction of air available to her, Ruth coughs again. A chunk of dark tissue resembling raw liver lands with a loud smack a few inches from Ferorrelli's tasseled loafer. The catharsis is so horrifying it borders on the comical. Tears are pouring from her eyes; the pain is unspeakable, but air is finally making its way into her lungs.

Ferorrelli steps toward her gingerly and inserts a new tube into her throat; it is identical in length to the original. Then he steps away, plants his back firmly against the wall, as if awaiting another explosion of blood.

When nothing happens, all three doctors depart the room wordlessly, leaving the patient, her daughter, and husband alone. I try to wipe the blood from my mother's freshly laundered jeans and suede shoes. A nurse enters to deliver another shot of Dilaudid, and leaves again. The pages of Ruth's notepad are stuck together with blood. Her hand, still clutching a pen, remains motionless. Any movement will trigger the cough and enhance the pain.

Suddenly Ferorrelli enters the room, clad in a fresh white coat. He hands are clasped in front of his waist, like a priest. His expression suggests he bears important news.

"You have throat cancer," he tells Ruth, who is watching him with something like awe through her haze of pain. "What happened here was to be expected. I feel a responsibility to let you know that the final event will no doubt be exactly like this one, and it's probably going to be very soon. I just wanted to be sure you fully understand that."

Three people stare at him in stony silence. Ferorrelli waits a beat, then leaves the room. Ruth and her husband look at each other in astonishment, as if wondering how their love, their life together, could possibly be ending in this surreal, bloody way, punctuated by the heartless meandering of a callow twit from central casting. Ruth's oncologist tries to locate Ferorrelli some hours later; he's trying to learn how a resident of such apparent brutishness could be working in the county hospital. It turns out that Ferorrelli is gone, not merely from the hospital but from the city. He is on his way to Kansas, where he is to join a private ENT practice. This was the final day of his residency, Ruth his last patient, before entering the brotherhood of board-certified healers.

❖ ❖ ❖

The game plan is unraveling. Ruth had been promised she would never spend a night in a hospital again, but a room is being readied for her. She's struggling for control over events, but pain keeps clouding her focus. Soon she finds herself in a steel bed in a crowded room, her daughter is hovering as usual, and the obese patient in the next bed is speaking loudly to a group of residents about what she likes to drink (Mogan David wine and 7UP) when she has no cocaine to shoot. When the doctors hear the woman uses needles, they immediately take several generous steps back, jostling the bed of the cancer patient. Whispering, her daughter tells Ruth that the noisy patient bears a surprising resemblance to a neighbor who lived next door on Girard Avenue, a bossy, meddlesome mother of four who used to peer disapprovingly from her windows into Ruth's house. "I knew it was someone we knew," Ruth writes to her daughter. "Of course. The very one."

Ruth's oncologist appears, dressed in a white Izod sport shirt, khaki Bermudas, and white Nikes. He has come from his son's soccer game. The oncologist is going to try to establish an intravenous line that will deliver a steady dose of morphine round the clock to his patient for the rest of her life. His forehead is beaded with sweat. He crouches at Ruth's bedside until their faces are at the same level. "Hello, Ruth," he says. She smiles at him in a way her daughter has rarely seen: There is no irony, no undercurrent of comedy or shared humor. Curiously, there is something else. As wounded as she is, the woman continues to exude a languid, earthy sexuality. The doctor feels it; the two exchange looks as if there were no one else in the room, and he lays a hand protectively over her bare shoulder. The daughter watches, enchanted by her mother's power. The woman is dying, and he alone is going to help her.

After completing the procedure, the oncologist talks to Ruth in private for a while. Before he leaves the hospital, he writes his orders: Ruth will be moved to a private room; she will remain in the hospital until her pain is quelled and an effective morphine dose is established, at which point she will be released into the care of her family; she will go home by ambulance. Contravening hospital policy, he also writes that residents, medical students, and interns may not enter her room at any point during her stay. This last order is posted outside Ruth's door; over the next twenty-four hours, several residents try to enter her room and are intercepted by nurses, who seem to enjoy performing this particular duty.

It is nine P.M. David, a man with a long blond ponytail, is taking care of Ruth. Every half hour, he asks her to rate her pain on a scale of one to ten. Sometimes it is six, sometimes it is ten; sometimes it drops to three. He continually readjusts the intravenous morphine drip. The pain is mostly in her ears, her neck, and her jaw, but for a while it is so universal that even the weight of her hospital gown against her body and the friction of the sheets is too much. David helps her to stand and delicately removes the gown until she is wearing nothing but her white panties. He stands close by in case she falls. The woman jokes with gestures and written notes until he is laughing; he calls her by her first name, as if he has known her a very long time. When she is ready, he helps her back into her bed, gently lifting her legs onto the mattress and drawing the sheet up carefully.

It is four A.M. Ruth finds she can only sleep for ten or fifteen minutes at a time. Awake, she feels agitated. She senses that what happened the previous afternoon has altered her view of the world. It has stolen something from her she never thought could be stolen. There is a new nurse, Marie. She begins to write, and when she finishes, she hands her notepad to this stranger:

> "Marie—I can find no pleasant
> Images—no—nothing to
> look forward to—
> I've never felt this
> way before.

I think this afternoon was
so traumatic it seems to have taken all the satisfaction out
of my life. I see my husband
(as he was this afternoon) shocked
paralyzed, grieved & Impotent
and my daughter, whose life
is in a bad place right now,
in a rage that this idiot
intern who could only
preside in a pompous way
as some woman he didn't
know strangled——Do
you know Marie, he actually
asked me—I can't speak—so it
was silly but—he asked
me—for how long have you been troubled by this shortness
of breath?"

Eventually, at a loss to explain the immensity of her feelings to the nurse, Ruth writes simply, "Marie, I'm having a bad day."

Early in the morning, her oncologist comes to her room, pulls a chair to her bedside, and seats himself. To him she writes:

"Yesterday was so
shattering——
I truly was like
a dancing bear—that young man asking
vaudeville questions—
While I choked
to death for
my husband & daughter
& three strangers.

Am I going through
all of this to end that way again?
Didn't I earn a
little bit of something
yesterday?"

They have discussed it many times; he has promised, and he promises her once again: It will not go down the way Ferorrelli predicted. "Ruth, you and I have talked about this and it's not going to be that way. You have a lot of pain-free living to do," he tells her.

Later that morning, she writes to her husband, "You do still love me don't you? I did dance w/out me gown for young David last night—but I kept my panties on."

The next day, when she is home, she writes to her husband and daughter, "Last night was the worst. But if you both want me to I can do it." She was talking about staying alive for a while longer. "Shall I? I want to but I can't if you don't care. You have to care, too, don't you?"

Two days later, Ruth lies in bed staring ahead at the gray cedar deck just outside the sliding glass doors of her bedroom while her daughter slumbers a few inches away. It is very early; the sun rose less than an hour ago. She is the only person awake in the house; even her dog, who has continued to shun her, is sleeping, and she feels very lonely. Her pen is poised above her legal pad. She is waiting. She has something urgent to tell her daughter. At last her daughter moves, then opens her eyes.

The woman purses her lips and writes in large, deliberate letters: "It's true."

"What is true?" I ask when I see the words.

"I'm sick," she writes. A long pause ensues. I say nothing.

The woman writes: "Will you help me with today?"

"Yes," I say.

"Thank you darling. I knew you would."

That afternoon, Ruth writes, "I am stronger than your stepfather is but you are stronger than I am. Remember this about yourself. You have to be strong for me. This is really going to help you out, now that you can know what you can do. I am so proud of you and in such need of you. You are not leaving me. You will just keep on going, needing & doing till that's over & then—& then we will just keep on doing and being. I don't think it's going to be many days, do you?"

June is drawing to a close.

"Hillary—I am very hot. I would like to have my head shaved."

Ruth asks for a bolus of morphine, a surge of the drug over and above the steady dose that can be given at her request no more than once an hour. The bolus is delivered with the touch of a keypad on a computer smaller than a paperback book. The first night the woman was home and receiving morphine in this fashion, she suffered a nightmare in which she awoke believing that her eyes were bleeding and her face was on fire. It took several minutes to convince her neither was true, frantic minutes during which she asked her daughter to wake her husband and bring him into her bedroom. When he arrived, Ruth embraced her daughter and husband for some time. She was trembling. She began writing. She had been dreaming of the Four Horsemen of the Apocalypse. She was in a great cave where acts of violence were being plotted, as if at a political convention. An Antichrist figure was laughing maniacally at her, causing her eyes to bleed. He indicated to her that he was planning, in Ruth's words, "male violence on this world. Not male versus female violence like rape—I mean war, and faulty distribution systems. He kept laughing and saying, She doesn't know we've been doing this for centuries! The horror was cosmic." As Ruth writes, she grows calmer, falling into a more analytical, jaundiced style. "I have long believed that the four horsemen needed to be renamed—something more accurate for Famine. I will give you that 'faulty distribution' is not the old grabber that Famine always was, however."

Her pen is still for a while. Finally she writes, "Never accuse me of not sharing! Go to sleep." But before she herself sleeps, she hallucinates that her son is standing over her bed; he reaches over her and gently pulls the tracheostomy tube out of her throat in order to better examine it. "He was room colored," she explains to her daughter afterward, signaling that the figure was transparent. "I have been writing to Ethan. It might have been Ethan. He was just kind of interested in it. He removed it painlessly and was just looking at it."

Ethan has been on her mind, but she holds his request to see her at bay. "A serious reason I have not wanted to see many people—people I love, who want to come here—is I don't think they could handle it," she had written in explanation some weeks before. In addition, the act of crying triggered pain and seemed to cause her throat to swell, making breathing even more difficult for her. Ethan presents a special challenge, however. She wants to touch him, to comfort him, but she feels vulnerable, too. Might her son, Bible in hand, return her to that state of impotency she felt as a child with Mabel? She lacks the strength to defend herself against an eleventh-hour effort to bring her into the realm of the righteous. More profoundly, she is still searching for a way to perform that most difficult task: telling the child—the one she fears she has failed—good-bye.

In her letter to Ethan, which she begins and stops, then begins again, and ultimately never sends because she can find no pleasing way to conclude, she writes,

> Bad times here—as bad as times can get—King size, double dose, beyond imagining and repeatedly. . . . There is a modest bonus in the drug therapy, however, in that colors and textures that art school taught me to be aware of become rich and brilliant and pleasing beyond previous comprehending. A simple crease in a fabric becomes a great cascading sweep of hills & valleys that one can control by simple manipulation of scale—what if that third pleat were a half-mile cascade?—and someway the drug makes that kind of manipulation a manageable trick. Of course, all the senses are affected. . . .

I have been raking my poor, tired, ratty old brain, to see if I can uncover a previously overlooked grain of wisdom— something to pass on to my son from what I guess is rather like a bully pulpit—my position just now being, for however long it lasts, and just now I don't think the odds are for long. You would think just this once I might be able to come up with something swell. But all I can think of is what I always only can think of—Do what you can, darling, and just keep on doing it and doing it and sometimes it turns out to be rather a lot. And sometimes it doesn't but there you are. Never stop caring.

Since those difficult days, Ruth has grown better accustomed to the morphine, and the hallucinations and dreams are less threatening. Now her mother, Mabel, keeps appearing in them.

"I cannot remember the dreams and they don't seem too bad— pleasing ordinary things going on in routine places," she writes. "Where my mother *is* isn't relevant of course although she does seem to be in the dreams pretty often. In no unpleasant ways. And so—actually I don't summon her. She simply turns up."

Very late one night she writes to her daughter,

I said that I didn't need to go to my mother when she was dying because she was getting perfectly good care (and she was) and there was nothing I could do for her—I was *so* wrong. But my mother never liked me as much as I have liked you so perhaps there really was nothing I could have done.

I *couldn't* have helped her because she didn't like me. She was ashamed of me in front of the nurses because of my bad language. I wouldn't have sworn, but she thought I might. . . .

I do & did forgive her—but we might have had sweet times. A pity she missed them . . . Of course—I think that love is a given in certain relationships—mother-child being one. How that love is expressed is the difference.

"Why are we having this conversation at 2 am Sunday morning?" she writes abruptly. "Go to bed darling and take your silly dog with you."

The next day, however, Ruth returns to her musings.

"I keep coming back to my mother is dead & I did not treat her as you have me," she writes. "But I do think that I was a better mother to you than she was with me. You—let's don't do this anymore. She did the very best she could."

❖ ❖ ❖

I had suspected but hadn't realized just how thoroughly Ruth had submerged the knowledge that she was leaving the life and the people she loved. By early July, she began writing frankly about dying: what it would feel like, when it would happen, and what would happen afterward, especially to me. One night, seemingly out of the blue, she wrote in bold letters that took up an entire legal-sized page: LEAVE MINNEAPOLIS. She looked at me sternly, tapping the page with her pen. She herself was leaving, after all; the time when I would need to get on with the business of my life was fast approaching.

Mostly she wrote about love. She would write, again and again, about how much she loved me and her husband, singly and together. She also sought reassurance from us. "Hillary," she would begin, "I love you very much. Thank you for loving me too. You do love me though too?"

Would I miss her? she wanted to know. Did her husband still

love her, even though she had cancer? Did I love her husband? Did he love me? She put these questions to us again and again. Our antipathy was intolerable to her.

"If you guys would just shape up I would be prepared for anything," she wrote us. Another time: "I am shocked to learn that you are all uneasy and suspicious of each other. I want you to know that I still have faith in the system."

Toward the end, she would beseech us on her notepads, "Won't you please, please love each other? Pleeessee?," her script becoming more indecipherable each day. She could not understand why the two people she loved and trusted most seemed not to love or trust each other at all.

Ruth clarified for me in a moment our absurd struggle over how much liquid nutrition she should receive when she wrote one day, "All that smartass avoiding of Attain—I thought that if I got my bod all pepped up and looking kind of smart I could get a little—this is so pathetic it will make you cry—4th of July party on the deck and maybe a little lunch." She enumerated the guest list she had held in her mind for months and the delicacies she had planned to offer her guests. In short, she had been trying to diet since February in anticipation of one of her favorite holidays. From here on out I was welcome, she notified me, to deliver the amount of Attain to her bod that her doctors had prescribed.

The more completely she embraced the stark fact of her death, the more stripped of inhibitions Ruth became. She seemed to have entered a world in which only the most basic truths could be spoken because time was collapsing into itself. Day and night were indistinguishable; hours rushed by in the space of minutes, yet tasks remained. She suddenly wanted to see her son. Her wish, once established, was quite urgent, although on a Wednesday before Ethan's scheduled arrival that weekend, she asked me to call Rank for a bedside consult.

"TELL HIM THAT I NEED HIM TO HELP ME SAY GOOD BYE TO ETHAN," she wrote urgently. "ASK HIM IF HE CAN

TALK TO ME SO I KNOW WHAT TO SAY. MAYBE RANK KNOWS SOME WORDS THAT WOULD JUST SOUND SOOTHING FOR HIM."

Rank came, of course. He sat by her bedside in a sweltering July heat as Ruth wrote page after page of musings about her relationship with her son. As she ripped the pages off her pad and handed them to him, he studied them carefully.

"It's my last scene w/ him—I should make my best effort to play it right," she explained to Rank. "We have never been exactly estranged and I am not so silly that I imagine some bit of pop psych you picked up in Med school could help. I want him to know that he does the best he can with what he has which is all I have ever done & all anybody I ever respected did. No apologies no regrets . . . I'm very ill. Will I die this weekend? I would like to get this done with Ethan but I don't want to wear Hillary out. She is doing it all now."

Rank offered no advice; he sat with her and read what she wrote, his face a study in sympathy and concern.

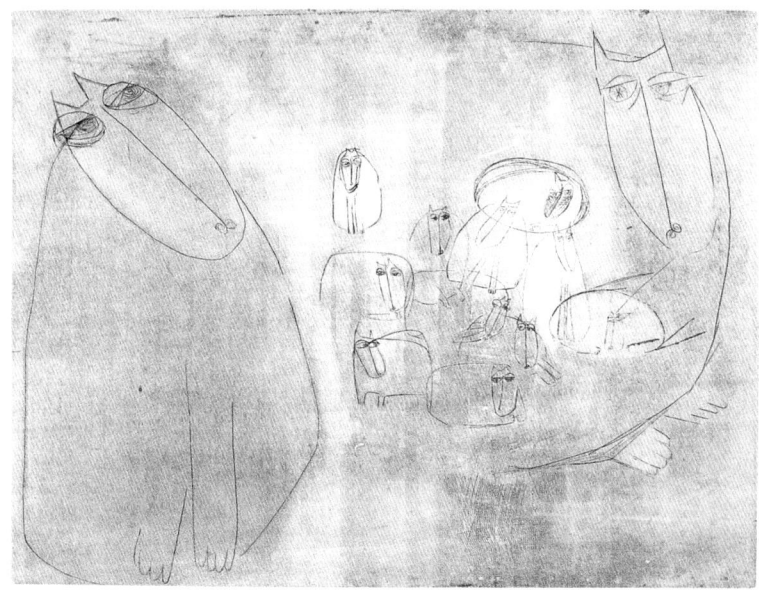

Ruth's fears about what to say and how to behave seemed to disappear in an instant when Ethan arrived. She was thrilled when her son entered her room, leaned over her, and kissed her warmly. Ethan was shaken by the machines, the tubes, the tabletop packed to its edges with family-sized bottles of controlled substances, the syringes, the bloody bandage at Ruth's throat, her silence. She did not cry, nor did he. "I needed you," she wrote, and looked at him tenderly. Ethan gathered up her fragility, her sense of mission. He placed his hand on her arm and waited. This was her time.

"Say goodbye to my three beauty grandsons and tell them I love them and wish them health and happiness all their lives," she continued. When Ethan told Ruth he had tried to raise his three sons as he had been raised by her, with attention paid to artistic expression in all matters, she responded, "Ethan, that is so lovely to hear. You could not have brought me a finer message. I haven't been entirely ignorant—I could tell that there was an impact and was always so flattered when little bits of me turned up in the boys. But I think I have not offered as much as I might have."

When Ethan told her that he loved her, she wrote, "I feel like a big coat has just melted off my body." When Ethan asked if she had *always* known he loved her, she wrote, "I know you love me—it has never crossed my mind. That's a stupid question. It's like how many toes do I have or something. You were a special person and important to me." Then she wrote for my benefit, "Ethan and I feel just fine. We're going to be so easy. I am melting like lobster butter."

Ethan complimented her on her pretty bedroom. "It's so lovely to die at home," she answered. "And since I've taken five years to die of this I'm so proud to have made such a lovely place to do it in. It's quite lovely. And this illness that I have, I could not go through in a hospital. I've been in *so* many—all so awful. But how fortunate I am to have a room to do all these things in. . . . I know it hurts, Ethan," she continued after studying her son's face for a moment, "but it's going to be all ok ok. I really am just liking it here. My bed, my stuff—just how it seems best."

Ruth asked her husband to write three checks for Ethan to take home to his sons, a last gift from their grandmother. Ethan thanked her, and promised she would receive a thank-you note from each of his boys. "You know, dear heart," Ruth responded, "I never cared about thank you notes. I'll tell you what I think persons who care about Thank You should do—make it a happy thing and part of the agreement. So, I think they should enclose a stamped, self-addressed envelope, don't you? You could open the package and train the heart to be as big as the body."

Ethan had returned to Minneapolis for brief visits just four times in his adult life; he was nearing forty-five. Ruth suddenly decided that she wanted to have a photograph taken of herself with her children. "It is still possible to prove to Ethan that he is part of this family," Ruth wrote to me privately. "We have to. It is the *most* important thing. Let Ethan know once and for all that we are a family & he is part of it. ETHAN NEEDS documentation." A photographer friend of Ruth's came immediately. "Bring me my eye make up," Ruth commanded. With difficulty, she applied eyeliner and mascara, and asked for one of her patterned scarves to be tied at her neck. She combed her hair. As the photographer, positioned at the foot of the bed, snapped away without speaking to us, Ruth began writing on her notepad: "I just want our children and grandchildren to know that we loved each other and had faith and confidence for all the years past and to come. Do the best to do right."

When Ethan left the next day, her final message to him was:

"I do not go from this life with regrets. I spent my life with the people who wanted to be with me and with whom I wanted to be. I might not have chosen them all in the same proportion but, regarding the matters with which I would be dealing it might have been just as well as it went. On balance I liked my life. I am leaving it as I might have chosen.

"Let me say one more thing," Ruth added after a pause. "It is ending, I think. We had some aggravation that stirred up a bad patch and I can't seem to get beyond it. I'm afraid I can take no more. Go & jump on your plane, my love, you are needed in another place. Take care and continue to be interested. We need your ongoing concern. If things work out, it is all going to have a happy ending. The difficulty is that the pain is taking over."

Ruth wanted to see Frannie, and her brother, John, too. Each of them flew to her, Frannie from California, and John from Texas, within twenty-four hours of her requests. Their stays were brief and ended bravely. "Dreadful as *much* of it has been—I think I want this time," Ruth wrote to Frannie. "And it's not all bad. Some of the time has been sweet indeed." Frannie had left her husband and two adolescent children behind in Newport Beach; she was fifty. The two women parted tearlessly, with a simple embrace and a happy wave. John, too, parted from his sister with a kiss, an embrace, and a final message from Ruth: "You know, Johnnie, I hadn't much wanted to die, but since I am, I don't want to find out that while I am actually dying that I am doing it carelessly or in a lost or frightened way. I want to feel like I am in control. And I believe that I am. Thought I would share what I've got—let you all examine and admire me. Grace & your help when it was so needed."

A few days after these visits, I lay with my mother on her grandly carved mahogany bed, her writing tablet uncharacteristically limp, her eyes seeming to stare at nothing. We were holding hands, as we often did then. The moment was relaxed, devoid of any particular medical crisis. Ruth's temperature was 98.6 degrees, her pain was under control, she had enough oxygen.

"Mom—remember when I invited you to New York and I promised to introduce you to all my friends and said I would have a party, and that we would spend our days at the Met, and—" Before I could go on, she interrupted me with a dreamy smile. "Yes, darling, I do," she wrote. She closed her eyes as if envisioning the days we might have shared in a city that had captured her imagination since her childhood, looking at art together, having tea at the Stanhope; the two of us, at peace. Indeed, it turned out that was exactly what she was doing. "We would have done it just the way you wanted it done," she wrote. "Pretend it happened and love it. Can we do that? I think it's fair. Flesh out day dreams & love them. Denial has helped me through so much of this ordeal—now that denial is not possible, let's embrace fantasy."

There was something else for which I needed to apologize, though twenty years had passed. "Remember when you gave me all those beautiful parties and you would always pop into conversations to say how pretty I was and—" I stopped suddenly when my mother's radiant smile emerged again. It was as if someone had pulled back the draperies and sun poured into the room. "Yes, dear heart," she wrote, looking at me fondly. Once more, she closed her eyes, as if this time she were reliving the parties, one by one, in their entirety: the fantastic menus, the devastating one-liners that fell effortlessly from her lips, the braless, sexy cotton dresses she wore, the mint juleps served in Mason jars and homemade lemonade on the deck in the summer, the aquavit by the fireplace at Christmas, the way she danced the lindy with men not her husband, the innocent flirtations, the cries and moans of delight as her guests indulged in their first tastes of the meals she served. ("Ruth!" they would exclaim, without further elaboration.)

"*That* is how I want you to remember me," she wrote on, with some urgency. "I want the picture you have of me to be that party picture—the house clean, me dressed up— pretty food & music— the nicest people I know at a party for my Hillary come home to visit."

On July 10, Ruth feels in the mood to tell her favorite nurse a story. It is Betsy, "my sweet violet," as Ruth inevitably calls her, who brings quilting projects along each time so that Ruth can feast her eyes on the fantastic montages of fabric. The "scrap" fabrics, pieced together at random in clever ways to form a larger, more eloquent pattern that gives definition to the quilt, swirl in front of her face like some psychedelic hallucination. She begins writing to Betsy about her daughter.

"When Hillary was 15 she took up smoking and I was very poor," she writes. "Mayonnaise was $1.00 a jar. So I kept buying mayonnaise, Hillary would make a sandwich, spread it with mayonnaise, smoke a cigarette and leave the mayonnaise uncovered, walk out of the kitchen. A day later I'd come into the kitchen & there would be the mayonnaise, all edges curled up and I would have to throw the whole thing away and buy a new bottle of mayonnaise. Well, she couldn't find her cigarette lighter. Her boyfriend had to buy her a new one—it turned out that what I had done was I found that scene one time too often. I just poked the lighter down in there, covered it up & threw it out with appropriate warnings it would happen again. She carried on but never did it again either.

"That all of story."

❖ ❖ ❖

There aren't rooms, or even specific areas of rooms, anymore. There are only theatrical sets, wherever Ruth looks.

"My illness and fever keeps me confused," she writes to her visiting hospice nurse, Katie. "Maybe my cancer has changed in the last few years. I seem, Katie, to be in a movie. I feel like I just look at those spaces and they are like sets. I am not in pain. I am in a very strange situation. I don't think my husband likes me any more. It was that vile E.N.T clinic and I had a notion that I was at a movie. See if you can imagine that. Something had gone very wrong, and it was like a movie set. The doctor kept saying to the people in the room, HOW DO YOU FEEL ABOUT RUTH—on a scale of one to ten? It seemed at some point that three came, and I CRRRRIIIEEE & Oh! No—oh no, all that no no sccrremenn. I can't do that. And now I have to follow you aarrouunn saying oh please, pplpeeaase love me. Oh Katie, tell my husband to make the dreams go away."

Sometimes she hallucinates, sometimes she is asleep and dreaming, and sometimes she is simply awake. She's having difficulty sorting it out. Emerging from sleep is especially difficult. Instead of an abrupt change of consciousness, it has become a period of reentry that needs to be undertaken slowly and warily. Over a period of several minutes, she must carefully put each object and person in the room into some kind of order that makes visual sense. Otherwise, what she sees is too bizarre, too frightening. She describes it as a "hideous violent pitching into weirdness."

In addition, she frequently finds herself in a state of panic, thinking some terribly important event has slipped her mind and she has only just then remembered it. She has invited twelve guests to dinner, but can't recall who they are or what she has planned to feed them; fifty people are about to arrive for an elaborate breakfast buffet, but there is no food in the house; she is sitting for her Latin final shortly and expects to fail. "I'm so worried about my Latin final," she writes again and again, close to tears. She can't be consoled on this matter; she is going to fail, and the despair she feels about this inevitability is potent.

"Hillary—is it true that Ethan is in Vietnam?" she asks. "Honey—I seem to be going silly. How can we rate what is going on in my mind? Try counting backwards from one-hundred by sevens?"

"We don't have any guns do we?" she asks her husband. When he says no, she writes, "I really knew that. The dreams I have are very realistic. NO guns were used that I remember but there were a number about casually—displayed in a cabinet, on the coffee table—not necessarily our house, really—just these sets where I spend some of my time."

The pain in her throat is mostly gone, but she can't rid herself of the absurd conviction, which started as a dream, that "the persons responsible for the Texas Chainsaw unpleasantness" have sown a patch of water lilies there. "The roots are clogging my trache tube," she writes. How could such a thing be, she wonders, and yet they are thriving and vibrant now; there's no stopping these luscious plants. "We all have to get used to this, you know," she writes to her daughter. "I am not accustomed to visions & horror dreams. In my drinking days I was never troubled by D.T.s—you know—lost weekend kind of stuff. I really have always felt myself to be in pretty firm control of my mind. I don't think of myself as a *nervous* person. Not stolid, but not subject to visions, either."

To quell the pain she is now experiencing, however, a great deal of morphine is required, and the visions and horror dreams keep coming.

She tugs her husband awake and writes, "I woke up afraid that [her former husband] had got hold of Rodger and was doing something hideous and cruel to Rodger. I had got annoyed with Rodger and he was hurting him and it was all my fault. The drug had powered Rodger over there. Hillary was trying to figure out my head so we could retrieve Rodger. Well, it's all right now and there's no emergency. Go back to bed sweet darling. I'll get used to this."

On another day, she writes to her daughter, "I woke up under the impression that I am running for Governor of the State of South Carolina. But I guess I'm just dying of cancer so I guess I better get somebody to figure me out an agenda." Later she writes, "I dreamt I was being pushed down into a black cellar hole to prepare a great supper for P–[her architect]. I woke up by grabbing your shirt. Sorry.

P– had an idea that would make us all rich. Replace snails in French menus with walnut-size furry spiders that are crisped in garlic butter & served with Kir."

Her oncologist is on her mind a great deal. In a life filled with strange and sometimes brilliant characters, Ruth has never met anyone like him. She thinks he may be a genius. "I don't know. I would like to know," she muses. She says she feels certain he is religious. It is the first time her daughter has heard her mother discuss religiosity as if it were a virtue. "I would be amazed to learn that Rank does not consider himself the possessor of certain kinds of powers & I do not think he is in any way a crank or lunatic. I think he believes that there is a lot of stuff out there.

"Is he perhaps a Quaker?" she continues. Her daughter looks puzzled, and Ruth explains, "His attitude about his work & his life. He seems to have great reverence for life and a commitment for what he means to do with his own."

The doctor comes and goes like a favored guest in her reveries. "Hillary, I have an impression of a large auditorium in which I am to make a presentation. It does seem to be a campus. I am perhaps the subject of a Brian Rank sermon. He is there and it's very jolly. Except to get on stage, one must wear shoes and I haven't got mine." She stops writing suddenly, then resumes, confessing with evident embarrassment that she must have been having another hallucination. She continues, "I will only, in passing, remark that if you were to pass a pair of white tennis shoes with yellow trim, I would ask you to fetch them along on spec—discreetly, of course."

She has felt herself to have been abandoned by so many doctors over the years, she seeks reassurance every few days: "Is Rank hanging in?" "Do you think Dr. R. still likes us?" And once: "I suppose Brian is mad at me."

The scene with Ferorrelli, won't go away. "I do not feel that I am building up," she writes. "I hit so near bottom that afternoon and sloped even lower with the midnight to morning nurse that I think it all got too late. . . .

"I feel like a bit of detritus that has broken off from the main body of some varied but more or less ordered & explicable progression."

I have stated that my mother was not a religious person, that she viewed Christianity, in all its permutations, as little more than a blunt-force instrument used by one party to harm another. As regards her art, however, Ruth followed Shaker tenets. Shakers believe art comes to its makers as a gift from the spiritual world; therefore, it must be given away rather than exchanged for tender like other commodities. I have rued the loss of so much of Ruth's work, but my mother's art was part of another economy, one more sacred than barter. Her art was an expression of her love. She made art precisely so that she *could* give it away—to those she loved, to those who admired it. At the end, she simply threw away that which had gone unclaimed, that which she deemed unworthy.

Very late—almost too late—I found two small pieces of my mother's art and had them framed before she died. Ruth had printed the pieces from the same etched plate. She had inked one in black; she inked and then added color to the second. The image was of a woman—not a smug or puzzled woman, but a nude whose long hair fluttered behind her as she looked into the wind, her body and face communicating a sense of soaring freedom, as if she had been caught in mid-ascent by a camera lens.

I told Ruth one morning that I had a surprise for her. She smiled eagerly. I drove to the nearby frame shop and picked up the finished pieces, then quickly returned. She watched with curiosity as I unwrapped the brown paper taped around the art and let if fall to the floor. I held both pieces up as steadily as I could so that she could see them clearly without moving her head.

She was so stunned, it was if she lost her breath for a moment. Then she wrote, in enormous block letters,

"I LOVE THEM BOTH! I AM THRILLED THAT I MADE THEM AND DELIGHTED THAT YOU FRAMED THEM IN THE SUPER BEAUTIFUL WAY THEY ARE DONE. IT'S PERFECT. IT'S JUST A BEAUTIFUL, PERFECT JOB."

It was a modest effort on my part, but I had so little to work with. Nevertheless, I felt I had been able to tell her in this humble, eleventh-hour way that I loved her art.

❖ ❖ ❖

Ruth is fighting hard to sustain her communication with her husband, her daughter, and the ever-changing cast of visiting hospice nurses. Death is coming now—she knows that with a certainty she resisted for a long time. Unfortunately, the drugs keep interfering with her "mentation," as her oncologist once described the problem to her. "Life is difficult, dear, for those of us whose mentations have been tampered with," she had written a friend when the phenomenon began in earnest. To her brother, she wrote, "My mentations are so very difficult Johnnie. I get a thought started and then someway it just rolls off the work table. Bad feeling."

Her missives are increasingly basic. She writes whenever she can organize her mind to send the proper messages to her hand, but she is puzzled and frightened much of the time. No one seems able or willing to answer the important questions she has: When will she die? What will it be like?

"Is this the way it is supposed to be happening??" she asks her daughter, late in July, but her daughter doesn't seem to know.

"Will I die soon?" she asks the hospice nurse who is taking her blood pressure.

And then she writes, "Why is Hillary crying? Does she know?" A few minutes later, she writes, "OH PLEASE HILLARY LOVE ME. LOVE ME."

"Put me asleep," she writes to her daughter. "Pleese, I *Must*. See, I want life & I can't breathe. WILL YOU Kill Me?"

Her daughter doesn't comment; instead, she kisses her and then leaves the room for a little while. Ruth drops her notepad on her lap, frustrated and still confused. Why won't anyone tell her anything?

"I am very weak," she writes to her husband. "When are we having our party? I dreamed we were planning a great party. Things are going down hill very quickly. Is it near the end? Does Hillary know? What shall I die of?" Her husband leaves the room for a few minutes, too. Why on earth does everyone keep running from her?

To her daughter, another time: "I have been trying to imagine what it might all be like and I can't. It all seems a dream. I'm sorry. I seem to be recovering. I may not be going to grieve—it may have been a hoax, I feel." To her husband she writes simply, "I may not be dying."

Sometimes she begins her notes to her daughter as if she were starting a letter:

Dear Hillary,
    I PLAN TO STAY ALIVE . . .

But then the letters trail off into indecipherable marks that look like a child's efforts.

She has moments of lucidity that seem startling perhaps because they are increasingly rare. "Dear Hillary," she begins one morning. "I am writing to thank you for the care and concern and deep tact and attention to my feelings that you have shown to me. . . . I hope we will all giggle over this some day. If we don't, then it's not funny."

One evening, she is sitting alone with her husband; the television set is on, but he has fallen asleep. She writes to him, "Darling, do wake up—I am finding this such a beautiful movie. Please wake up and watch it with me. My dearest heart, I love you, I love you, I love you. Please ignore any parts of Woody Allen that annoy you. We have so little time. I am so manic. I am happy. Please wake up and love me and please me. If we try to love each other, we don't fail. Please. My darling. I love you."

Writing to herself another day, she asserts, "I deserve to be loved. I am a very nice person. I like who I am. I have a cute dog."

On another evening, she is in an unusually gay mood. "Somewhere there is a little red car," she writes to her daughter. "A Corvette? No—a Corvair. Maybe it was *my* Corvair. I *drove* that Corvair. I had sensational legs. I should have gone & got some money & champagne & Hors'd & made a nice party.

"I was going to tell you about the symphony days & how swell & honest & pretty I was," she continues, taking note of her daughter's enthusiasm. "Should you like to hear? Shall I tell you? Will you promise to be amused? All the men wanted to sleep with me because I was so pretty and honest and—" She stops for a moment, her train of thought utterly derailed by the memory of a summer day she shared with a lovely redheaded woman named Beverly.

"Beverly was so jazzy. Is she here?" she scribbles on her legal pad, her face glowing with anticipation. When her daughter tells her Beverly isn't with them, Ruth shrugs lightheartedly; she has suffered worse disappointments. "She was a funny, *funny*, lady," she writes.

"We seem to need a games director," she continues. "I want to get started playing or else send everybody home."

Games director or no, she asks her daughter if she would like to hear a limerick she learned as child. She writes effortlessly in clear block lettering:

> There were three girls from Birmingham
> And I'll tell you a story concerning them
> They lifted the frock
> and played with the cock
> of the bishop who was confirming them.

Well the bishop he was no fool
He had been to the public school
He lifted the frock and played with the cock of the
bishop who was confirming him.

"I don't think that's the end of the story, my dear," she con-
cludes, "but I am old and it is not working out as well as it might be."

Her oncologist comes to visit her. She is surprised, and smiles graciously when she recognizes his imposing figure sitting at her bedside, one of his hands placed lightly on one of hers. She begins to
ask him how much longer she will live, but she stops in midthought
and asks him instead if he will be coming to her service. The sentences run together without punctuation. Her handwriting is so difficult now, the doctor makes a rare mistake and interprets the word
service as survive. He tells her that her spirit is keeping her alive
now, that she may live for days, or for weeks, but that she has the
permission of everyone in the room to let go if the struggle becomes
too hard. It is unclear whether the meaning of his words has registered with her. She tries again to learn whether he will be coming to
her service; it is obvious she very much wants him present at the
event, but her writing has deteriorated into near-obscurity and the
doctor remains unaware of her query.

The following day, Ruth is still planning her funeral service, although before she fell seriously ill, she had insisted on immediate
cremation and nothing more elaborate than a small party in her
memory. She writes to her daughter, "Mother is dying," but her
daughter is uncertain whether the woman is referring to herself or
her own mother. Ruth continues, "Will there be a service? Fix me so
I look pretty. Make up. Black mascara. Pearls. Black dress . . . Just a

few snacks and a nice fruit punch. Just little treats. Funny dress. Is Brian Rank to come? It's not going to be too much longer."

A few moments later, she looks at her husband and daughter, studying their faces carefully. "Are you guys feeling down? You still think I'm going to die? Soon, in a week or so? Will you send for Ethan and pay his fare? I thought Ethan should read something. When I DIE. What's the date? Will I be happy? Will Hillary be rich?

"Is he still here, sweetest Dr. Rank?"

"I look at my Sweet DARLING Hillary," Ruth writes one day soon after. "I love you the most. I love you the best of everything. I love your every bad thing you ever did. Eight times more than I am cross about. SHOOT. So that's a whole lot of forgiving." When her daughter studies the words, a shadow seems to cross her face. She looks up at her mother, tears starting to form. Ruth quickly adds, "And you didn't *do* any bad things—that the dumb part."

Pasiphaë on the Colorado Plain

My writing look like drawing, dont it?" Ruth wrote to me one day toward the end of July. "It's hard to know—is this a movie I am writing or tee vee or something to please some kinds of folks? Am I just making this story up? . . . It is true that I have cancer & that I am dying, right?"

Her face was worried, bleak. She wanted me to call Rank; she needed to see him. "I have a bed depression, a feeling that I've let everyone down. Ask if that Ativan [an antianxiety drug] can be given in a form that might cheer me up like Valium. I have, I believe, no more serious reason to be depressed than anybody else does. (Anybody else in my situation, that is.) I am as comfortable as I can be made to be."

"I am easier about my daughter than I have had reason to be," she wrote to the doctor when he arrived. "Obviously, she must read this to you and I believe it is information you should have. We are nearer than we have ever been and her performance in my desperate situation here has given me a deep *confidence* in her ability to *perform well* in a career challenge. I know from the sure touch that takes over from the 'I don't know' whine I would hear or not useful outrage. I can be sure that part of my goal (How can one person's success be a part of another's goal?)—" And for a moment she lost her direction, then reclaimed her topic, "Nevertheless I am deeply confident with Hillary."

❖ ❖ ❖

On July 27, Ruth asks, "Did I *ever* have cancer???"

On July 28, she pleads to see a doctor. The source of the illness that has laid her so low is a mystery to her now. She is especially confounded by a certain heaviness and numbness in one arm. "I am afraid there's a kind of paralysis taking hold of my hand and arm. That make any sense to you?"

She writes to a person in her room who might be a nurse, "You must tell my doctor that he must save his Hillary's mother. The arm is weak and there is no strength there. Tell him I know surely he can mend the difficulties. What is our doctor's name? Yes! Brian Rank can help fix Hillary's mother's arm. I have to see Dr. Rank—see if he can fix me. . . .

"I'm going out of here," she says when the younger woman hesitates. "Get me some clothes on."

The oncologist comes quickly. Ruth is enormously relieved when he appears in her room, well dressed, confident—in stark contrast to the tattered, tearful staff usually attending her. At last there is a professional on the premises. Surely he will be able to answer her unanswered questions, mend her arm, heal the wound at her throat. She smiles as if a person she holds in high esteem—Saul Steinberg, Julia Child—had arrived for lunch.

Afterward, outside Ruth's room, the oncologist tells her daughter that the loss of function in her mother's right arm suggests the cancer is probably "central"—it has metastasized to Ruth's brain. This is a rare but not unheard-of development in throat cancer, he notes. There is little left to do, he says.

Later that day, Ruth writes to no one in particular, "This must be what it's like to be dying. I don't hurt anywhere. I just feel alone."

❖ ❖ ❖

Very early in August, Ruth's eyes followed me as I moved about her room. I can't remember what I was doing—the usual nursey lady duties. She handed her notepad to me. She was saying good-bye:

"Oh you my beautiful best daughter friend—
Hillary of whom
I love her—
so lovely—
my lovely Hillary—
How did I get so sick?
Didn't mean to hurt your writing—
Thank you for not be too mad
funny ending—
You gonna finish the book—
weird cancer—
you gonna finish the book."

❖ ❖ ❖

When I look back on those final weeks, I cannot point to smooth transitions from one particular stage to another in my mother's dying. Instead, time simply passed as a succession of hours and eventually days—days when Ruth was confused and frightened, days when she was satisfied with herself and her "Tender Loving Dork" caregivers, days when she was overwhelmed with worry that her long dying spell—her "lingering" on the "brink of death," as she often called it—was ruining my life or her husband's.

"Do I really linger?" she had mused some weeks before. "I mean, could not what I'm doing more properly be described as 'loitering'? It *has* gone on for a very long time. Or so it seems some of the time. Actually, in my heart of hearts, what I accuse myself of doing—some of the time—is lurking. But 'lurking on the brink of death' has a kind of shiftless ring to it. I can hear my mother—'Edna Ruth! Little Dorothy would *never* have lurked on the brink of death!'"

Dorothy was the impeccable child next door with whom Mabel had often contrasted her wicked daughter Ruth.

Some days she simply wanted it to be over:

"GREAT PAIN
CAN YOU
HELP
CHILDREN
CAN
YOU
HELP,"

she wrote to me and her hospice nurse Katie during one horrific
bout of pain.

"I
am
GOING
AWAY,"

she wrote when the pain had subsided.

Other days, or even the very next minute, she would change her
mind, as long as we assured her that we loved her. There was a
broader pattern, of course, that of decline—although never submission—but as we were living out those days with Ruth, none of us
saw it with particular clarity. My own grief kept me hovering, worried, in the moment, besieged with powerful emotions. Ruth's temperature was 101 degrees; she was suddenly in pain; she was
overdrugged; she defiantly had attempted to stand when no one was
in her room and tumbled into a corner; the arm she used to write
with was becoming numb and uncoordinated; she needed to pee, an
undertaking that required the preparation and organization of an
army assault it sometimes seemed, except there was usually just
Ruth and me to manage.

Ruth's personality, always dominant in some form no matter
how severe her problems, frosted the days with a certain black com-

edy and gaiety. You saw it in the hospice nurses' smiles of anticipation as they entered Ruth's bedroom. "I am being shorted in the kisses direction," she would write them. "Tell my husband I need many more. Ask him if he would kiss me about one hundred times." She called them "darling child," "my sweet violet," or, in the case of a woman named Phyllis, who reminded her of Frannie, "my love." Soon after meeting Phyllis, Ruth wrote to her husband and me, "I tell you, there is a lot of stuff you don't know when you start out in life. In my case, it turns out to be quite surprising but in no way ominous or even particularly disturbing. The fact is, I have fallen in love with a lady named Phyllis. Hospice nurse by birth & trade. Lovely. It's just one of those things that I thought we should share."

Upon completing this sentence, Ruth awarded my stepfather and me a generous smile, as if urging us to join her in her newfound happiness. She was having us on, of course; her use of the word *share*—a cliché she would have avoided in serious conversation—was the tip-off. Yet we knew there was some portion of sincerity in her sentiment. Phyllis had attended the terminally ill for more than a decade. Phyllis was handling my mother's predicament quite nicely. Indeed, she had a remarkably calming influence on Ruth. My stepfather and I, on the other hand, were weeping alone at odd hours in far corners of the house. Where were we at such times? Had we stopped loving her?

"Phyllis would never run away from me, would you Phyllis?" she wrote to the hospice nurse one day. "I keep making my husband and Hillary cry so they don't stay very long. But WHAT ON EARTH HAVE I BEEN DOING TO DRIVE THEM OFF? I do not recall making any fusses or ado. If your whole family had set out to cry, you would look troubled too. What am I to do for those desperate people? I'm just bewildered. Rank said I was doing fine. I love them all so. If Rank knows what to be brave about then he must tell them."

Her mind rambled, leading her into dark corners she didn't want to find herself in, but couldn't seem to leave. "Hillary," she began one afternoon. And then suddenly, out of nowhere: "I was such a bad mamma. . . . If you could stand it, call up Ethan & tell him I always loved him and the boys and did not show it because, see, I couldn't help him. See, sometimes I could help you, Hillary, so I didn't feel so bad when I tried to help up and couldn't. . . . When I woke up a little bit ago and couldn't find you I was afraid you'd run away cause this time I really couldn't help you. I almost never had any money of the kind you needed. . . . I think that if your father had stayed home with you and Ethan—be what they call a house husband, and let me go to law school we would have made out better when you were little. Should have been a lawyer . . . But I did love my babies."

In a solitary moment with her husband, she wrote, "I don't want to die. Help me not die. Fix me so I don't. Keep me by you some longer. I want to be here. I like to touch and feel you. Keep me darling. It's a nice evening. You are the love of my life. You are the love of my LIFE. We have had a long time. And we would not have had much if you had not chosen to be together. The Hospital would have done me in some time back. I thank you for the beauty time."

Then she asked her husband to find me and bring me to her.

"Hillilllary," she wrote to me, "I feel thankful and grateful that there is still time. I have days and weeks yet to spend with my loved ones. I want to spend time with all of you Every day. I'm going to stay alive and be around for you guys to pinch and love. So be nice tonight and I'm going to live as long as you will have me." She told me that she wanted me to sleep on the sofa that night. "I would like to wake up in the morning with my husband, if you would not mind."

Another day, when her husband's daughter came by to visit, a woman Ruth had known and loved since she was a child of three, Ruth suddenly poured out her heart:

"We are not managing very smoothly," she began. "Every day we say now surely THIS will be the last and it never is. ITS HARD TO DIE," she continued, her lettering becoming larger and more emphatic. "AND POOR HILLARY IS WORN OUT AND HER

BOOK NEEDS TO GET WRITTEN . . . AND MY LIFE IS OVER AND HILLARY IS BEING RUINED AND I CAN'T DIE AND PLEASE HELP ME. I GET SO SCARED AND SO IMPATIENT AND WANT IT TO END. I DIDN'T WANT IT TO GO THIS WAY."

Afterward, to her husband, she wrote simply, "How long am I going to go on in this dumb bluffin way?"

❖ ❖ ❖

Near the very end of her life Ruth insisted that she wanted to draw an ink-and-water color study of cats to present as a gift to Betsy, her "sweet violet," the quiltmaker and nurse who helped me care for my mother. Ruth had been planning elaborate tea parties in Betsy's honor for quite some time, but as death neared, her passion for Betsy escalated. Ruth could barely stand, and yet one evening in early August she said to me, "We have perfect weather—the deck is ideal for drawing—you want to try tomorrow? Let's give it a shot or two?"

The next day, the plan was still very much on her mind. "Do you love me now?" she wrote. "I seem to get so tired. I have so little energy. I stay here of course," she said, gesturing at her bed. Then, accidentally substituting "you" when she meant "I," she wrote, "What did you use for a pen when you made some cat drawings—years ago—a stick of bamboo—sure, just cut the end with a razor or a blade."

We had no bamboo. I gathered pens and drawing paper and jars of ink, and we made the journey in slow motion, hissing machines and all, from her bedroom to her deck. The lake was very blue and evenly striated by the white tops of choppy waves. We sat together at the table she had designed and built, an enormous blank page between us. She began drawing, her face taking on a look of extreme concentration. I watched her transformation with a sense of awe.

She was not dying at that moment; she was as alive as anyone could possibly be. Further, consciously or not, she was telling me at last by resolutely *showing* me that she was not merely my mother, she was an artist; that this is what she did.

When she accidentally jostled a jar of ink and its contents spread over the top of the page, she was unperturbed. The spill was not a calamity; it was an interesting development. She began to incorporate the stain into the extremely intricate, if mysterious, subject she was drawing. She pressed on in this way for some time. Suddenly she was tired. She needed to be horizontal again and we returned to her bedroom. She was satisfied. She had done what she needed and wanted to do.

After my mother died, I fell into the habit of meeting her friend and former teacher, Bill Roode, at Lake of the Isles. We talked mostly about Ruth as we made our way around the lake during those autumn afternoons. We were in no particular hurry; there was nothing left to do then but remember her. I told him that Ruth had suddenly requested drawing materials immediately after the surgery that rendered her mute—the exact point at which her fate was finally stripped of all ambiguity. Her first and most pressing desire had been to complete a series of drawings of the life span of a flower, from closed bud to fallen petals. I told him how she had spent hours sketching self-portraits of the internment camp prisoner she suddenly perceived herself to be once she returned home. "She was overwhelmed, then," Roode said. "Art became her main way of communicating."

He was powerfully affected when I described Ruth's effort to draw a series of cats just before her death. The impulse that drove my mother to make art, Roode had always sensed, was comparable to a biological need; my tale confirmed his sense of things. The will to make art was profound, he said, and so invincible in Ruth's particular case that it had comprised her final conscious effort, superseding every obstacle.

"Part of what I loved about Ruth was that she was an artist," Roode said on one of those walks. "She was *really* an artist," he reiterated, "and not many people actually are."

❖ ❖ ❖

By August 7, Ruth's handwriting had become unintelligible to everyone, even perhaps herself. It had started weeks before, when she had written, "The letters get mixed up—they make anagrams on their own. Like I wanted to write EYES & I wrote yes. Never noticed that about writing." The problem had surged way beyond unbidden anagrams and dyslexia and spelling I would describe as emotional rather than by the book. The problems had to do more with achieving mastery over her disabled arm and hand, and remembering how and perhaps even why written language was actually executed. The first two or three letters of a word were always legible, and then her script would begin its wild spinning and tumbling down the length of the page. She would stare at the marks with puzzlement and deep frustration, then turn the page and try again.

I wanted more than anything to know what she had to say. It all had meaning, of that I felt certain. One evening, she made a small mark on her notepad, then handed it to me. I looked at it without comprehension. I gave it back and urged her to try again. She took the pad back and made another mark. Her eyes were sparkling. I looked again. The mark was as mysterious as the first. She made a third mark and returned the notepad. Suddenly I understood. Shorn of her ability to communicate by speech and written language, she was enticing me into the world of art, as was her habit when I was barely able to speak or write myself. Her husband was in the room, and I explained the game to him. Ruth smiled with relief, and nodded as if to say, "Finally I am understood." We played at that game

226

until she grew tired. We tried but failed to create an intelligible representation of anything. I was too old now, too inhibited, my imagination stripped away by years of living in the world. Her capability was limited as well: Her arm and hand simply wouldn't do what she wanted them to do. For an hour or so, however, we communed as we had when I was three and she was twenty-five. Then Ruth put the pad down and closed her eyes.

❖ ❖ ❖

In time, Ruth lost patience with me and with her husband as her ability to write deteriorated. Finally she abandoned the struggle. Sometimes she tried to simply mouth words, but we could rarely understand those efforts. Often, Ruth would stare at me intently, mouthing the words of a single sentence again and again; whatever she was trying to say, it was vitally important to her and, in her mind apparently, equally important to me. I was unable to understand a word of it. I would offer her an expression of apology, feeling on the verge of tears. Eventually she would look at me coldly; she had raised an idiot.

After a while, Ruth began to have rages. Seemingly defying laws of physics, nature, and probability, she would sit up in her hospital bed, swing her feet to the floor, stand for a minute to catch her balance, all the while supporting herself by gripping a steel pole on which hung a computerized feeding pump and a morphine pump. She was a mother ship to which satellites were bound by thin plastic tubes, but she cared nothing for these accoutrements; she had other things on her mind. The pole was on wheels and Ruth, using this stalk as her support, would lurch dizzily from her bedroom. Once she tipped into a wall; I broke her fall by inserting my arm between her body and the wall, and although I felt no pain, my wrist turned black and blue and remained that way for months. She was incredibly strong at these times; I could no more dissuade her from her purpose than I could deflect a meteor from colliding with the earth, and so I would trundle behind her, wheeling the oxygen tank that was attached by a narrow tube to the clear plastic mask at her neck. I'm sure she would simply have let the heavy tank drag along the floor behind her had I not tended to it.

She wanted to be in the open space of the main room of her house, a room that had been the footprint of the original structure before she decreed that the walls and ceilings be torn down. She would stand in the center of this room in which she had read hundreds of books, served thousands of dinners, and warmed herself for twenty-four winters in front of crackling fires, and look around imperiously, as if to assure herself everything was in its proper place. Afterward, not wishing to return to the prison of her bedroom, she would soldier on, passing through the great space and into a smaller room. There was nowhere to go after that, and having come to the edge of her world, she would collapse on a leather sofa, her face knotted in a degree of physical pain and frustration I wouldn't presume to quantify. She was spent. She required a wheelchair and a bolus of morphine to get back to her bed.

It was increasingly apparent that Ruth believed she was being held prisoner by two maniacs, me and her husband. Once she pushed her way past me and went off in search of her wheelchair. I rushed to gather the satellite machines together. When she was settled, Ruth demanded, by means of blunt, angry gestures, to be taken downstairs. We descended in her glass, one-story elevator to the ground floor. She then insisted that we head out, she in a nightie, bathrobe, and bare feet. Just as I opened the front door, the woman who lived directly across the street stepped out of her house. Catching the woman's eye, Ruth began waving frantically. The neighbor waved back, got into her car, and drove away. Ruth had always suspected the lady across the way was loopy; surely a sane person would have come to her rescue. Jabbing her finger into the air in front of her, Ruth demanded we continue down the sidewalk; she was in search of a sane person. I respected Ruth's struggle to save herself from the madness inside her household. Eventually I pushed Ruth and the machines attached to her around the entire block. It was slow going. We didn't see another human being.

The next morning, Ruth managed to write a recognizable word on her legal pad: It was "doctor." Over the course of hours, I recognized a few more words; taken together, they were "If you love me, take me to Hennepin County General. Please!" I called her oncologist. He arrived two hours later. He sat on her bed and covered her hands with his own. "How are you, Ruth?" he asked. Her eyes widening, she mouthed the word "*Moi*?," in homage to Miss Piggy. "I'm *fine!*" she added, as if surprised by the question. "Good," he said, smiling. "My dog is sick," she wrote. "They won't let me see him." Then, suddenly remembering something far more important, she wrote, quite legibly, "I seem to be injured." She gestured at the bandage covering the tumor at her neck. "Do you want to go to the hospital?" he asked. Ruth nodded emphatically. She wrote, in large letters, "Pleassseesse." "Let me call an ambulance," Rank said immediately, standing. "I would take you with me right now, but I'm driving a small car and you wouldn't be able to lie down in the backseat." Ruth nodded; she understood his dilemma; she could wait. He looked at me and we left the room together.

He told me, "Ruth is gone. She won't be coming back." The paranoia she was exhibiting, Rank said, was a symptom as horrible as the pain. Were she in the hospital, the nurses would control the paranoia with "pharmacology." She required little more than compassionate care at this point. I asked if he thought we should send Ruth back to the hospital. He said it was unnecessary. "She'll be fine now," he added. We were to increase Ruth's antianxiety drugs.

I agreed to let Rank prepare a "Do Not Resuscitate, Do Not Intubate" request on my mother's behalf because he seemed to feel it was important and because he had yet to hurt Ruth or err in her care. Yet I still could not get it clear in my mind—the notion that Ruth's life was ending and nothing could be done. I studied the document anxiously after he left, looking for escape clauses; there weren't any.

Ruth never tried to leave her bedroom again, never raged against her captors again. But she withdrew to a private sphere all her own, a place where we no longer mattered. Sometimes when I was giving her a sponge bath, she would shoot me a disapproving glance: Where was my sense of decorum? Mostly, I was just a body that moved around the room, one that did little but break her concentration in countless annoying ways.

When I sat by her bed in middle of the night, she was wide awake, too, looking up at the white wall in front of her as if a movie were being projected there. She would watch intently, her face frequently breaking into its room-brightening smile. Sometimes she would appear to laugh, even cry out with approval. On occasion, she would raise her hands high in clumsy applause, wearing a look of triumph and pleasure, as if she were encouraging a troupe of actors, or circus performers, or puppeteers, letting them know she appreciated their remarkably fine performance. I sometimes wondered if she was rewriting her life, or my life, or my brother's life, fine-tuning the script, righting wrongs, fashioning her children into better people, expunging villains and missteps from her own history. I wondered, too, if instead she had passed into an unearthly realm where everything was new and delightful, the past buried and irrelevant.

On one of these occasions, when the performance appeared to be over, she lay quietly, a half-smile on her peaceful face. Standing over her bed, I asked her gingerly, "Are you having a good time?"

"I'm having a perfectly *awful* time!" she answered, mouthing the words quite clearly.

In the second week of August, a friend called me. I was ten feet from Ruth, and so I spoke softly, but I was growing lax about what I did or didn't say in her presence. Ruth was somewhere impenetrable, there but not there, apparently conscious but not of me or the things I perceived to be real. Or so I thought. In addition, I felt near collapse. I sat next to her bed from hour to hour, latex gloves on my hands, measuring and cutting strips of cotton twill with which to replace her bloodied trache ties, and readying fresh bandages to apply over the tumor that had slowly pummeled its way through the flesh of her neck. It was quite large now. Ruth, herself, had months earlier ceased to examine its progress. I, who dressed the wound, kept the horror of its emergence to myself, like the child who tells no one about the monster making its home in her closet. Increasingly worried about infection, I cleaned the site and replaced the ties and bandage as often as four times a day. The mass of red tissue bled at the slightest provocation, especially when I cleaned the area and replaced the bandage. It also bled for no apparent reason at all. One night it bled for two hours. Ruth's neck and pillowcase were covered in blood; I was glad she couldn't see the gore. As the minutes passed, I felt more defeated than ever before. It was perhaps the lowest moment. I found my stepfather. I told him Ruth was bleeding to death, that there was nothing I could do. He looked at me like a sleepwalker might, without expression, and I turned and went back to Ruth's bedroom. The bleeding stopped a few minutes later.

The next morning, I was in the process of tying fresh trache ties at her neck after having applied a fresh bandage. Ruth, lying on her back, simply pulled the metal tracheostomy tube out of her throat and held it high in the air before I could tie the bow, her face registering surprise, then glee as she glimpsed it in her hands. Her husband and I were standing on either side of her, stunned. She encoded the fear on our faces and looked at us with deep affection and calm, as if to say, "Finally, my dears, we may now say good-bye." My stepfather seemed frozen. I freed the metal device from Ruth's hands, rinsed it in saline water, and carefully reinserted it. Ruth seemed not to notice. A few days later she stood and began tugging violently on the tube leading into her stomach until I interceded. Her gestures left no room for misinterpretation.

"Have you given your mother permission to die?" my friend asked. "No," I answered. My friend expressed her disapproval. I needed to end Ruth's suffering by giving her my "permission" to die, she explained. I had spent every waking hour of the last six months trying to stave off Ruth's death. I wanted her to have every second of life left to her, but I can't deny the element of selfishness: I was terrified of the moment when I would be forced to face life in a world without my mother in it.

My friend was insistent, but I was uncertain, my judgment wavering wildly. Nevertheless, I thought at the moment I hung up, maybe she was right. Rank had carried this same message to my mother weeks before. Maybe I had done Ruth a disservice by withholding "permission" to die. I walked to her bed, sat on its edge, and looked into her face. It was okay for her to "let go," I assured her. Everything would be "all right" if that was what she wanted to do. I tried to sound confident, but saying these things made me feel queasy; I had no commitment to the principles behind the words. I asked if she understood what I had said. She had. Her ear for bullshit was still finely tuned. Her eyes turned icy and prideful upon hearing my best sellerdom-ese come rattling at her like a garbage truck through the morphine and the brilliant reveries. Afterward I wished I could somehow disassociate myself from this callow person who had foisted what suddenly seemed like little more than New Age psychobabble on Ruth, of all people, promoting her demise as if it didn't matter one way or the other, as if some copyrighted notion about what to tell a dying person had anything to do with Ruth. She didn't deserve this.

Years passed before I fully understood. Ruth had needed something very much just then, but it wasn't the voguish "permission to die." She was awaiting an end to the conflict between those two people she loved so fiercely and completely, a conflict that was blocking her path like a massive boulder, menacing and disorienting. The resolution never came.

Exactly one week later she mouthed a sentence and the words were plain as day. "You're very wrong, you know," she said. "I'm *not* going to die." "Good!" I said immediately, but the sentiment must have seemed hollow, arriving as it did after the "death and dying" prattle. Ruth looked at me scathingly. I was further punished for my lapse: As things turned out, it was the final lucid exchange I ever had with my mother.

Two days later, on a Friday, in spite of her best intentions, Ruth's blood pressure dropped. On Saturday morning, she cast a look of irritation in my direction when I raised her arm to bathe it. "*Really*, Hillary!" her expression said. I stopped immediately. It was odd and exceptionally painful, this new phase we were in, in which her love for me seemed to be a thing of the past, and I had become her tormentor, just as surely as any of the myriad nursey ladies who had tended her in hospitals. I didn't want our relationship to end this way, but my exhaustion was so overwhelming I felt drugged, my thoughts and actions nearly mechanical. Although I wanted to reestablish our bond, I was too tired to discover the mechanism.

I was in my own dreamworld; there would be no more "phases." Ruth was in the business of dying that day. She was so still and quiet, in fact, I left her alone and sat in the living room in a quiet stupor for nearly three hours; I may have even slept. It was perhaps the longest period I had left her side in the previous two months. When I came into her bedroom, she was remarkably still; even the position of her hands had remained unchanged since I last saw her. I touched her arm. Her skin was cold. I suddenly realized it was chilly in the room and that I had left her covered with only a flannel sheet. Her shoulders and arms were bare. Her temperature was a degree below normal. My heart began to race. I called the hospital; the doctor on call said to pile on as many blankets as I could. Sick with guilt, I placed down comforters and even Ruth's fur coat on top of her, but an hour later she was too warm: She had a fever. I took away some of the blankets and gave her a Tylenol and codeine mixture to bring the fever down. The drugs worked, and her temperature returned to normal, but by five P.M., I noticed her eyes were just half open and covered with a thick film of tears she made no attempt to blink away. Her body was almost motionless, except that her breathing had become a coarse, sonorous gasp. I called the hospital again, but the staff was fresh out of ideas. A doctor offered to send an ambulance; after I said no, we were both silent for a moment; then he said that he and his colleagues would be thinking of us that night. I had suspected Ruth was dying, and now it was clear that this doctor thought so, too.

At midnight, I awoke my stepfather, who had gone to bed at ten P.M. I couldn't see how Ruth could possibly continue much longer in this state. He and I sat on either side of her; I held her hand. I gave him a book, one of Ruth's favorites, and he read aloud, beginning with the first page, from *The Portrait of a Lady*. At five A.M., a thunderstorm blew out the electricity and for the first time in months the machines in the room fell silent. I lit candles so I could see my mother. Her bedroom was transformed by warm flickering light and dark shadows; the room looked very beautiful. I wondered if she had ever seen it this way. I thought that she was dying as one of Henry James's heroines might have died: in her own bedroom, unhampered by machines, her face lit by candlelight.

My stepfather went back to sleep on the leather sofa. Ruth continued to gasp loudly for breath. At six A.M., the sun rose, the electricity returned, and I sat next to Ruth, half-perusing the Sunday real-estate ads in the *Minneapolis Tribune* classified section as had been my vain habit for years. At seven A.M., I heard my stepfather in the kitchen frying lamb chops for his breakfast.

A sudden absence of sound caused me to raise my head and look at Ruth. No breathing. Two belabored intakes of air. No breathing. I stood over her and wrapped my fingers around her wrist. Her pulse was surprisingly strong—pounding, in fact—but erratic. Then her pulse stopped, too. "I'm here with you," I heard myself saying. "I'll miss you very, very much. You were a wonderful mother. I'm here with you. I'm here with you." I felt three more pulse beats, but they were very slow. They were her last.

I wanted to sit with her, just the two of us, alone, but after a minute, I rose and followed the scent of lamb chops to the kitchen. I was crying. My stepfather turned from the stove and looked at me. "Clay," I managed, "Ruth is dead." "Oh—Hillary—" he murmured, surprising me with a look of sympathy, as if I had suffered the greater loss. We embraced then. Neither of us would be loved with such wild extravagance again; no one else would grieve as we would grieve. We stayed that way for a while, and then we disengaged.

It was August 22, 1993.

Cat in August

A few days after Ruth died, I received a condolence letter from the pulmonary chief at the county hospital, the first doctor Ruth ever saw at this institution. He wrote:

> It was a great pleasure to know Ruth and to have experienced her wit, intellect and joy in life. She seemed to have this joy despite the most difficult physical problems.
>
> I did want to share with you some of the concerns she raised when we first met. As she first faced the loss of her voice and her diagnosis of recurrent cancer she seemed to be searching for reasons that she wanted to press on. During one of her clinic visits she told me that she had discovered something that would provide her with real importance to continue. I am sure it was one of many efforts to provide some meaning for her life and some purpose for what had happened. She said she wanted to provide her daughter with the best example of dignity and courage that she could. And it seems she did just that by dying with dignity and grace—one of the last gifts our parents can provide for us and perhaps the most unselfish of all.

Each of the senior doctors and even a few of the residents who attended her eventually remarked upon these qualities to me. They weren't being polite. They wanted me to understand that Ruth had been different, had touched them in a fashion not every dying patient had.

Ruth succeeded very well at this, her final gift to me. In her dying, I recognized she had not only faced her death with enormous courage, she had led her life with courage and grace as well. Her incredible physical strength in the face of such devastating illness, her powerful will to live, had been another revelation. She was not spun sugar. She was not the same woman who at thirty, the mother of two children, had sought death out. She had not been that person for a very long time. I had harbored that ancient event inside me for a lifetime. I had incorporated it into my version of my mother exactly the way one snaps a piece of a jigsaw puzzle in place to advance the myriad senseless parts toward a recognizable image. During the years I spent with her, I had to sacrifice that piece, throw it away; it was part of some other puzzle.

❖ ❖ ❖

In the last days of my mother's life, I was launched on a highly personal investigation. I began by searching for whatever might remain of her art in the whitewashed basement studio. What I found as she lay in her bed directly above me on the next floor were pieces that were little more than scraps—rejects she had cast out years earlier, likely even before the great purge of 1989, that perhaps had missed the rim of the waste bin and found a silent resting place on the floor under the studio's free-standing shelves, still densely packed with painting supplies and lithography paper. There they would have remained undisturbed for years no doubt but for a daughter's desperation. I found a delicate etching of a sheep, its solid body suggesting a ram in fact, but its face thoroughly human; my mother had cut the creature out of a larger print using bold, careless scissor cuts, then she had taken a watercolor brush to the cutout, leaving most of it white, but parts of it streaked with sea-colored green.

I sighted a small white scrap of paper behind the washing machine, another tiny etching; the plate mark was visible at the top. I named it *Madame Recamier*. A voluptuous nude was reclining, her breasts in perfect, charming repose. Madame was attended by three mice the size of cats; she was looking brightly, with Betty Boop innocence, at the one nearest her, an eager, bright green mouse. A dab of red watercolor lay on the floor below. I wondered if it was meant to be blood, but decided the scene was too idyllic; the red was just a burst of color, an artist's mysterious, unimpeachable decision.

Tucked inside cardboard tubes that had lain hidden for years behind wall shelving units were large paint-on-paper portraits of women, of strange, friendly-looking beasts, and densely painted abstracts. These were created, I was to learn, in her first painting class with Roode. In the corner of one a pencil mark remained: .25. Ruth had chosen neither to erase nor paint over the price of the paper. Sometime afterward, I would encase this painting of a grinning blond woman in a purple sun hat, what I have come to feel certain is my mother's self-portrait, in an eight-hundred-dollar frame. I made certain the twenty-five cent mark remained visible.

Hugely encouraged, I pored through the pages of dusty sketchbooks resting under half-empty tubes of ink, my determination akin to animal instinct. I found just one drawing amid hundreds of blank bound pages. I might have been Leakey placing his hand on the skull of Lucy. It was an idly drawn, perhaps long-forgotten ink sketch of a sturdy Greek maiden. The subject's hair was piled prettily on her head, her eyes were startled and wondering; one arm reached to cover her pubis, the other was outstretched as if to wave away the wild-haired, flute-playing creature with cloven hooves intent on luring her toward what could only be a lascivious conclusion. On the reverse side, roly-poly angels floated in the air. One angel stood with his wings at rigid attention, his hand raised to his lips, not to blow a kiss but to wickedly thumb a row of fingers.

My mother's art is meaningful to me for its clarity, its playfulness, its refusal to obscure reality with sentimentality. She possessed what a friend of mine once characterized as a "wild hand." She was bold and uninhibited when she drew, just as she was in conversation and in the choices she made. Her paintings and prints, with their strong lines, their unambiguous point of view, their enchanting wash of colors, their often wicked, cartoonish humor, and their dark, worldly underside, were a remarkable, intensely realized expression of who she was. That enigmatic process—the act of imagination and interpretation that produces not only the image but insights into the artist as well—was exceptionally finely tuned in my mother.

Through her art, I could begin to understand who she was—exclusive of me, her husbands, her son, exclusive even of the pain she had been seeking to deaden since girlhood. In the creation of her art, she revealed herself to be someone quite different from the woman I had known only as my mother three decades before. Her art restored her to her original self, the raucous, joyful self of early childhood, a self that existed long before I existed. It allowed her to tell those stories she had stored up, her morality plays about love—appropriate and inappropriate; the human pecking order; parents and offspring; bigotry; evil; and, above all, survival.

I continue to study her work. I am struck again and again by the brilliant light she possessed. Like a beacon at the edge of a dark ocean, it circles round in bright, dependable bursts of illumination, showing me the way, reminding me that I was loved. When I am beset by the terrible silence her death has left behind, I can, if I concentrate, hear her soft, seductive voice: "Hi, darlin'. It's your mamma."

AFTERWORD

Five years to the day after Ruth's death, I began reading the more than one hundred uncensored pages of her county hospital records, awarded me at my request by Brian Rank two years earlier. Staff in the oncology department had kept written records of every phone call I had made to the hospital. The calls had gone on for months, and the staff had come to know my voice. Initially I was "Patient's dtr" in their notes, then, "dtr." Toward the end, I became simply Hillary. "Hillary says her mother is delerious," one note began.

The official medical account of my mother's decline was as difficult to read as I had imagined it would be. Neither Ruth's suffering nor my own ostentatious lapses of judgment could be viewed lightly. I discovered that the cardiac resident with whom I had fought had chosen to write a lengthy, two-page addendum in his case notes about my unruly behavior in his unit, even quoting me—to my recollection, inaccurately—and emphasizing repeatedly the fact that I had insisted on telling him and his staff how they should care for my mother. As I studied his complaint, I couldn't help but feel remorse, and sorry for this young doctor whose deeply held sense of decorum and personal authority I had shattered that weekend. In the end, my foot-stamping and outrage accomplished nothing. Ruth had died anyway.

The oncologist who stood with her back against the wall of the little room where Ruth nearly choked to death one summer afternoon in 1993 had something to say as well. Concluding her muted clinical description of the high-stakes drama she had just witnessed, the doctor offered her subjective assessment of the patient: "Pleasant woman in pain." The comment struck me as profoundly true and beautifully stated, like haiku.

Arriving at the end of this journal of savage, helpless medicine—and its subtext of rage and grief—I found a page that was clearly out of place. It was Ruth's hospital admittance form, completed the morning she entered the building for tracheostomy surgery. Next to my mother's name, under "Profession," someone had printed "Artist, Homemaker." Those words, which were obviously among the very last my mother had spoken, struck me with a force unlike anything else that came before. Ruth knew who she was, even if I hadn't always known. She might have been headed for oblivion, but should anyone wonder later on, she was determined to set the record straight for the keepers of records on that particular morning near the end of her life.